THE MODERN SPAIN SOURCEBOOK

THE MODERN SPAIN SOURCEBOOK

A CULTURAL HISTORY FROM 1600 TO THE PRESENT

Edited by Aurora G. Morcillo, María Asunción Gómez, Paula De La Cruz-Fernández and José Manuel Morcillo-Gómez

Bloomsbury Academic
An imprint of Bloomsbury Publishing Plc

B L O O M S B U R Y
LONDON · OXFORD · NEW YORK · NEW DELHI · SYDNEY

Bloomsbury Academic

An imprint of Bloomsbury Publishing Plc

50 Bedford Square	1385 Broadway
London	New York
WC1B 3DP	NY 10018
UK	USA

www.bloomsbury.com

BLOOMSBURY and the Diana logo are trademarks of Bloomsbury Publishing Plc

First published 2018

British Library Cataloguing-in-Publication Data

A catalogue record for this book is available from the British Library.

ISBN:	HB:	978-1-4742-6897-4
	PB:	978-1-4742-6896-7
	ePDF:	978-1-4742-6898-1
	eBook:	978-1-4742-6899-8

Library of Congress Cataloging-in-Publication Data

Name: Morcillo, Aurora G, editor. | Gómez, María Asunción, editor. |
Cruz-Fernández, Paula de la, editor. | Morcillo-Gómez, José Manuel, editor.
Title: The modern Spain sourcebook : a cultural history from 1600 to the
present / edited by Aurora G. Morcillo, María Asunción Gómez,
Paula de la Cruz-Fernández and José Manuel Morcillo-Gómez.
Description: London : Bloomsbury Academic, an imprint of Bloomsbury
Publishing Plc, 2017. | Includes index.
Identifiers: LCCN 2017018019| ISBN 9781474268974 (hb) | ISBN 9781474268967 (pb)
Subjects: LCSH: Spain—Civilization—Sources. | Spain—History—Sources.
Classification: LCC DP48 .M54 2017 | DDC 946—dc23 LC record available
at https://lccn.loc.gov/2017018019

Cover design by Irene Martinez Costa
Cover image: JOEL-PETER WITKIN, LAS MENINAS,
1987 (Toned Gelatin Silver Print, 28 x 28 inches, JRFA #10668).
Courtesy of Jack Rutberg Fine Arts

Typeset by RefineCatch Limited, Bungay, Suffolk
Printed and bound in Great Britain

CONTENTS

Contents

Contents

ILLUSTRATIONS

INTRODUCTION

This work was born out of our discussions about how to make sources for the study of Spanish history and culture more accessible to non-Spanish language students. In preparing materials for teaching and discussion for our multi-ethnic American classrooms, we face a challenging scarcity of Spanish primary sources translated into English. Awareness and reciprocal appreciation of other cultures involves an effort to read and understand their cultural and historical heritages. While graduate students in Hispanic studies programs across disciplines will need to master Spanish for their research and scholarly work, it is also important to expose undergraduate upper-division students, who do not speak or read Spanish, to translations of important primary sources, cultural symbols, and artifacts. We believe this exposure to the richness of the Spanish world will encourage students to pursue further studies and research in the field. Moreover, this compilation of translated and contextualized sources will be useful for scholars and students outside the Spanish field of research, by offering comparative perspectives to historical analysis in the twenty-first century global society. We are convinced that translating primary sources is instrumental in creating a global learning community.

The collection of documents included here stems from our practice of interdisciplinary research in the fields of gender studies, literary criticism, and cultural history. In Spain, cultural history has been influenced by French historiography; specifically, by the work of Roger Chartier, who has had a significant impact on early modern Spanish historiography.[1] The modern period (nineteenth and twentieth centuries), however, is still more focused, with some exceptions, on social and institutional history. Anglo-Saxon Hispanists from the fields of philology and Spanish literary criticism have been the most influential for the study of gender and cinema, as well as the press and popular culture. The seminal works of Jo Labanyi, Lou Charnon-Deutsch, and Noël Valis have impacted the literary field and have also brought forth an alternative way of writing history.[2]

English departments spearheaded cultural studies throughout the country, but not necessarily with a focus on Spain. Cultural history is not even part of the university curriculum, although it has been gaining ground since the mid–1990s, thanks to the work of a few scholars interested in modern Spanish intellectual history, such as Octavio Ruiz Manjón, Elena Hernández Sandoica, and José Alvarez Junco.[3]

For the most part, the approach to cultural studies and its influence on historical narrative comes from American and British literary critics in language and literature departments, following the model of what has been called the "linguistic turn" and with emphasis on semiotics. In other words, there has been an interest in decoding cultural symbols that inform social practices and define individual and collective identities, not only through prescriptive texts (legislation, school curricula, medical treatises, conduct manuals) but also through counter discourses (everyday life practices, fiction, cinema, and popular culture). Therefore, cultural critics (historians) have at their disposal familiar images, texts, and objects that are nevertheless left outside the realm of primary sources in the traditional positivistic historiography. In the last few decades, there has been a multidisciplinary "cultural turn" that has revealed an interest in the elusive and concealed corners of cultures, which provide insight into the subject, in addition to a reciprocal understanding because of the current global intellectual exchange.

The fruitful collaboration between the literary critic and the historian occurs when the former pays attention, not only to the literary text, but also to the historical context in which it is produced, and the latter pays attention to the cultural production of the historical period she or he is immersed in studying. To better accomplish such interdisciplinary goals, this work is organized thematically, rather than chronologically or geographically. The criteria utilized to select the documents are rooted in cultural and gender history and, therefore, some of the materials are found outside of the traditional archive. We refer here not only to the physical, but also to the theoretical and historiographical archive, following the ideas that Jacques Derrida introduces in "Archive's Fever:"

> There is no political power without control of the archive, if not of memory. Effective democratization can always be measured by this essential criterion: the participation in and the access to the archive, its constitution, and its interpretation.[4]

In citing the work of French scholar Sonia Combe, Derrida further elaborates:

> [S]he asks numerous essential questions about the writing of history, about the "repression" of the archive [318], about the "'repressed' archive" as "power ... of the state over the historian" [321]. Among all of these questions, and in referring the reader to this book, let us isolate here the one that is consonant, in a way, with the low tone of our hypothesis, even if this fundamental note, the (patri) archive, never covers all the others.[5]

The term "patri-archive" is particularly important for us, as gender analysis guides many of our selections. When co-author Aurora Morcillo began her career as a historian in Spain in the mid–1980s, her professors pointed out to her how nearly impossible it would be to find records on women's historical experience in the archives. What they meant was that there were no "legitimate historical records" (only those found in the archive) that would allow for the writing of any serious history. All they anticipated she could find was anecdotal information buried in the mainstream records, or marginal at best, and some representation in censuses and government. Certainly, much of the materials on women's experiences were relegated to customs and folklore inside the traditional archive. This is the result of what Derrida also discusses in his article: "The archontic principle of the archive is also a principle of consignation, that is, of gathering together."[6] The authority to decide what to keep and what not to keep, responds to nationalist narratives, which have been proven to be gendered ever since the inception of national archives in the late nineteenth century, and the professionalization of history. This is also a debate about official historical narratives versus secondary ones, as much as a debate between what constitutes History and Memory, objectivity or subjectivity and, in the final analysis, absolute truth.[7]

We have come a long way. In the process, we have realized that the historian is an archeologist of her surroundings, a genealogist of knowledge in a Foucaldian sense; we realize we carry history in our DNA. Our environment is saturated with traces of history everywhere—the archive is within and around us.

Structure and how to use this volume

This book is divided into ten modules or chapters organized thematically. Each module opens with a short introduction and historical context relating documents diachronically from the sixteenth century to the present. The modules contain a wide variety of sources, including visual and material culture, as well as texts. In addition, the authors have prepared questions to guide the reading, and a selection of secondary sources in the final bibliography to further future research on Spanish history and cultural studies.

This volume is geared toward undergraduate and graduate level courses in History, Literature, Cultural, and Gender Studies. As a compilation of historical sources—not only on the history and culture of Spain, but as a supplementary reading for comparative approaches in other regions and disciplines that have an interest in global understanding as part of the learning process—it serves as a complementary text for upper division college courses, as well as graduate seminars. A growing number of history departments in the United States are offering courses such as "Women and Gender in Europe since 1750" or "Women and Gender in Latin America." Despite the increasing interest in this approach and in these courses, Spain and Spanish primary sources are absent from the textbooks available on the market. This lacuna in the available curriculum materials contributes to keeping an important piece of knowledge excluded from the mainstream curriculum, turning it into an incomplete instruction for future global citizens.

The sources gathered here aspire to highlight historical and cultural experiences from a democratic, inclusive, and innovative perspective. The narrative they may aid to construct would be one built from below. Therefore, the selection of written and visual materials in this volume, while representative and significant, exemplifies only a minimal assortment. We hope readers will explore further and beyond these pages to interpret and gain insight into new multidisciplinary and diachronic research topics, which, although Spanish in focus, are imbued with universal value.

Miami, October 2016

MODULE 1
LITERATURE AND ART

ABSTRACT

Literature and art hold clues that help us understand history. We are including in this module fragments from different representative Spanish writers as well as two art pieces. Miguel de Cervantes' (1547–1616) *Don Quixote* (1605), a founding novel in modern Western literature, is followed by a prologue that María de Zayas (1590–1661) wrote for her *Exemplary Tales of Love and Disillusion* (1637). In this piece, she deals with women's inferiority, a topic that Benito Feijóo (1676–1764) addresses a century later in, "A Defense or Vindication of Women" (1726). Cervantes and Zayas show how women are not intellectually inferior by nature, and claim this myth is the product of a social system that insists on keeping women in a subordinate position—politically, economically, and culturally. In the sixth document of this module, a fragment from *For A History of Mercy* (1989), a text by Spanish philosopher María Zambrano (1904–91) where she claims that we tend to look at history in a "scientific" rather detached way, leaving aside the life of anonymous people who represent an authentic and important part of history. In her view, literature, and more specifically poetry, reflects the truth about the lives of people and their innermost feelings better than the clinical historical knowledge inherited from the age of reason. Zambrano proposes a poetic reason to better understand the depths of human experience.

The two art pieces chosen for this module are the artists' personal reaction to the social and political turmoil that Spain was going through at the time. The etching, "The Sleep of Reason Produces Monsters" (1797–9), is Francisco de Goya's response to Ferdinand VII's reactionary policies. These regulations started with the establishment of an absolutist monarchy upon his restoration to the throne in 1814, and the rejection of the short-lived liberal Constitution of 1812 (a fragment of which is included in Module 6). The last document in this first module is a poster created during the Spanish Civil War (1936–9), chosen as a good example of propagandistic art.

DOCUMENT 1
MIGUEL DE CERVANTES SAAVEDRA.
EL INGENIOSO HIDALGO DON QUIJOTE DE LA MANCHA (THE INGENIOUS GENTLEMAN DON QUIXOTE OF LA MANCHA, 1605)

Miguel de Cervantes Saavedra (1547–1616) is the creator of *Don Quixote*, one of the most celebrated characters in world literature. Most likely of *converso*[1] descent, Cervantes had to endure many adversities and financial hardships. As a young man, he fought against the Turkish fleet in the battle of Lepanto (1571), where his left hand was maimed. Four years later, he was captured by Ottoman corsairs and was held captive in an Algiers prison for five years. After being ransomed, Cervantes became commissary of provisions in Seville, and in 1597, irregularities in his accounting sent him to jail again.

Cervantes wrote several novels, sonnets, and two plays, but he is best known for his collection of *novellas* (short stories) entitled *Novelas ejemplares* (Exemplary novels, 1613) and, above all, for *El ingenioso hidalgo don Quijote de la Mancha* (The Ingenious Gentleman Don Quixote of La Mancha). Published in two volumes, in 1605 and 1615, and translated into more than sixty languages, it is considered one of the most widely influential novels in the world. Cervantes' masterpiece tells the adventures of a *hidalgo* who, after reading too many chivalric romances, decides to become a knight-errant. Accompanied by Sancho Panza, a farmer he makes his squire, Don Quixote wanders the fields of La Mancha trying to undo wrongs and bring justice to those who suffer abuse. There have been multiple interpretations of this multifaceted and radically original novel. Before the nineteenth century, it was mainly read as a humorous parody of the outdated, but still popular, chivalric romances; the Romantics transformed Don Quixote into a tragic hero and started to address the historical critique of Spanish imperialism. In the twentieth century, criticism also focused on the metafictional strategies used in the novel to show the impossibility to separate facts from fiction, appearances from reality.

The validity, vitality, and universality of *Don Quixote* is in part due to the complexity of meanings portrayed in the novel. In a continuous fluctuation between nihilism and idealism, Cervantes shows a profound understanding of human nature and this novel can be read as a cry for tolerance and good faith. Therefore, turning the text into a key primary source to understand cultural values of the early modern era that aid the historian of contemporary times to see the impact of the arts in the political and social fabric. *Don Quixote* is the artistic representation of a new worldview where reality is contradictory and where medieval institutions and values such as chivalry and honor are substituted by modern society values where personal relations are based on material interest. These two opposed worldviews are incarnated by Don Quixote (the idealist) and

Sancho Panza (the materialist). The clash between the two worlds is also apparent through language. For example, in the selection below, we see that Don Quixote is well versed in the language of the romances of chivalry, but does not understand the slang that prisoners use and is frequently in need of "a translation."

EL INGENIOSO HIDALGO DON QUIJOTE DE LA MANCHA (THE INGENIOUS GENTLEMAN DON QUIXOTE OF LA MANCHA)

Chapter XXII

In regards to the freedom Don Quixote conferred on several unfortunates, who against their will, were carried where they had no wish to go

Cide Hamete Benengeli, the Arab and Manchegan author, relates in this most grave, high-sounding, minute, delightful, and original history, that after the discussion between the famous Don Quixote of La Mancha and his squire Sancho Panza (which is set down at the end of chapter twenty-one), Don Quixote raised his eyes. He saw some dozen men on foot, coming along the road, strung together by the neck, like beads, on a great iron chain and with manacles on their hands. With them, also came two men on horseback and two on foot; those on horseback with wheel-lock muskets, and those on foot, with javelins and swords. As soon as Sancho saw them, he said:

"That is a chain of galley slaves, on the way to the galleys by force of the king's orders."

"How by force?" asked Don Quixote; "is it possible that the king uses force against anyone?"

"I do not say that," answered Sancho, "but that these are people condemned for their crimes to serve by force in the king's galleys."

"In fact," replied Don Quixote, "however it may be, these people are going where they are taking them by force, and not of their own will."

"Just so," said Sancho.

"Then if so," said Don Quixote, "here is a case for the exercise of my office, to put down force and to succor and help the wretched."

"Recollect, your worship," said Sancho, "Justice, which is the king himself, is not using force or doing wrong to such persons, but punishing them for their crimes."

The chain of galley slaves had by this time come up, and Don Quixote in very courteous language asked those who were in custody of it to be good enough to tell him the reason or reasons for which they were conducting these people in this manner. One of the guards on horseback answered that they were galley slaves belonging to his majesty, that they were going to the galleys, and that was all that was to be said and all he had any business to know.

"Nevertheless," replied Don Quixote, "I should like to know from each of them separately the reason of his misfortune;" to this he added more to the same effect to induce them to tell him what he wanted so civilly that the other mounted guard said to him:

"Though we have here the register and certificate of the sentence of every one of these wretches, this is no time to take them out or read them; come and ask themselves; they can tell if they choose, and they will, for these fellows take a pleasure in doing and talking about rascalities."

With this permission, which Don Quixote would have taken even had they not granted it, he approached the chain and asked the first for what offenses he was now in such a sorry case. He made answer that it was for being a lover.

"For that only?" replied Don Quixote: "Why, if for being lovers they send people to the galleys I might have been rowing in them long ago."

"The love is not the sort your worship is thinking of," said the galley slave; "mine was that I loved a washerwoman's basket of clean linen so well, and held it so close in my embrace, that if the arm of the law had not forced it from me, I should never have let it go of my own will to this moment; I was caught in the act, there was no occasion for torture, the case was settled, they treated me to a hundred lashes on the back, and three years of gurapas besides, and that was the end of it."

"What are gurapas?" asked Don Quixote.

"Gurapas are galleys," answered the galley slave, who was a young man of about four-and-twenty, and said he was a native of Piedrahita.

Don Quixote asked the same question of the second, who made no reply, so downcast and melancholic was he; but the first answered for him, and said, "He, sir, goes as a canary, I mean as a musician and a singer."

"What!" said Don Quixote, "For being musicians and singers are people sent to the galleys too?"

"Yes, sir," answered the galley slave, "for there is nothing worse than singing under suffering."

"On the contrary, I have heard say," said Don Quixote, "that he who sings scares away his woes."

"Here it is the reverse," said the galley slave; "for he who sings once weeps all his life."

"I do not understand it," said Don Quixote; but one of the guards said to him, "Sir, to sing under suffering means with the non-sancta fraternity to confess under torture; they put this sinner to the torture and he confessed his crime, which was being a cuatrero, that is a cattle-stealer, and on his confession they sentenced him to six years in the galleys, besides two hundred lashes that he has already had on the back; and he is always dejected and downcast because the other thieves that were left behind and that march here ill-treat, and snub, and jeer, and despise him for confessing and not having spirit enough to say nay; for, say they, 'nay' has no more letters in it than 'yea,' and a culprit is well off when life or death with him depends on his own tongue and not on that of witnesses or evidence; and to my thinking they are not very far out."

"And I think so too," answered Don Quixote; then passing on to the third he asked him what he had asked the others, and the man answered very readily and unconcernedly, "I am going for five years to their ladyships the gurapas for the want of ten ducats."

"I will give twenty with pleasure to get you out of that trouble," said Don Quixote.

"That," said the galley slave, "is like a man having money at sea when he is dying of hunger and has no way of buying what he wants; I say so because if at the right time I had had those twenty ducats that your worship now offers me, I would have greased the notary's pen and freshened up the attorney's wit with them, so that to-day I should be in the middle of the plaza of the Zocodover at Toledo, and not on this road coupled like a greyhound. But God is great; patience- there, that's enough of it."

Don Quixote passed on to the fourth, a man of venerable aspect with a white beard falling below his breast, who on hearing himself asked the reason of his being there began to weep without answering a word, but the fifth acted as his tongue and said, "This worthy man is going to the galleys for four years, after having gone the rounds in ceremony and on horseback."

"That means," said Sancho Panza, "as I take it, to have been exposed to shame in public."

"Just so," replied the galley slave, "and the offense for which they gave him that punishment was having been an ear-broker, nay body-broker; I mean, in short, that this gentleman goes as a pimp, and for having besides a certain touch of the sorcerer about him."

"If that touch had not been thrown in," said Don Quixote, "he would not deserve, for mere pimping, to row in the galleys, but rather to command and be admiral of them; for the office of pimp is no ordinary one, being the office of persons of discretion, one very necessary in a well-ordered state, and only to be exercised by persons of good birth; nay, there ought to be an inspector and overseer of them, as in other offices, and recognized number, as with the brokers on change; in this way many of the evils would be avoided which are caused by this office and calling being in the hands of stupid and ignorant people, such as women more or less silly, and pages and jesters of little standing and experience, who on the most urgent occasions, and when ingenuity of contrivance is needed, let the crumbs freeze on the way to their mouths, and know not which is their right hand. I should like to go farther, and give reasons to show that it is advisable to choose those who are to hold so necessary an office in the state, but this is not the fit place for it; some day I will expound the matter to some one able to see to and rectify it; all I say now is, that the additional fact of his being a sorcerer has removed the sorrow it gave me to see these white hairs and this venerable countenance in so painful a position on account of his being a pimp; though I know well there are no sorceries in the world that can move or compel the will as some simple folk fancy, for our will is free, nor is there herb or charm that can force it. All that certain silly women and quacks do is to turn men mad with potions and poisons, pretending that they have power to cause love, for, as I say, it is an impossibility to compel the will."

"It is true," said the good old man, "and indeed, sir, as far as the charge of sorcery goes I was not guilty; as to that of being a pimp I cannot deny it; but I never thought I was doing any harm by it, for my only object was that all the world should enjoy itself and live in peace and quiet, without quarrels or troubles; but my good intentions were unavailing to save me from going where I never expect to come back from, with this weight of years upon me and a urinary ailment that never gives me a moment's ease;" and again he fell to weeping as before, and such compassion did Sancho feel for him that he took out a real of four from his bosom and gave it to him in alms.

Don Quixote went on and asked another what his crime was, and the man answered with no less but rather much more sprightliness than the last one.

"I am here because I carried the joke too far with a couple of cousins of mine, and with a couple of other cousins who were none of mine; in short, I carried the joke so far with them all that it ended in such a complicated increase of kindred that no accountant could make it clear: it was all proved against me, I got no favor, I had no money, I was near having my neck stretched, they sentenced me to the galleys for six years, I accepted my fate, it is the punishment of my fault; I am a young man; let life only last, and with that all will come right. If you, sir, have anything wherewith to help the poor, God will repay it to you in heaven, and we on earth will take care in our petitions to him to pray for the life and health of your worship, that they may be as long and as good as your amiable appearance deserves."

This one was in the dress of a student, and one of the guards said he was a great talker and a very elegant Latin scholar.

Behind all these there came a man of thirty, a very personable fellow, except that when he looked, his eyes turned in a little one towards the other. He was bound differently from the rest, for he had to his leg a chain so long that it was wound all round his body, and two rings on his neck, one attached to the chain, the other to what they call a "keep-friend" or "friend's foot," from which hung two irons reaching to his waist with two manacles fixed to them in which his hands were secured by a big padlock, so that he could neither raise his hands to his mouth nor lower his head to his hands. Don Quixote asked why this man carried so many more chains than the others. The guard replied that it was because he alone had committed more crimes than all the rest put together, and was so daring and such a villain, that though they marched him in that fashion they did not feel sure of him, but were in dread of his making his escape.

"What crimes can he have committed," said Don Quixote, "if they have not deserved a heavier punishment than being sent to the galleys?"

"He goes for ten years," replied the guard, "which is the same thing as civil death, and all that need be said is that this good fellow is the famous Gines de Pasamonte, otherwise called Ginesillo de Parapilla."

"Gently, señor commissary," said the galley slave at this, "let us have no fixing of names or surnames; my name is Gines, not Ginesillo, and my family name is Pasamonte, not Parapilla as you say; let each one mind his own business, and he will be doing enough."

"Speak with less impertinence, master thief of extra measure," replied the commissary, "if you don't want me to make you hold your tongue in spite of your teeth."

"It is easy to see," returned the galley slave, "that man goes as God pleases, but some one shall know some day whether I am called Ginesillo de Parapilla or not."

"Don't they call you so, you liar?" said the guard.

"They do," returned Gines, "but I will make them give over calling me so, or I will be shaved, where, I only say behind my teeth. If you, sir, have anything to give us, give it to us at once, and God speed you, for you are becoming tiresome with all this inquisitiveness about the lives of others; if you want to know about mine, let me tell you I am Gines de Pasamonte, whose life is written by these fingers."

"He says true," said the commissary, "for he has himself written his story as grand as you please, and has left the book in the prison in pawn for two hundred reals."

"And I mean to take it out of pawn," said Gines, "though it were in for two hundred ducats."

"Is it so good?" said Don Quixote.

"So good is it," replied Gines, "that a fig for 'Lazarillo de Tormes,' and all of that kind that have been written, or shall be written compared with it: all I will say about it is that it deals with facts, and facts so neat and diverting that no lies could match them."

"And how is the book entitled?" asked Don Quixote.

"The 'Life of Gines de Pasamonte,'" replied the subject of it.

"And is it finished?" asked Don Quixote.

"How can it be finished," said the other, "when my life is not yet finished? All that is written is from my birth down to the point when they sent me to the galleys this last time."

"Then you have been there before?" said Don Quixote.

"In the service of God and the king I have been there for four years before now, and I know by this time what the biscuit and courbash are like," replied Gines; "and it is no great grievance to me to go back to them, for there I shall have time to finish my book; I have still many things left to say, and in the galleys of Spain there is more than enough leisure; though I do not want much for what I have to write, for I have it by heart."

"You seem a clever fellow," said Don Quixote.

"And an unfortunate one," replied Gines, "for misfortune always persecutes good wit."

"It persecutes rogues," said the commissary.

"I told you already to go gently, master commissary," said Pasamonte; "their lordships yonder never gave you that staff to ill-treat us wretches here, but to conduct and take us where his majesty orders you; if not, by the life of—never mind; it may be that some day the stains made in the inn will come out in the scouring; let everyone hold his tongue and behave well and speak better; and now let us march on, for we have had quite enough of this entertainment."

The commissary lifted his staff to strike Pasamonte in return for his threats, but Don Quixote came between them, and begged him not to ill-use him, as it was not too much to allow one who had his hands tied to have his tongue a trifle free; and turning to the whole chain of them he said:

"From all you have told me, dear brethren, make out clearly that though they have punished you for your faults, the punishments you are about to endure do not give you much pleasure, and that you go to them very much against the grain and against your will, and that perhaps this one's want of courage under torture, that one's want of money, the other's want of advocacy, and lastly the perverted judgment of the judge may have been the cause of your ruin and of your failure to obtain the justice you had on your side. All which presents itself now to my mind, urging, persuading, and even compelling me to demonstrate in your case the purpose for which Heaven sent me into the world and caused me to make profession of the order of chivalry to which I belong, and the vow I took therein to give aid to those in need and under the oppression of the strong. But as I know that it is a mark of prudence not to do by foul means what may be done by fair, I will ask these gentlemen, the guards and commissary, to be so good as to release you and let you go in peace, as there will be no lack of others to serve the king under more favorable circumstances; for it seems to me a hard case to make slaves of those whom God and nature have made free. Moreover, sirs of the guard," added Don Quixote, "these poor fellows have done nothing to you; let each answer for his own sins yonder; there is a God in Heaven who will not forget to punish the wicked or reward the good; and it is not fitting that honest men should be the instruments of punishment to others, they being therein no way concerned. This request I make thus, gently and quietly, that, if you comply with it, I may have reason for thanking you; and, if you will not voluntarily, this lance and sword together with the might of my arm shall compel you to comply with it by force."

"Nice nonsense!" said the commissary; "a fine piece of pleasantry he has come out with at last! He wants us to let the king's prisoners go, as if we had any authority to release them, or he to order us to do so! Go your way, sir, and good luck to you; put that basin straight that you've got on your head, and don't go looking for three feet on a cat."

"'Tis you that are the cat, rat, and rascal," replied Don Quixote, and acting on the word he fell upon him so suddenly that without giving him time to defend himself he brought him to the ground sorely wounded with a lance-thrust; and lucky it was for him that it was the one that had the musket. The other guards stood thunderstruck and amazed at this unexpected event, but recovering presence of mind, those on horseback seized their swords, and those on foot, their javelins, and attacked Don Quixote, who was waiting for them with great calmness; and no doubt it would have gone badly with him if the galley slaves, seeing the chance before them of liberating themselves, had not effected it by contriving to break the chain on which they were strung. Such was the confusion, that the guards, now rushing at the galley slaves who were breaking loose, now to attack Don Quixote who was waiting for them, did nothing at all that was of any use. Sancho, on his part, gave a helping hand to release Gines de Pasamonte, who was the first to leap forth upon the plain free and unfettered, and who, attacking the prostrate commissary, took from him his sword and the musket, with which, aiming at one and leveling at another, he, without ever discharging it, drove every one of the guards off the field, for they took to flight, as well to escape Pasamonte's musket, as the showers of stones the now released galley slaves were raining upon them. Sancho was greatly grieved at the affair, because he anticipated that those who had fled would report the matter to the Holy Brotherhood, who at the summons of the alarm-bell would at once sally forth in quest of the offenders; and he said so to his master, and entreated him to leave the place at once, and go into hiding in the sierra that was close by.

"That is all very well," said Don Quixote, "but I know what must be done now;" and calling together all the galley slaves, who were now running riot, and had stripped the commissary to the skin, he collected them round him to hear what he had to say, and addressed them as follows: "To be grateful for benefits received is the part of persons of good birth, and one of the sins most offensive to God is ingratitude; I say so because, sirs, ye have already seen by manifest proof the benefit ye have received of me; in return for which I desire, and it is my good pleasure that, laden with that chain which I have taken off your necks, ye at once set out and proceed to the city of El Toboso, and there present yourselves before the lady Dulcinea del Toboso, and say to her that her knight, he of the Rueful Countenance, sends to commend himself to her; and that ye recount to her in full detail all the particulars of this notable adventure, up to the recovery of your longed-for liberty; and this done ye may go where ye will, and good fortune attend you."

Gines de Pasamonte made answer for all, saying, "That which you, sir, our deliverer, demand of us, is of all impossibilities the most impossible to comply with, because we cannot go together along the roads, but only singly and separate, and each one his own way, endeavoring to hide ourselves in the bowels of the earth to escape the Holy Brotherhood, which, no doubt, will come out in search of us. What your worship may do, and fairly do, is to change this service and tribute as regards the lady Dulcinea del Toboso for a certain quantity of Ave-Marias and credos which we will say for your worship's intention, and this is a condition that can be complied with by night as by day, running or resting, in peace or in war; but to imagine that we are going now to return to the flesh-pots of Egypt, I mean to take up our chain and set out for El Toboso, is to imagine that it is now night, though it is not yet ten in the morning, and to ask this of us is like asking pears of the elm tree."

"Then by all that's good," said Don Quixote (now stirred to wrath), "Don son of a bitch, Don Ginesillo de Paropillo, or whatever your name is, you will have to go yourself alone, with your tail between your legs and the whole chain on your back."

Pasamonte, who was anything but meek (being by this time thoroughly convinced that Don Quixote was not quite right in his head as he had committed such a vagary as to set them free), finding himself abused in this fashion, gave the wink to his companions, and falling back they began to shower stones on Don Quixote at such a rate that he was quite unable to protect himself with his buckler, and poor Rocinante no more heeded the spur than if he had been made of brass.

Sancho planted himself behind his ass, and with him sheltered himself from the hailstorm that poured on both of them. Don Quixote was unable to shield himself so well but that more pebbles than I could count struck him full on the body with such force that they brought him to the ground; and the instant he fell the student pounced upon him, snatched the basin from his head, and with it struck three or four blows on his shoulders, and as many more on the ground, knocking it almost to pieces. They then stripped him of a jacket that he wore over his armor, and they would have stripped off his stockings if his greaves had not prevented them. From Sancho they took his coat, leaving him in his shirt-sleeves; and dividing among themselves the remaining spoils of the battle, they went each one his own way, more solicitous about keeping clear of the Holy Brotherhood they dreaded, than about burdening themselves with the chain, or going to present themselves before the lady Dulcinea del Toboso. The ass and Rocinante, Sancho and Don Quixote, were all that were left upon the spot; the ass with drooping head, serious, shaking his ears from time to time as if he thought the storm of stones that assailed them was not yet over; Rocinante stretched beside his master, for he too had been brought to the ground by a stone; Sancho stripped, and trembling with fear of the Holy Brotherhood; and Don Quixote fuming to find himself so served by the very persons for whom he had done so much.

Questions for discussion

1. What is the narrator's position toward the galley slaves? Can you identify any sign of empathy?

2. Ginés de Pasamonte says that he has started writing an autobiographical account of his life, and predicts that it will surpass the picaresque novel *El Lazarillo de Tormes* (1554). Discuss the main characteristics of the picaresque genre, and why is the *Lazarillo* so important from both a literary and historical point of view.

3. The social and political criticism that underlies throughout the whole novel can sometimes be lost for some contemporary readers. For example, a seventeenth century reader was aware that the Spanish Crown was bankrupt, leaving no money to pay for men who would row on the galleys. Therefore, people who committed petty crimes paid for them in an excessive way, by being sent to the galleys for long periods of time. In what ways can Don Quixote's actions be considered an allegorical attack to the Spanish political and economic state of affairs? What is Cervantes' implicit criticism of the government, judicial and penitentiary systems, and of Spanish society in general?

4. In the sixteenth and seventeenth centuries, free will became a disputed theological problem. What is Don Quixote's position on this topic?

DOCUMENT 2
MARÍA DE ZAYAS Y SOTOMAYOR. *NOVELAS AMOROSAS Y EJEMPLARES* (EXEMPLARY TALES OF LOVE AND DISILLUSION, 1637)

Little is known about the life of María de Zayas y Sotomayor (1590–1647?), apart from the fact that she was born to an upper-class family and participated in the literary life of Madrid, where she was referred to as the "Tenth Muse." Like Cervantes, she cultivated the Italian genre of the novella, very popular in Europe at the time. Although she was widely read, she also received harsh criticism. Her writings were considered morbid and inappropriate, most probably because it was unacceptable for a woman writer to include sensual and intimate passages, in addition to overly graphic descriptions of gender violence. María de Zayas was later excluded from the nineteenth century literary canon and her writings did not receive much attention until recently, when she was recovered as a pioneer of Spanish feminism.

Her two collections of *novellas—Novelas amorosas y ejemplares* (Exemplary Tales of Love and Disillusion, 1637) and *Desengaños amorosos* (Disillusion in Love, 1647)— challenge the patriarchal mind-set and the social view towards women prevalent in Counter-Reformation Spain. Many of the stories depict women and children wronged or victimized by cruel men. Zayas usually portrays strong women trying to seek independence, regain their honor and escape the oppression of devious men. Paradoxically, they are usually not successful in achieving their goals. The only escape for women in this misogynistic society seems to be the convent and the only support they can find is other women. The mistreatment of women at the hands of men takes, at times, a dark tone and, at others, an extremely violent turn, especially in *Desengaños amorosos*.

In this prologue, entitled "To the Reader," Zayas shows her awareness of the hurdles she might encounter by using a woman's voice in a crushingly male literary tradition, and at the same time, she defends women's right to equality with men, arguing that souls do not have a gender and that women are not intellectually inferior, but have been treated as such by men, whose best interest was to hamper their access to education.

NOVELAS AMOROSAS Y EJEMPLARES
(EXEMPLARY TALES OF LOVE AND DISILLUSION)

To the reader
Who would doubt, dear reader, that you are surprised that a woman would have the wit, not only to write a book, but also have it published, which is the crucible where the purity

of ingenuity is tested. Until what is written appears in letters of lead, it has little value (as the senses are easily misled, so that poor eyesight sees pure gold, whereas in the light of fire, it is only a piece of polished brass). Who doubts, I say again, there will be many who attribute madness to my virtuous resolution in bringing to light my scribbling, since being a woman, according to some simpletons, is the same as being incapable. But anyone, if only out of courtesy, will neither view it as novelty nor lament its folly, because in this matter of which we are made, both men and women, whether it be the union of fire and clay, or the dough of spirits and lumps of earth, there is no more nobility in men than in us women. After all, it is the same blood, senses, faculties, and organs, where their effects work one and the same; and our soul is the same as theirs, because souls are neither men nor women. What reason exists that men are the learned ones and presumes that we, women, cannot be the same?

In my opinion, there is no other answer than men's wickedness or tyranny in confining us and denying us teachers. Thus, the real reason that women are not learned is not deficient intellect, but rather lack of study, because if in our upbringing instead of putting fine linen on our sewing cushions and embroidery patterns in our frames, they would give us books and teachers, we would be just as qualified for the positions and university professorships as any man. And, maybe we women would be even sharper, since we are of colder nature and understanding consists of humid quality, as can be seen in our quick answers and in our artful thinking, and what is done with craftiness, although not a virtue, it is ingenious. And if this reason is not enough for our reputation, then history will show us what women who fortuitously participated in literary endeavor did, and although it is no excuse for my ignorance, it illustrates my daring.

The poet Lucano acknowledges that his wife Argentaria helped him correct the three books of the *Pharsalia* and composed many of the verses attributed to him. Themistoclea, the sister of Pythagoras, wrote an erudite book of aphorisms. Diotima was venerated by Socrates for her eminence. Aspano gave many lectures in the academies. Eudoxa wrote a book of political advice. Zenobia left a compendium of oriental history. And, Cornelia, Africanus' wife, wrote family letters with great elegance. And, there are many more women both in antiquity and in our times, which I pass over in order not to protract, because you already have heard of this, even if you might be a layman and have not studied it. And since there are polyantheas in Latin and collections of moral principles in the vernacular, the laymen and women can be lettered. Indeed, if all this be true, then what reason exists that we lack aptitude for books? That is true especially if women have my inclination; whenever I see a new or ancient book, I set my sewing aside and do not rest until I have read it. From this disposition knowledge was born, and from knowledge, good taste, and from this followed composing in verse, until the writing of these tales. It could be that many non-erudite books tend to be well received because they deal with an easier or more pleasurable topic, while other books, which are available for sale are filled with subtleties but no one buys them because their subject matter is unimportant or vapid. It is unnecessary to warn you of the compassion you must have, because if the work is good, it will cost you nothing to praise it and if it is bad, then you will show respect out of the courtesy due to any woman.

With women there is no rivalry; whoever does not esteem them is a fool, because women are needed, and whoever betrays them is an ingrate who fails to recognize the hospitality women had given them in their earliest day. Thus, you do not wish to be discourteous, foolish, rude, or ungrateful. I offer this book certain of your gallantry and confident that if it displeases you, you could excuse me since I was born a woman, without any obligation to write good tales, but greatly wishing to please you.

Farewell.

Questions for discussion

1. What is María de Zayas' purpose in writing this prologue? Whom is she addressing?

2. In Counter-Reformation Spain, feminine inferiority was defended by discourses, which asserted that gender differences were grounded on divine or natural laws. How does María de Zayas present her case to prove women's disadvantaged position in society?

3. Could this prologue be considered completely transgressive or defiant?

4. What are the apparent contradictions that modern feminists can find in this prologue?

DOCUMENT 3
BENITO JERÓNIMO FEIJÓO Y MONTENEGRO, "A DEFENSE OR VINDICATION OF WOMEN," 1726 FROM *TEATRO CRÍTICO UNIVERSAL* (UNIVERSAL THEATER OF CRITICISM. FIRST VOLUME. 16TH TREATY, 1726–40)

Benito Jerónimo Feijóo y Montenegro (1676–1764), referred to as the "Spanish Voltaire," was born to a noble, Galician family. Yet, at the age of fourteen, he renounced his inheritance and entered a Benedictine monastery. There, he spent the rest of his life, becoming one of the most polemical scholars of his time. Feijóo introduced Enlightenment ideas in Spain, while trying to debunk the scholastic system that was still prevalent in a country where the Enlightenment was never as strong and widespread as in France. In his writings, Feijóo confronted the traditional values defended by the majority of the Spanish people and the clergy. Instead, he promoted critical thinking, the scientific method, and radical education reform. Although he incessantly attacked superstitions and criticized some rituals and religious practices, he never defied or questioned the Catholic dogma, as he considered that faith could not be an object of scientific analysis.

Feijóo's writings were compiled in two major publications—the eight volumes of *Teatro crítico universal* (Universal Theater of Criticism), published between 1726 and 1740 and the five volumes of *Cartas eruditas* (Intellectual Letters), published from 1742 to 176—which are a good example of Spanish enlightened encyclopedic writing, due to their comprehensive nature and widely-spread readership. In his essays, Feijóo deals with a variety of topics, ranging from philosophy, education, history, literature, and religion, as well as natural and physical sciences, medicine, mathematics and astronomy. The essay, "Defensa de las mujeres" ("A Defense or Vindication of Women"), published in 1726 (translated to English in 1765), introduces revolutionary ideas for its day and it predates Mary Wollstonecraft's *A Vindication of the Rights of Woman* (1792), another ground-breaking publication that advances the cause of women's access to education, as well as women's moral, physical, and intellectual equality to men.

A DEFENSE OR VINDICATION OF WOMEN

I enter upon a serious and difficult undertaking. In such prosecution, it is not only one ignorant and vulgar person I shall have to contend with; for setting about to defend all the women, amounts to pretty much the same thing as resolving to offend all the men (there being one scarce among them, who, in order to give precedence to his own sex, does not endeavor to bring the other into disesteem). To such an extravagant length has this custom of abusing and vilifying the women by common consent been carried, that in a moral sense, they load them with defects, and in the physical one with imperfections, will hardly allow them to possess a single good quality. Still, they lay the greatest stress on the scantiness or limitation of their understandings; for which reason, after briefly vindicating them in other respects, I shall discourse more at large their aptitude, for attaining all forts of science and sublime knowledge.

The false prophet Muhammad denied the women entrance into the ill-laid-out and absurdly-disposed paradise, which he had devised and appropriated to be possessed by his followers, limiting the felicity of the females to beholding from without, the glory and happiness enjoyed by the men within; and it certainly must give the women great pleasure, to survey their husbands in that scene of delights, composed all of turpitudes, clasped in the arms of other comforts, which were feigned to be newly created for this particular purpose by that great artist in fabricating chimeras. Such a delirium being admitted and received by a great part of the world, sufficiently shows, to what a degree mankind is capable of running into error.

But it seems as if these, who deny the women almost every kind of merit in this life, do not differ much from those who deny them happiness in the next. The vilest among the vulgar, very frequently represent that sex as having a most horrible propensity to vice; and would insinuate, that the men are the sole repositories of the virtue. It is certainly true, that you will find these species of sentiments loudly trumpeted forth in an infinite number of books; in some of which, the invective is carried to such a point, as scarcely to admit there is one good woman, and asserting, that their blush, which has been generally considered as an addition to their beauty, and a token of modesty, is the effect of the lewdness of their souls.

Aspera si visa est, rigidasque imitate Sabinas Velle, fed ex alio dissimulare puta.

Instead of replying to such insolent malevolence, the best method is, to treat it with contempt and detestation. Not a few of those, who are most addicted to paint the sex in the blackest coloring, have been observed to be the most felicitous about obtaining their favor and good graces. Euripides, who was exceedingly satirical upon them in his tragedies, as Athenaeus and Stobaeus inform us, was excessively fond of them in private. He execrated them on the theatre, and idolized them in the chamber. Boccace, who was excessively addicted to women, wrote a satyr against them, entitled, *The Labyrinth of Love*. What was the mystery of this? Why is most probably was, that, under the disguise of having an aversion to them, he endeavored to conceal his passion for them; or it might be, that the brutal satiety of the torpid appetite had brought on a loathing, which caused every thing appertaining to the other sex to appear hateful and disgusting. This sort of abuse, may also sometimes proceed from a refusal to lend a kind ear to entreaties and solicitations; for there are men so malevolent, as to be capable of saying a woman is not good, because she has refused to be bad. This unjust motive for complaint and resentment, has sometimes vented itself in the cruellest acts of revenge, an example of which may be instanced in the unhappy fate of that most beautiful Irish lady madam Douglass, against whom, William Leout was blindly irritated, for having refused to comply with his lewd felicitations. To be revenged he accused her of high treason; and procured the calumniating and false charge to be proved by suborned witnesses. She suffered capital punishment; and la Mothe de la Vayer, who (in his Opuse. Scept.) gives the relation, says that Leout himself afterwards confessed the falsity of the accusation, and the wicked means used to prove her guilty.

To this instance, may be added that of a most virtuous and beautiful French lady, the marchioness of Gange. Her two brothers-in-law made dishonorable propositions to her, and successively tried many arts, to prevail on her to gratify their base inclinations; but, not with standing one of them, who was an extreme cunning man, and governed the marquis her comfort entirely, threatened to instill into the mind of her husband suspicions of her fidelity, she vigorously rejected their entreaties. Finding themselves in spite of the menace, repeatedly repulsed with scorn and indignation, they resolved to carry the threat into execution; and, having prevailed on the credulous husband to entertain doubts of his wife's honor and constancy, he consented that the two brothers should take away the life of the innocent marchioness; which they did in a barbarous and cruel manner, by first forcing her to swallow a poisonous draught, but afterwards, doubting of the efficacy of the potion, they gave her several desperate wounds. Although she survived both the wounds and the operation of the poison for the space of nineteen days, and, by means of her relation of the matter, which was corroborated by other circumstances, the officers of justice and the public were informed of the whole transaction, and measures were taken for apprehending the delinquents; yet they, finding themselves discovered, fled the kingdom, and escaped the punishment due to their crime. This tragic event happened in the year 1667, and is related by Gayot Piteval, in his fifth volume of *Remarkable Cafes*.

I don't deny that many of them are vicious; but, alas! If we were to trace their flips and irregularities to their source, I fear we should find them originate in the obstinate and persevering impulse or felicitations of our sex. He, who would wish or endeavor to make all the women good, should begin with converting all the men. Nature implanted modesty in the sex, as a fence wall to resist the attacks of appetite; and it very rarely happens, that a breach is made in this wall by force applied on the inside.

The declamations against the women, which we read in some parts of holy writ, should be understood as pointed and leveled at the perverse ones, as there is no doubt but there are such; and, although they should be supposed to have an eye to the sex in general, nothing could be inferred from thence; because the physicians should declaim against women, as the physicians of the body declaim against fruit, which although it is good, beautiful, and useful in itself, the abuse or excess of it is pernicious: besides this, allowance should be made for the latitude permitted to oratory of magnifying the risqué, when it is used to divert or turn people from dangerous courses.

Let them, who suppose the female sex to be more vicious than ours, tell me, how they can reconcile this, with the church having in an especial manner, bestowed on them the epithet of devout? How with the words of many of the most grave and eminent doctors, who have declared it as their opinion, that there are more women saved than men, even having regard to the proportion, in which it is generally thought the number of females exceeds that of the males which opinion, they do not, nor cannot found on any other thing, than their having observed in them a greater inclination to mercy.

Methinks I already hear, in opposition to our undertaking, that proposition of much noise, and little or no truth, that the women are the cause of all evil; and, by way of providing it, the vulgar, down to the meanest and most contemptible of them, endeavor to inculcate at every turn, that La Caba occasioned the ruin of all Spain, and even that of all mankind.

But the first instance is absolutely a false one. The count Don Julian was the person who brought the Moors into Spain, but was not persuaded to it by his daughter, who did no more than make known to her father the affront and injury she had received. How unhappy is the lot of women, if, in the case of being trampled on by an insolent ravisher, they are to be deprived of the relief of unbosoming themselves to their fathers, or their husbands! The aggressors, in these cases, would gladly deprive them of this relief and benefit; though if at any time an unjust vengeance should be the consequence of the complaint, the fault would not lie at the door of the innocent offended person, but would rest with him who did the execution with the sword and the man who committed the insult; and this the whole blame and crime would be imputable to the men only.

If the second example proves, that the women in general are worse than the men; by the same mode of reasoning it may be proved, that the angels in general are worse than the women; because, as Adam was induced to sin by a woman, the woman was seduced by an angel. It is not yet decided whose sin was the greatest, that of Adam, or that of Eve, because the fathers are divided in their opinions; and, in truth the excuse which Cayetane makes in favor of Eve, that she was deceived by a creature of much superior intelligence and capacity to herself, is a circumstance that cannot be urged on behalf of Adam, and greatly abates her crime in comparison with his.

But passing from the moral to the physical, which is more applicable to our present purpose, we shall find the preference of the robust over the delicate sex is a point settled, and any claim or pretensions to equality on the part of the women is set aside, and treated with contempt; and to such a length has depreciating the women been carried by some, that they have not scrupled to call them imperfect, and even monstrous animals, asserting, that Nature, in the work of generation, never intended to produce any thing but males, and that it was only by mistake, or in consequence of some defect in the matter or faculty, that females were produced.

O admirable adepts in physics! It would follow from hence, that Nature conspired to work its own destruction, because, without the concurrence of both sexes, the species cannot be preserved. It would follow also, that Nature in this her principal work, is more frequently mistaken than right because it is allowed, that she produces more women than men. Nor when we see females the offspring of parents who are healthy, robust, and in the flower of their age, can we attribute the formation of them to debility, want of vigor, or a defect in the matter; nor is it probable, that if man had preserved his original innocence, in which case there would have been nor of these defects, we should have had no women born, and that the human lineage would have been kept up or continued without propagation.

I know very well there was an author, who, for the sake of indulging his malice, and supporting his envious insinuations against the other sex, swallowed so palpable an absurdity. This was Almaricus, a Parisian doctor of the twelfth century, who, among other errors, asserts that, if the state of innocence had continued, all the individuals of our species would have been males, and that God would have created them immediately himself as he did Adam. Almaricus was a blind follower of Aristotle, insomuch that all, or very near all his errors, were produced by conclusions, which he had drawn from the doctrines of that philosopher; and, seeing that Aristotle, in more than one part of his works, gives it to be understood, that a female is a defective animal, its generation accidental, and out of the design of nature, he concluded, that there were no women in the state of innocence; and thus it comes to pass, that an heretical theology is very frequently occasioned by a mistake in physics.

But the great and avowed adherence of Almaricus to Aristotle, was rather unfortunate to them both; because the errors of Almaricus were condemned by a council held at Paris in 1209; and, in the same council, the reading of the books of Aristotle were prohibited, which prohibition was afterwards confirmed by Pope Gregory IX. Almaricus had been dead a year when his dogmas were proscribed; but his bones were afterwards dug up, and thrown into a jake.

This shows, that we should not lay any great stress upon the opinion of a few doctors, who, though they were in other respects discreet men, have asserted, that the female sex is defective (...) It is certain, that Aristotle's treatment of the women proceeded from spite for he not only proclaimed with vehemence their physical defects, but was more vehement still in blazoning their moral ones; some instances of which, I shall point out in another place. Who would not suppose from all this, that his disposition inclined him to shun the sex? But nothing so opposite to him, for he not only tenderly loved two wives which he married, but his affection for the first, named Pythais, who, as some say, was daughter, others niece of Hermias, tyrant of Atarneus, carried him so far beside himself, that he franticly offered incense to her as a deity. They also give us relation of his loose amours with a little servant girl, though Plutarch does not incline to credit the tale; but in this business, the testimony of Theocritus Chio, who was contemporary to Aristotle, for his obscenity. From this influence we may perceive, that men's seeming malignity to, and inveterate abuse of women, is, as we have observed before, frequently accompanied with an inordinate inclination for them.

From the same physical error, which condemned woman for an imperfect animal, there sprung another theological one, which is combated by St. Austin, in *Lib. 22, de Civit. Dei cap. 17*. The authors of this system say, that, at the universal resurrection, this imperfection is to be remedied, by converting all women into men; and that then, grace is complete and finish the work which nature had only began.

This error is very like that of the infatuated Alchemists, who, relying on the maxim, that nature in the formation of metals, never intended to produce anything but gold, and that it was only from some obstruction, or from some defect of vigor and virtue, that she fabricated other imperfect metals; also pretend, that art is afterwards capable of carrying the work to perfection, and making gold of that which was originally produced iron. But, after all, this error is most sufferable of the two, because it does not interfere with matters of faith; and because also, let the intention of nature in the formation of metals, and the imaginary capacity of art, be what they will, it is a fact, that gold is the most noble of metals, and that the others are of a much inferior quality compared to it. But, in our present question, the assertion, that Nature always intended the production of males, and that her producing females was the effect of a bastard operation, is all false and erroneous, and much more so is the affirming, that this is to be amended at the resurrection.

I would not, however, be understood to approve of what is thrown out by Zacuto Lusitano, in the introduction to his *Treatise De Morbis Mulierum*, where, with frivolous reasons, he attempts to give the preference to the women, and to persuade us, that their physical perfections greatly exceed those of men. Such an opinion, might be supported by much more plausible arguments that are used by him; but my view is not to persuade a superiority, but only an equality.

And to begin, setting aside the question of their understandings, which I mean to discuss separately and more at large in this discourse, let us consider the three endowments, in which the men seem manifestly to have the advantage of the women, to wit, robustness, constancy, and prudence; but, although this should be granted by the women, they might pretend to a competition, by pointing out other three qualities, in which they excel the male sex, to wit, beauty, gentleness and simplicity.

Robustness, which is a bodily perfection, may be considered as counterpoised by beauty, which is so likewise. Many people are disposed to give the last the preference; and they would be right, if that was esteemed the most valuable, which is the most flattering or pleasing to the sight: but the consideration of which is most useful to the public, should, in the eye of sound judgment, weigh most in deciding the question; and, viewing the thing in this light, robustness must be preferred to beauty. The robustness of men, furnishes the world with three most essential benefits, which may not improperly be termed the three columns, which support every state, to wit, arms, agriculture, and mechanics. From the beauty of women, I do not know what important advantage can accrue, unless it comes by accident. Some will argue, that beauty, so far from producing benefits, occasions serious mischiefs, by causing unruly amours, which inflame and excite competitions and strife, and which involve those who are charged with the custody of women, in cares, uneasiness's, and anxiety.

But this accusation, as it originates from a want of reflection, is ill founded; for supposing, for argument's sake, that all the women were ugly, and those who were blemished with the fewest deformities, we should experience the same attraction, which we do at present in the handsome ones, and they would consequently occasion the same mischief. The least ugly placed in Greece would have caused the burning of Troy, as Helen did; and placed in the palace of King Roderigo, would have been the ruin of Spain, as la Caba was. In those countries where the women are the least tempting, there are no fewer disorders than, there are in those where they are more genteelly, and more admirably formed: even in Muscovy, which in number of handsome women exceeds all the other kingdoms in Europe, incontinence is not so unbridled as in other countries, and conjugal faith is observed there, with more exactness than in other places.

Beauty therefore of itself, is not the cause of the mischiefs which are attributed to it; notwithstanding which, in the present question, I must give my vote in favor of robustness, as I esteem it a much more important quality than beauty, and therefore, in this particular, must give the preference to the men. There is, however, saved and remaining to the women, if they chose to avail themselves of it, an objection to this decision, which may be founded on the judgment of many learned men, and which was assented to and admitted by a whole illustrious school: this judgment, recognizes the will for a more noble faculty than the understanding, which is rather favorable to their cause; for if robustness, as being of the most consequence, is, in the general opinion, most prized and valued, beauty, as the more amiable quality, has most control over will.

The virtue of constancy, which ennobles the men, may be contrasted with docility, which is resplendent in the women. But it will be proper here to remark, that we do not treat of these or other qualities, as formally considering them in the state of virtues, because in this sense, they are not of the lineage of nature, but only as they are grafted into, and displayed themselves in temperament or habit; and, as the embryo of information is indifferent to receive good or bad impressions, it would be better to call them flexibility, or inflexibility of disposition, than constancy or docility.

I may be told, that the docility of women degenerates many times into levity; to which I answer that the constancy of men as frequently terminates in tenaciousness. I confess that firmness in a good cause is productive of great benefits; but it can't be denied, that obstinacy in a bad one is also productive of great evils. If it is argued, that an invincible adherence to good or evil is a quality appertaining to angels only: I answer, that this is not certain, for many great theologians deny it; and many properties, which in superior beings spring from their excellence, in inferior ones proceed from their imperfection. The angels, according to the doctrine of St. Thomas, are more perfect, the fewer things they understand; in men, their knowledge being confined to a few particulars, is considered a defect. In angels, study would be regarded as a diminution of, or a reflection upon their understandings; although it is known to be absolutely necessary, to illustrate and adorn those of men.

The prudence of men may be balanced by the simplicity or gentleness of the women; and I was even about to say more than balanced, for, in reality, simplicity or gentleness, is more beneficial to the human race, than the prudence of all individuals; for nobody has ever described the golden age as composed of prudent, but of candid men.

If it is objected, that much of that which is called simplicity in women, is thoughtlessness or inattention: I reply, that much of that which is called prudence in men, is fallacy, duplicity and treachery, which are much worse qualities. Even that very indiscreet frankness, with which they sometimes incautiously unbosom themselves, is a good token, considered as a symptom. No person is ignorant of his own vices; and whoever finds himself loaded with them to a large amount, is very careful to shut the crevices of his heart, to prevent the prying of curiosity: whoever commits criminal disorders within his house, does not leave his doors open at all hours, and by that means expose himself to be detected. Reserve is the inseparable companion of a bad heart. (...) Considered then in this light, the simplicity or candor of the women, is always a valuable quality; but, when conducted with good sense, it approaches to perfection; and, when it is not, it may always be looked upon as favorable symptom. (...)

I shall conclude this discourse, by endeavoring to set aside an exception that may be made to the undertaking; which is, that persuading mankind of the intellectual equality of both sexes, does not seem to be productive of any utility to the public, but is rather likely to occasion mischief, as it tends to foment in the women, presumption and pride.

I might reply to this scruple, by only saying, that, in whatever matter that may present itself to our reflection, knowing the truth, and setting aside error, is an utility which is apparent, and of itself sufficient to justify our enquiry. The right understanding of things, is of itself estimable, without regard to any other end or object in the creation. Truths have their intrinsic value, and the stock, or riches of the understandings, does not consist of any other money. Some pieces are more valuable than others, but none are useless. Nor can the truth we have proved, of itself, induce in the women vanity or presumption. If they, in the perfections of the soul, are truly equal to us, there can be no harm in their knowing, or being sensible to it. (...) The women then, by knowing what they are, if they don't estimate their qualifications above their real value, can never become vain-glorious, or presumptuous; but by attending to the thing, it will be found, the deception this chapter is calculated to remove, will rather have a different effect; and instead of adding presumption to the women, will take it away from the men. (...)

I have not yet told all the utility, which, in a moral sense, will result to both the men and the women, by extricating them from the error they lay under, with respect to the inequality of the sexes. I firmly believe, this error is the cause, of many marriage-beds having been dishonored and contaminated with adulteries. It may seem that I am entangling myself in a strange paradox, but this is not the case; I having done no more, than assert an established truth. Attend.

A few months after the souls of two consorts, are united together by the matrimonial bond, a woman begins to lose that estimation, which she at first obtained, as a delectable object, newly acquired, and recently possessed. The man, passes from tenderness to lukewarmness, which luke-warmness many times, comes to end in contempt, and positive misestimating. When the husband arrives at this vicious extreme, he presuming on the advantages which he supposes to be annexed to be superiority of his sex, begins to triumph over, an insult his wife; instructed by, and versed in those sentences, which pronounce, that the most which a woman can attain, may be attained by a boy of fourteen years old, and that it is in vain, to seek for either sense of prudence in them, together with other ridiculous, and injurious reflections of the same kind; treating every thing he observes in his wife with the utmost contempt. In this situation, if the poor woman attempts to remonstrate, she is accused of raving; all she says is impertinent, and foreign to the purpose; all she does is wrong. If she is handsome, the attraction of her beauty stands her in little stead, for its charm is dissolved, and the security of possessing it, has made it of no value. The husband only recollects that his wife is an imperfect animal; and if he neglects her, will upbraid the most spotless woman with being a vase of impurities.

When the unhappy woman is in this humiliating and dejected state, a gallant casts fond, or, as we commonly say in Spain, good eyes on her. To her, who at all times is condemned to see nothing but a frowning brow, it is natural to suppose, a pleasant countenance appears very delightsome: and such a leading circumstance conduces much to bring on, and facilitate a conversation between the parties; in which, the woman hears nothing but what is flattering and pleasing to her. Before this, she used to be accosted in naught but terms of reproach and contempt, and now, she is addressed in expressions of tenderness and adoration. She lately was treated as something beneath a woman; and now, she is elevated to the sphere of a divinity. She was accustomed lately to be called nothing but fool; and now, she is told that she possesses a sublime understanding. In the language of her husband, she was all imperfections; in that of her gallant, she is all charms and graces. The partner of her bed, lorded it over her like a tyrant master; the other, throws himself at her feet as an humble slave; and although the lover, if he had been her husband, would have acted just as the husband did: this reflection escapes the miserable wife, and she only sees that sort of difference between them, which there is between an angel and a brute. She views in her husband, a heart full of thorns; and in her gallant, one crowned with flowers. There a chain of iron presents itself to her sight; here a golden one. There slavery; here dominion. There a dungeon; here a throne.

In this situation, what can the most resolute woman do? How can she resist two impulses, directed to the same point, one that impels, and the other, which attracts her? If heaven does not stretch forth a powerful and a friendly hand to support her, her fall is inevitable. And if she does fall, who can deny that her own husband forced her over the precipice? If he had not treated her with indignity and abusive railing, the flattery of the lover would have been of no avail. It was his ill treatment, which occasioned her downfall. All this mischief, most frequently proceeds from the mean opinion, which married men are apt to entertain of the other sex. Let them renounce these erroneous maxims, and the consequence will be that their wives will become more faithful and constant. Let them cherish and esteem them, for God has commanded they should love them; and I can't understand, how love and contempt, with respect to the same object, can be entertained, and accommodate themselves together in one and the same heart.

Questions for discussion

1. Who is the intended audience for this essay?

2. "On Defense of Women" was extremely controversial for his contemporaries. Identify which, in your opinion, would have been the most provocative points of this essay, by means of the Enlightenment discourse in eigtheenth-century Spain and beyond.

3. The notion that women's bodies spoke to their weakness and inferiority was widely spread European lore. It appeared in essays such as "*Examen de ingenios*"

("The Examination of Men's Wits," 1575) by Spanish humanist, Huarte de San Juan. How does Feijóo question the inadequacy of this widespread belief?

4. How does the content of this document affect the political and social opportunities of women in the centuries ahead? Is there any value in reading this document today?

DOCUMENT 4
FRANCISCO JOSÉ DE GOYA Y LUCIENTES. *EL SUEÑO DE LA RAZÓN PRODUCE MONSTRUOS* (THE SLEEP OF REASON PRODUCES MONSTERS, 1799)

Francisco de Goya (1746–1828) is the most remarkable Spanish painter of the late eighteenth and early nineteenth centuries. His early paintings, drawings, and engravings depict both aristocratic and popular pastimes, as well as other scenes of Spanish contemporary life. Goya had a long career at court. It started in 1775 with a series of more than sixty cartoons for the Royal Tapestry Factory, under the direction of German painter, Anton Raphael Mengs (1728–79). From the simplicity of European Neoclassical style, Goya evolved to a more personal one, which was in part a result of Velázquez (1599–1660), and the expressive realism present in his work. In 1786, he was appointed royal painter to the enlightened Bourbon king, Charles III, and later to Charles IV. He painted the portraits of both kings, as well as many other court officials and members of the aristocracy. He drew with astonishing results on realism, and a type of characterization that is not always flattering, producing at times a caricature-like effect.

At the height of Goya's career, Napoleon's troops invaded Spain (1808) and both Charles IV and Ferdinand VII went into exile. Goya's sympathies for the French ruler, José Bonaparte, helped him retain his position as first court painter, but upon the restoration of Ferdinand VII, Goya had to prove his allegiance to him through two large, dramatic paintings that commemorated the heroic response of the people of Madrid to the French invasion: "The 2nd of May 1808: The Charge of the Mamelukes" and "The 3rd of May 1808: The Execution of the Defenders of Madrid." In response to the violence and numerous atrocities, degradation, and tragedies that the War of Independence brought about to soldiers and the civilian population alike, he also painted a vivid series of prints entitled, "Los desastres de la guerra" ("The Disasters of War" (1810–20). In his last years, he became deaf and he started to isolate himself while painting a series of expressionistic frescoes in the walls of his country house, the so-called "Quinta del Sordo," which show his state of despair, his misanthropy, his skeptic negativity, and his overall disillusion. He died in exile in Bourdeaux, France.

The etching below, entitled *El sueño de la razón produce monstruos* (The Sleep of Reason Produces Monsters), belongs to the series *Los Caprichos* (The Whims), a collection of eighty etchings that dates from Spring 1797 to Fall 1798, a period of social and political instability in Spain. In many of these etchings, Goya depicts distorted creatures with bestial and diabolic faces that are, nevertheless, infused with human features. "The Sleep of Reason" has been considered by art critics to be one of Goya's

Figure 1. Francisco José de Goya y Lucientes. *El sueño de la razón produce monstruos* (The Sleep of Reason Produces Monsters, 1797–9).

many self-portraits, but there is no agreement in the meaning of the title and the etching itself.

Questions for discussion

1. The ambiguity of the title of this etching rests in the fact that the word "sueño" can mean "sleep," but also "dream." Is Goya trying to say that when reason is not present, the imagination produces monsters and chaos; or rather that reason alone may lead to madness? What is, in your opinion, the meaning of this etching?

2. Goya was a great admirer of Cervantes, and Don Quixote was his favorite character. Do you think Don Quixote is a good example of the prevalence of imagination over reason? In what ways, does Cervantes' message differ from Goya's?

3. This etching has often been compared to Goya's portrait of Gaspar Melchor de Jovellanos, one of the most renowned figures of the Spanish Enlightenment. We will learn more about his views on education in Module 5. For now, describe Goya and Jovellanos' common views on political ideas.

4. Goya was initially a supporter of mild Bourbon reformism, but soon became a convinced liberal. Was this ideological shift akin to that of other Spaniards of the Enlightenment period?

DOCUMENT 5
XAVIER BADIA-VILATÒ, POSTER "AMBITION, MILITARISM, WAR. THIS IS FASCISM. UNITE TO DESTROY IT," 1936

The Spanish Civil War (1936–9) is one of the most significant events in contemporary European history, and is widely considered by many to be the prelude of World War II. On July 18, 1936, the government of the democratically-elected Second Republic (1931–9) suffered a *coup d'etat* led by the right-wing forces of the army. What could have been a short conflict, turned into a bloody civil war, when civilians took to arms to assist soldiers loyal to the Republic. The Republican army incorporated a mixed coalition of groups with conflicting ideologies (anarchists, socialists, and communists, among others), and was aided by the Soviet Union and the International Brigades (military units made up of volunteers from various countries). The rebels called themselves "Nationalists," led by the General Francisco Franco, and aided by Fascist Italy and Nazi Germany. They won the war in 1939, after three years of intense fighting which devastated the country's economic and social structure.

War posters are invaluable historical documents that help us visualize the landscape of the Spanish Civil War and how people experienced it. Eyewitness's correspondence and memoirs mention the omnipresence of propaganda art in prominent public spaces of most Spanish towns. Both sides used imagery to convey political messages, condemn an attack, or defend the righteousness of their cause. Most posters are very large, display huge contrasts, and hold an optimistic tone. The poster below has a focused agenda and was designed to attract the sympathy of the viewers toward the anti-fascist Republican forces.

Most of the Spanish Civil War posters are anonymous. Although we can identify the designer of the piece included here, not much else is known about his life. Xavier Badia-Vilatò (1916–2012) was an anarchist artist who designed propaganda posters to aid the Republican cause. After the war, he lived in France where he became a militant of the group, International Antifascist Solidarity. In 1947, he published a series of anti-Francoist lithographs entitled *Imágenes de la España franquista* (Images of Fascist Spain).

Figure 2. Xavier Badia-Vilatò. *Ambiciones, militarismo, guerra. Esto es el fascismo. Destrúyelo uniendo tu esfuerzo al de los demás* (Ambition, Militarism, War. This is Fascism. Unite to Destroy it, 1936).

Questions for discussion

1. Through a collage-like layering of images, the poster contrasts two ideologies. Explain how this is done. What is the symbolism of the dove and the hand? In what ways, does color reinforce the pacifist message? What is the color that represents peace in this poster?

2. The influence of surrealism in Badia-Vilatò's work is apparent in *Images of Fascist Spain*. Can you also find some surrealist traits in the poster (p. 32)?

3. Republican propaganda posters used loaded messages and images to change the attitude toward its cause not only in Spain, but also abroad. What do you think about propagandistic art? Is it justified to manipulate human emotions for a good cause?

4. Many Republican war posters had to show an optimistic message to avoid defeatism. Do you think this is one of them?

DOCUMENT 6
MARÍA ZAMBRANO, *PARA UNA HISTORIA DE LA PIEDAD* (FOR A HISTORY OF MERCY, 1989)

María Zambrano (1904–91) is one of the most radically original Spanish philosophers of the twentieth century. Her genealogical critique on discursive reason and metaphysics unveils what she described as "Western philosophical impostures." She was influenced by the secularization and innovative educational reforms of the *Institución Libre de Enseñanza* (Free Pedagogical Institute). She attended the classes of José Ortega y Gasset and held a position as assistant to the Chair of Metaphysics at the University of Madrid from 1931 to 1936. Her political involvement with the Republican government during the Spanish Civil War forced her into an exile that lasted for almost fifty years. During this time, she taught at different universities in Cuba, Mexico, Puerto Rico, Chile, Italy, Greece, France, and Switzerland. Upon her return to Spain in 1984, she was recognized for her intellectual work by receiving the *Premio Cervantes* (1988), among other prestigious awards.

As Ortega y Gasset's disciple, her philosophy presents a personal approach to ratiovitalism. For Zambrano, philosophy's goal is to reach the knowledge of the spirit and philosophers' aim should be the construction and interpretation of the mysteries and symbols directly related to the transcendence of human beings and their relationship with the divine. She explores the relationship between philosophy and Christianity, philosophy and poetry, and philosophy and history. In *Filosofía y poesía* (Philosophy and Poetry, 1939), she analyzes the ways in which both aim at achieving eternity and immortality; philosophy does it through meditation and poetry through intuition. In *El hombre y lo divino* (Man and the Divine, 1955) she approaches mercy as a philosophical problem and claims that we can reach the divine through what she terms "poetic reasoning." Throughout her more than twenty volumes of writings, Zambrano insists on the importance of personal responsibility, and the need of compassion in human relationships, while reflecting on the notions of hope and the connection of human beings to the divine. She also urges philosophers to recognize the importance of instinct, passion, poetry, and the irrational to achieve alternative ways to philosophize. Hers is a constant strive for the authentic being in human experience. Perfectly aware of her historical condition, Maria Zambrano's work is an essential reading to understand how the intellectual must engage art in the pursuit of peace and understanding.

PARA UNA HISTORIA DE LA PIEDAD (FOR A HISTORY OF MERCY)

Before history appeared, there was a prehistory of history: poetry. It is founded by certain poems like *The Iliad* and *The Odyssey*, as well as other poems. They featured the oldest of all civilizations, where the first stories and visions of human events appeared. These stories are poetic; therefore religious, and eminently dramatic. In such poems, only extraordinary individuals appear, and they are agents of large feats. History is the account of great and extraordinary actions; being in history itself means to enter a certain immortality that separates the heroes from the rest of the mortals.

This heroic sense of history has endured remarkably, like all the origins. History as an account of immemorial feats still persists, especially in the *naïve* consciousness of the people. It is the memory of what is wondrous. But history has also been science and, in this field, it went to pick up facts, mere events, that were decisive and transcendent, but that did not necessarily have to be heroic. To be transcendent means nothing but not ending in itself, that is, to trespass its own limits. Moreover, this scientific way of making history, left aside everyday life; the life that elapses without fanfare and forms the plot, the only scrim where one can draw the extraordinary action or transcendent event.

This anonymous life that did not reach the historical category has been the subject of the novel numerous times. Hence, the best history in some periods of Western culture has been the novel, the best history and the best sociology, since it corresponds to what is now known as the study of "life forms." That is the situation now; more than extraordinary and transcendent individuals and events, it is important to capture the forms of life, the way life is modeled through economic, social, and political relations, among others. But there is something else in the novel and in poetry.

Novel and poetry have reflected better than the historical knowledge, the true life, the truth about the things that happen to people and their inner sense. In order to be complete and truly human, history will have to descend to the most secret places of the human being, the so-called "insides." The insides are the least visible, not only because they cannot be seen, but because they resist being seen. And the insides are the seat of emotions. But the term "feelings" is so broad that we should stop there because within its field lies mercy, the feeling we are providing a brief history of.

Is it just a feeling? Perhaps, in the realm of the mental life, there is nothing more difficult to define than feelings. When we try to understand them, we realize that they constitute the entire life of the soul, that they are the soul. What would happen to a man if the capacity to feel could be removed from him? He would even cease feeling his own self. Every single thing that can be the object of knowledge, everything that can be thought of or subjected to experience, all that can be desired, or calculated, is previously felt somehow; this applies to the being itself because if it could only be understood or perceived, it would not address its own center, the person. Making an effort to imagine this state, we see it as a kind of abstract dream, a total alienation in which even the things themselves would not be perceived due to a lack of interest, due to the absence of someone who perceives them.

More than any other psychic function, the capacity to feel creates who we are; we could say that while we possess the rest of the psychic functions, feeling is what we are. Thus, feeling has always been the supreme sign of authenticity, of thriving truth; it has been the ultimate source of legitimacy for what human beings say, do or think.

With so brief an observation, we see that if something has the right and the necessity of history is, precisely this vast world of feelings, because its history will be the most accurate history of humankind. However, the difficulty is great, according to a law that seems to preside all human affairs: the greater the need, the greater the difficulty. Feelings are abundant and elusive; since they are the liveliest thing of our lives, they are also the most intangible; the most ready to escape, leaving us with a kind of effervescent vacuum, when we try to capture them.

They are the most rebellious to be defined. That is the reason why poetry and novel have been their best channels. Because what characterizes feelings is the capacity to be expressed, not analyzed. Expression is part of the life of feelings and, when it is achieved, far from fading, they acquire an adamantine kind of entity that makes them transparent and invulnerable to time. Since in our present time, a rationalist notion about the life of the soul has prevailed, knowing about feelings has been decreasing, finding shelter in the most hermetic places. One of the greatest misfortunes and hardships of our time is the inscrutability of deep life, of the true life of feelings, which went into hiding in less and less accessible places. Creating its history, albeit timidly, will be a liberating task.

But what is mercy in the immense and delicate world of feelings? It is perhaps the initial feeling, the widest and most profound; something like the homeland for the rest of the feelings. Although hesitantly expressed, this might seem a very bold assertion, but we hope that along these brief pages, this idea will gain power in the mind of the hypothetical reader. We have to start with an attempt to "present" this feeling, since a definition is, as we have indicated, the most inadequate and clumsy way to approach mercy. But, since feelings—especially mercy—do not have an adequate definition, they must have a history. The objects that have an adequate definition, to the point of coinciding with it, are called "ideal objects": a triangle, a character from a novel, a thousand-faced polygon, and a round square do not have a history. Instead, that which seems impossible to be captured in a definition, is expressed without losing any thing in its multiple and successive manifestations; that is, it is expressed in its history.

Mercy cannot be adequately defined, because it constitutes the epitome of a specific type of feelings: the amorous and positive ones. Mercy is not love itself in any of its forms and meanings; it is not charity either, a particular form of mercy discovered by Christianity; it is not even compassion, a more generic and diffuse passion. Mercy is like the prehistory of all positive feelings. And yet, it accompanies them in their history, and mercy itself has a history. And here we have to stop to see the specific form feelings take in their historical path.

The idea we have about the historical path, like any path where time is involved, is one of destruction: "the destructive time" is the image that lingers in the consciousness of almost all human beings; hence, the history of feelings or anything of what constitutes the intimacy of the human condition has not been attempted yet. History seemed to be a sequence of things that destroy the previous ones, a sort of parade of fleeting shining instants that are replaced by other shinning instants. The philosopher Bergson has provided a masterful criticism of this linear conception of the passage of time, which has been represented as a series of dots that follow one another and that they are consumed as they pass by. Time, according to Bergson, it is growth with multiple forms, in which every instant penetrates and is penetrated by other instants; instead of destroying, time creates. This fundamental thesis of contemporary metaphysics casts a bright light on our topic, since feelings, in their history, do not destroy each other. Therefore, Mercy can be the mother to all positive or amorous feelings, without being swept by them, as they come.

Moreover, it is also something that contradicts the common idea that feelings appear in history, instead of appearing all of a sudden. We still have the idea that human beings are formed once, and forever. Maybe so, but it is also true that the capacities or potencies of their being are revealed progressively, while manifesting themselves throughout History. That is why there might be, there is, a history of feelings; because humans have not shown suddenly from the outset of their appearance on Earth, all its fullness and complexity; these are revealed, unraveled. The horrors and sufferings that History is littered with, are "ultimately" justified. Through the vicissitudes of History, the human being unravels, is brought to light; that is, the human being is being born in History, instead of having been born once.

Mercy appears to us as the matrix where the life of feelings originates. Let's see why. Without trying to define it, as has already been said, we must form a certain idea of what we understand by it. To this end, we should dispose of the idea of feeling, since, as it happens with all elaborated and widely used concepts, it carries a load of misconceptions. Moreover, the very term "feeling" corresponds precisely to the stage of thought where mercy has been more unknown. Thus, if we approach it directly, it seems to escape us. But there is a very old way to get to these entities and it is what theologians have called the negative way. An ancient Hindu mystic referred to God by saying that it is "neither this nor that." This definition has reached throughout the ages the highest theology with Plotinus and the highest mystics. The subtle things that cannot be apprehended by their presence, can be perceived through their absence, through the gap they leave. And we should not be scared by such a procedure, because we surely have experienced it in our own lives: we feel what the loved person or the friend are when we lose them, because of the irreparable void they leave us with; the same goes with homeland landscapes, with health, and with the possessions that are indescribable because of their immensity. They overflow our soul, they flood our consciousness, and they possess us. How do you define them?

To define is to see distinctly the limits of one thing, and seeing it requires to have it at a distance, to distinguish the limits of what is seen, to see it among other things in the same plane, forming a set. Large goods and evils, by contrast, possess us; we feel that they exceed our life and our consciousness. Almost always we need to lose them or to have them concealed in order to recognize them through their absence.

Thus is mercy. Undoubtedly, it has suffered in recent times an intense eclipse which coincides with the rise of rationalism. Enthusiasm for reason and for its results, the light radiating from rational knowledge seems to have thrown its shadow over Mercy. Since this has been happening for quite some time, we can look with perspective and ask ourselves: what are we missing? That which the wonderful methods of science and technical creations could not give us. Which is our situation as human beings in the Universe? And the answer comes to our conscience immediately, as if it was there, before the question was posed: we are alone, alone as human beings and alone in front and among things: we dominate them, we handle them, but we do not communicate with them. If we were to take mercy as the act of treating people, animals and plants gently, it could seem that such communication exists. But mercy is not philanthropy, or compassion for animals and plants. It is something else: it is what allows us to communicate with them; in short, it is the diffuse and gigantic feeling that places us appropriately among all the planes of being, and among different beings. Mercy is knowing how to deal with what is different, with that which is radically other than us.

The idea that a man is, above all, conscience and reason has led us to consider that only another man can be equal to him. But the process does not stop there, because as differences exist between men and since there are races, nationalities, cultures, social classes, and economic differences, we have come to the quite apparent spectacle of current society. We only know how to deal with those, which are almost a reproduction of ourselves. When the modern man looks out to the world, he is searching for a mirror that reflects his own image, and when he cannot find it, he is puzzled and often he wants to break the mirror. We have become terribly incapable to understand that there are people different from us. To fill up this void, the word "tolerance" was invented, a favorite term in the vocabulary of modern society. But "tolerance" is neither understanding nor proper treatment; it is simply, keeping distance, respectfully, with everything we do not know how to deal with.

Other periods of time show us an opposite situation, like the Middle Ages for example, when mercy was not eclipsed. Naturally, without violence, without speeches or official organizations, medieval people knew how to deal with that which was different in a spontaneous way: in the human world it was the incurable patient, even the monstrous or the criminal. Beyond humanity, there were chimeras and ghosts, angels and Gods. God Himself was not conceived as a great consciousness, it was not reduced to humanity. Instead, the modern man has tried to reduce everything to what he can find immediately within himself; to what he believes is his essence: to conscience, to reason. Everything has been reduced to reason and conscience and that which resisted this transformation, became unknown, forgotten and, sometimes, reviled.

And that is how we ended up alone; alone and unable to deal with "the other." But if we put together the various kinds of "otherness," we realize that it is nothing but reality, the reality that surrounds us and where we are anchored. Thus, we perceive more clearly the vital problem, which was hidden under the problem of knowledge in the last stages of Philosophy. It is known that the problem was precisely reality, the apprehension of reality. It seems that consciousness and intelligence by themselves do not provide assurance that we are in contact with reality. And science, with all its splendid results, has also failed to give humans the deep conviction that they are knowing reality, that irreplaceable communion that human beings had in more *naïve* and pious ages.

Reality, and philosophers discover this fact again, occurs somewhere previous to knowledge, to the idea. The Spanish philosopher Ortega y Gasset developed the concept of "vital reason" based on his discovery that the reality is prior to the idea, contrary to what Idealism formulated. And if reality is prior to the idea, it has to be given through feelings. Mercy can be understood as the feelings experienced by a subject, by someone who feels reality not in a diffuse and homogeneous way, but distinguishes instead the "species" and type of realities that somehow must be favorable to him. That is, a subject who feels reality and at the same time feels himself heterogeneous from it. Awareness of solitude and, at the same time, consciousness of participation, sociability. The rationalist believes that reality is given through an idea or thought and that only by reducing reality to thought he can understand it. Mercy is the feeling of the heterogeneity of being, of quality of being, and therefore it is the yearning to find the ways of understanding and deal with each one of those multiple ways of reality.

This which is evident to us now by contrast, and as we stated above, by absence, was an ingenuous belief before rationalism; ingenuity and the further back in history we look, the stronger this ingenuity was, until we see it constitutes the mentality, the way of life of primitive peoples.

Does human progress inevitably condemn mercy? Modern ethics has sought to replace it with different virtues or values, such as philanthropy, cooperation, and justice. Today everything is asked on behalf of justice and what it is given is equally awarded on its behalf. Will it be enough? Will values such as justice or cooperation be able to fill that sentimental gap left by mercy, and feed the flame of creation? Will the heart and the entrails of humans be satisfied with nothing more but what is being granted by justice? Can the anguish that we feel today be dissipated with remedies born in the mind? Reason and justice are sisters, they walk together; one is in practice what the other is in knowledge. But their sole rule will assume that humans only need to know visible and tangible things and to feed from them. But since you do not live from bread alone, justice and reason are not enough.

Won't there be, away from distinct and clear knowledge, the necessity of other knowledge that is less distinct and clear, but equally indispensable? Are not there things and relationships so subtle, hidden and indiscernible that they can only by apprehended by feeling or intuition? Will we be able to dispense with inspiration? In sum, let's say the dreaded word that we have been concealing so far. Will it not be a bedrock of mystery supporting everything that is clear and visible, everything that can be enumerated? This would be the ultimate and abysmal bottom of the inexhaustible reality that man feels in himself, filling him up in the happy moments and in suffering; joy and suffering appear endless. And in them it is when we feel that reality not only touches us, but also absorbs us, it inundates us.

Mercy is knowing how to deal with the mystery. That is why its language and its ways have repulsed the modern man who has thrown himself frantically to deal only with what is clear and distinct. Descartes assigned to ideas the qualities of "clarity" and "distinction." Nothing can be challenged but, insensibly, we have come to believe that "clarity" and "distinction" are also the notes of reality. And the truth is that only very few realities can achieve that privilege, those to which we alluded earlier, saying that they are the ones that can be defined. However, there is a vast territory that surrounds us and hugs us that sometimes reject us, submerging us in anguish and despair, and these feelings are neither clear nor distinct. And there they are; we have to deal with them every instant. It is simply our own life. Mystery is not found outside; it is within each of us, surrounding and enfolding us. We live and we move within mystery. The guide to avoid getting lost in it resides in Mercy.

Questions for discussion

1. What does Zambrano mean when she says that "poetry" is the "prehistory of history"? What are the disadvantages of the "scientific way of making history"? How do we know reality? Why is science insufficient to understand human beings and the universe they live in? In what way is Zambrano's view of history different from the traditional one?

2. What is Zambrano's approach to explain the concept of "mercy"? Why does she say it cannot be defined? Explain the role "mercy" had in the Middle Ages, as well as its present-day role.

3. What are Zambrano's thoughts about the relationship among human beings? Why is communication difficult?

4. Read about Miguel de Unamuno's concept of *intrahistoria* and explain what it has in common with Zambrano's view of history.

5. Just as José Ortega y Gasset, Zambrano rejects deductive and inductive methodologies of analytic reason to understand reality. What is the relationship between Zambrano's "poetic reason" and José Ortega y Gasset's "vital reason"? How are these concepts different from Nietzsche's vitalism?

MODULE 2
LABOR AND BUSINESS HISTORY[1]

ABSTRACT

The texts included in this module are a selection of documents pertaining to Spain's labor history and the development of liberalism. Contrary to the commonplace assertion that Spain was a latecomer in bringing liberalism and reform to economic life, the two documents included here by Pedro Rodríguez de Campomanes (1723–1802) and Juan Álvarez Mendizábal (1790–1853) show how the country's intellectuals and politicians' plans to transform the economy and engage industrial advancement in the eighteenth and nineteenth centuries were in parallel to their European counterparts, and as in any other industrializing nation in the West, Spanish women were part of the service sector that boomed in the late nineteenth century. For example, the so-called "Chair Act," one of many labor bills passed at the beginning of the twentieth century, represented an attempt to regulate the growth of women's presence in the labor force. Although women in Spain had been engaged in a diverse range of economic activities before the nineteenth century, their economic participation was more and more visible as they became wage-earners at the turn of the twentieth century. After the Civil War (1936–9), Francisco Franco's dictatorship (1939–75) put a halt on women's work outside the home through the Labor Charter of 1938, enacted a year before the end of the conflict. The economic take off resulting from the Pact of Madrid[2] signed with the United States in 1953 changed the labor market. Spain's Law of Political and Labor Rights of Women of 1961 again opened the labor market to women. The last document in this module is a newspaper article regarding the MATESA financial scandal followed by a table showing Spain's workers' salaries in 1973. These two sources seek to make the reader reflect on the broader significance of Spain's so called model transition to democracy and the economic continuities and ruptures that ensued and linger to this day.

DOCUMENT 1
PEDRO RODRÍGUEZ DE CAMPOMANES, FROM "TREATISE ON THE PROMOTION OF POPULAR EDUCATION (1774) AND TREATISE ON THE POPULAR EDUCATION OF ARTISANS AND ITS PROMOTION" (1775)

Pedro Rodríguez de Campomanes y Pérez (1723–1802), Count Campomanes, was a Spanish politician during the reign of Charles III (1759–88). He studied at the University of Oviedo in Asturias, and like other Enlightenment thinkers of his time, such as Anne Robert Jacques Turgot, Baron de l'Aulne (1727–81), in France he was educated in law and philosophy and participated in government by directly counseling the king in fiscal matters. Campomanes wrote important manuscripts in fields like history, such as the *Dissertaciones historicas del orden y cavalleria de los templarios*, and geography, such as *Noticia geografica del reyno y caminos de Portugal*. The *Tratado sobre el fomento de la industria popular* (1774) was one of Campomanes' most popular works about the economy and how to tackle the country's industrial development. His main goal in this influential treatise was to encourage Spanish manufacturing by reforming the country's guild organization and educational system, which he saw as being stagnant and representing an impediment to Spain's commercial, industrial, and economic growth. In this text, Campomanes focuses on entrepreneurship and more extensive education to promote scientific innovation. His reformist ideas were the basis for the creation of the *Sociedades de Amigos del País* (Friends of the Nation Societies) an Enlightenment project to promote Spain's technical education. His latest post in government was as president of the Consejo de Castilla from 1788 to 1793.

PEDRO RODRIGUEZ DE CAMPOMANES EXCERPTS FROM *TREATISE ON THE PROMOTION OF POPULAR EDUCATION* (1774) AND THE *TREATISE ON THE POPULAR EDUCATION OF ARTISANS AND THEIR PROMOTION* (1775)

Popular industry

(. . .) Necessity was the guiding force for rational minds to give rise to the invention of Art, to provide refuge, sustenance, and comfort for their kind. According to their whims and talents, their tendencies, tastes and fashions varied at all times (. . .) This resulted in so much diversity in the nation's adornments and forms of dress.

Many trends were introduced as instruments of ambition or for the purpose of human security: that is, to attack or to defend each other. Other inventions are destined to take us by land and sea across all possible distances, to cross, block or to take advantage of rivers. Art is appreciated for its usefulness, its taste, its intrigue and its effect. This appreciation varies in men of society, according to sex, profession, class and age. The harmony and delight of the *ear* has resulted in the invention of musical instruments; and the necessity to distribute and enjoy time, in that of clocks.

Gluttony, and hunger before it, has led to the origin of many arts, and has also stimulated agriculture, the cultivation of trees and orchards: everything has been designed to satisfy the sense of *taste*. The preparation of scents and the variety in the cultivation of roses with different fragrances, the art of gardening, the distillation of spirits, as well as the manufacturing of cigars, are all intended for the recreation of the sense of *smell*.

Optics is a science, founded for this purpose, whose knowledge can result in many important discoveries for men. Painting and writing convey to those present and future through the same sense everything man is able to perceive, develop, or devise.

If we lack these two arts of painting and writing, the world would forget all it has learned and remembered until now.

Only sculptures with their shapes and carved letters could, by means of the sense of touch, substitute the lack of sight even though with more difficulty.

The roughness of metals and rocks has yielded to the art of men, to receive and give shapes, provided to the smooth sense of *touch*.

Touch is also what guides the hands in all, or at least the main maneuvers of the artisans. Without these arts and trades, human society cannot occur.

The Sciences have their auxiliary arts such as: writing, printing, engraving, the art of making punches and dies, casting letters, paper mills, and bookbinding materials. These arts thrive or wane depending on the progress of its instruction in the nation that employs them.

Perfection in the arts contributes to the facilitation and dissemination of different forms of human knowledge, since they all share a certain universal relationship among them; and provide humankind with more ways to live at the expense of the rich and wealthy, or of those who need the arts to satisfy their tastes or needs.

It is not enough to establish any kind of arts and trades in a country or to devote a lot of time to them. It is necessary to continually improve in competition with other nations. When Spain neglected this close vigilance, our manufacturing and artifacts lost their esteem: leading to foreign superiority. It takes a very short time for factories to go bankrupt if the lacking improvement and instruction are not introduced.

This gives rise to the first general challenge to fix the learning of trades; the subordination of disciples or apprentices to their masters; the study of drawing, to make proportionate and correct works; rigor and justification of the examinations; awards and appropriate support to the artisans by giving them the recognition they justly deserve as industrious citizens who are useful and necessary to the Kingdom.

The best are the foundations that support the call to work and reject idleness in any social class, including knights, *hidalgos*, commoners, and women of said hierarchies.

My intention with this speech is to encourage those who profess the arts and trades in Spain, so that they dedicate themselves to drawing, and exercise their respective trades per their rules, symmetry, and proportions.

(...)

In the past, Spain had many more factories and trades. If the ancients could surpass other nations, why now must we accept that we are unable to be equal?

(...)

Now we explore the state of the artisans, which are dedicated solely to their trades, and to working with raw materials, which were prepared by the scattered industries of the villages.

The craftsman can receive daily or weekly the product of his labor; and even if he has a considerable number of children, he can secure their future by teaching them and passing on his trade.

For the arts to be solidly established, superior and improved education for artisans is necessary; the administration of these professions also needs to improve so that the artisans can receive the due respect.

On learning

Learning each trade must have an appointed time, during which boys can become acquainted with the tools of their art, and in handling them equally and in order.

They should be instructed on basic operations of their trade, and to learn the more complex ones gradually.

Apprentices should not be treated like their teachers' servants; nor should they be distracted in other occupations other than their own. This would be exemplified in the bad policy practiced by the Romans, who abandoned their arts to their slaves.

Parents, relatives or guardians must not be able to get the students out of the tutelage of their masters on working days; and they should not allow them to be idle by way of misunderstood compassion, which would be very harmful to them in the future.

The teacher lacks rules, and since he was taught through pure imitation, he could hardly teach his apprentices.

If we, against the law, take away from companies' tariff-free benefits (...), they will move to other nations (...) Paris and London hold a great number of foreigners who have established themselves as tradesmen (...)

On drawing

If we exclude trades that concern the ordinary sustenance of men—transportation, tending the cattle and tilling the soil—the rest usually require art and rules. Art consists of rules. It is true that in the common manner of speaking, arts are usually deemed to be trades, since all arts are trades, but the reverse is not always true.

Arts and trades that do not immediately rely on drawing, certainly make use of it to make their instruments, machines, and operations known, a method through which the subject can become known to those who are not familiar with it.

The Academy of Arts facilitates this teaching process in Madrid, Seville, Valencia and other places. Where they are lacking, it is convenient to open patriotic schools of drawing managed by economic societies of friends of the country, using the form and methods proposed in the *speech on the promotion of popular industry.*

To Guild Masters

In these schools, not only do we need to provide general instructions on drawing and parts of the human body; it would also be convenient to delve into the designs of machines, instruments and proper operations of the respective art of the apprentice. Once they learn the basic principles of drawing, students should be divided into levels depending on how advanced they are in their art. They should not be moved ahead prematurely since that would be detrimental.

These designs can be found in *the books of art* and in others, which these schools should have along with other books that may be created: so that they can become familiar and available to the whole nation.

On Christian Morals, and Useful Knowledge, on Which the Youth Devoted to Arts and Trades Should be Educated

It should also be considered that these young apprentices of the arts need to be educated in Christian, moral and useful knowledge, which they will need for the rest of their life in order to act with integrity and decency.

Cleanliness and decency in dressing is generally lacking among these people, not just in apprentices, but also in professionals and masters. They go out on the streets looking disheveled, without combing their hair or washing their hands and face; and even with tears in their clothing resulting from not mending them in time. They could certainly occupy their spare time or their mothers' and sisters' on mending their clothing using patches of the same color. Besides, in diligently mending their clothes, people can maintain clothing properly and inexpensively.

The current untidiness of many of this class of citizens, although they are respectable, can be attributed to bad upbringing. Parents can be held accountable for the lack of personal grooming. Their children tear their clothing while playing rough and dangerous games, which is inconvenient for this rational argument.

Setting standards

The whole national system of jurisprudence, if we understand our interests, should aim to direct, encourage, and honor our work and skilled people.

Poor nobles should not lose their honor for being industrious. Otherwise in some provinces, where the nobles abound, they could not establish themselves in industry or the arts.

Basic education

Some would ask, "why should an artisan write?" Others, more compassionate, would add that an artisan is not a man of letters, but an excellent manual laborer in a professional in a trade. And still others will say, following the same reasoning, that overloading craftsmen with learning not only to read, but also to write, will distract many from embracing these occupations, even if they are honorable and useful professions.

EXAMINATION OF APPRENTICES

On the Journeymen Who Aspire to Become Masters and the Qualities They Should Acquire and Have Before Being Admitted to the Master's Exam

The apprentice that is approved should be given certification by the clerk of the council. To obtain this certificate and become a journeyman, he should only pay for the sealed paper and the clerk's services; and he shall be treated as such on record and by his masters, colleagues and parents; without asking or receiving, even if it was spontaneously offered, drinks or tips for this reason. In that case, the offenders should be penalized, and restitution should be double.

Questions for discussion

1. Like other Enlightenment thinkers, Pedro Rodríguez de Campomanes sought reform in various aspects of the economy. Who and why do you think would be opposed to his ideas?

2. It is common to depict Spain's eighteenth century as backwards in relation to other European nations. Even Campomanes implies in his text that Spain is behind other nations as regards technological innovation. Which old regime institution is he mostly pointing to when blaming Spain's lack of industrial progress?

3. Outline Campomanes' program for technical education. His focus on training diversification rather than on concentration of knowledge in the Guild's Master or higher education is key to understanding his plans. Would you side with Campomanes? If we look at the present, does this debate sound familiar?

4. Thinking in gender terms, Campomanes was not clear or specific about what to do in regards to female trades and economies. In fact, women were not allowed to be part of guilds before the end of the eighteenth century. How revolutionary would his reforms have been without concretely addressing the place of women in the economy?

DOCUMENT 2
DECREE OF DISENTAILMENT OF THE REGULAR CLERGY, 1836. SIGNED BY GOVERNING QUEEN MARÍA CRISTINA OF NAPLES, MOTHER OF ISABEL II. BY JUAN ÁLVAREZ MENDIZÁBAL (1790–1853). GACETA DE MADRID. N. 426. YEAR 1836. SUNDAY, FEBRUARY 21

Juan Álvarez Mendizábal (1790–1853), was a defender of liberalism and of a freer ownership system in a country that he thought was still immersed in Old Regime property laws. The old regime economy existed even after the Constitution of 1812 granted property as a basic civil right for the first time in Spain. These ideas sent him to exile during Ferdinand VII's reign (1814–34). Coming from a family of merchants, and a businessman himself, Mendizábal, along with other Spanish and European liberal thinkers, while in exile in England, further developed his ideas to promote liberalism in Spain. As the head of Spain's Treasury, his first plan for disentailment was passed on February 19, 1836. This law privatized underused convents and monasteries land. However, his intention to modernize Spain's access to land while trying to reinvigorate and fund the State's drowned finances after years of dynastic wars between *carlistas* and *Isabelinos* did not get the results that the promoters of liberalism expected. In addition to worsening the differences between the Catholic Church and the liberal governments, poor peasants were left without land as they had traditionally depended on public and Church lands. In addition, historians have demonstrated that land disentailment resulted in the accumulation of more land in the hands of only a wealthy few that had the means to buy property.

DECREE OF DISENTAILMENT OF THE REGULAR CLERGY (1836)

Her Majesty the Queen, her August Mother and Governing Queen, and the Infanta María Luisa Fernanda, continue without change in her valued good health in the Royal Palace of El Pardo ...

Madam:
Selling the properties that have passed to the hands of the State not only fulfills a solemn promise and gives positive assurance to the national debt through a repayment exactly

equal to the product of the income, but it also opens an abundant source of public happiness; reviving a dead wealth; unblocking the channels of industry and circulation; connecting the country through the natural and vehement love for what is ours; engaging the nation; creating new and strong ties that unify it; basically, identifying with the exalted throne of Isabel II, a symbol of order and freedom.

It is not, Madam, a cold commercial speculation or a mere credit operation, although this is the lever that moves and balances the nations of Europe in our time: it is an element of animation, of life and fortune for Spain. It is, if I may explain myself in this way, the complement of her political resurrection. (...) So that the most ingenious suspicions do not feed any qualms, where there is only a healthy intention, it is initially declared that all goods are for sale. (...)

Another measure of incalculable importance is that which sets on recommending the division of large estates, to reduce them to lots that are available to the honest and industrious citizens who are the strength and hope of the motherland. Without this system and without the commitment to execute it, the primary purpose of these sales would be distressingly disappointed, which, as I have mentioned to Her Majesty, is to create new ties that bind men to the homeland and its institutions.

Royal Decree

Given the need and desirability of reducing the consolidated public debt, and delivering the mass of real estate which have become the property of the nation, to private owners, so that agriculture and trade get from such properties the benefits that could not be achieved entirely in its current state, or that would be delayed at the expense of national wealth, for as long as the properties are not put for sale, let it be known that:

Art. 1. All real estate of any kind which had belonged to extinct religious corporations is declared on sale as of now, and other properties that were awarded to the nation by any title or for any reason, and also all those that will be awarded since the act of adjudication.

Art. 2. Exceptions to this measure are the government buildings intended for public service or to preserve monuments of the arts, or to honor the memory of national feats. (...)

Art. 3. Regulations on how to proceed with the sale of these assets shall be devised, maintaining, insofar as convenient and adaptable to current circumstances those regulations decreed by the courts in September 3, 1820 and adding the necessary rules for the implementation of the following measures:

1st: The auction shall be verified not only in the capital of the province where the farms or real estate would be based, but also in this court, within exactly one day. (...)

2nd: The official newsletters of the provinces, or a special print, shall be published the next day after the conclusion of the auctions (...) bidders' names will be omitted in these publications, circumstantially expressing the amount of the highest bid.

3rd: Within ten days of receipt by the court of the results of the auctions carried out in the provinces, the name of the bidder shall be published, who by offering the highest price for the property should be declared its buyer.

4th: All rural property subject to division, without reducing its value, or without serious obstacles to a prompt sale, shall be distributed among the largest number of parties as possible. (...)

6th: To make these divisions, which must include careful consideration of all circumstances that could lead to facilitating their sale, a committee of farmers and people of good knowledge in farming shall be appointed by the respective council, to designate land that can be divided by each village's jurisdiction.

7th: Once the division is made, it shall be published in the corresponding village and it shall be forwarded by the president of the town's council to the head of the province, who shall order the publication in its capital. (...)

Art. 4. Any Spanish or foreigner shall have power to order in writing to the governor of the province an appraisal of the farm or farms among those which have not yet been appraised or included in the published lists so that they can proceed to the auction. (...)

Art. 7. Fifteen days after publication of the price of the appraisal, at the latest, the sale of the designated farm or farms shall be announced, following the same rules laid down for the disposal of any other property of this class. (...)

Art. 10. Payment of the auction price shall be in one of two ways: consolidated debt securities or cash.

Art. 11. The consolidated debt securities which shall be delivered as payment of the amount of the auction, will be accepted at their full face value, but on condition that the required payment is made and executed under these terms: one third in already consolidated debt securities at 5 percent interest; another third in already consolidated debt securities at 4 percent interest; and the remainder in debt securities that will be consolidated again at 5 percent. (...)

Art. 17. The heirs of estate buyers shall be subrogated to the heirs for the fulfillment of all obligations pending payment of installments, until the total amount of the price for which the properties were auctioned is paid. (...)

Art. 20. Every month a statement of the verified sales paid in cash during the previous month shall be published and the amounts received pursuant to the fifth part to be satisfied before the formalization of the deed. The product shall be invested by third parties in the purchasing, through exchange agents in this capital of the kingdom, of debt titles consolidated at 4 and 5 percent and debt securities without interest, which, having been liquidated and recognized would have not been subject to consolidation, and which are amortized by publicly destroying them and announcing them in the Gazette and the number and value of the securities redeemed in this way.

Questions for discussion

1. Contrary to what was expected, municipalities were not the direct beneficiaries of Mendiźabal's plans or other disentailment programs enacted in Spain in the nineteenth century. Why do you think privatization of land in Spain was not favorable to small towns and cities? Why is it believed to be the origin of the country's high concentration of land in fewer hands than before the lands were made available?

2. Who do you think were mostly benefited by the reforms?

3. What other policies would have been more efficient in distributing the land?

4. Would you agree that Spanish liberalism lacked enough civil support within the country?

DOCUMENT 3
THE CHAIR ACT, 1912. WEDNESDAY FEBRUARY 28, 1912, *GACETA DE MADRID* 59, PP. 565-6. YEAR CCLI VOLUME I

The so-called "Chair Act" of 1912 declared that all businesses in the service sector must provide a chair so women workers could rest after standing up for periods of time. This act followed a European trend and it was part of a wave of labor regulations in the wake of the Second Communist Congress (Brussels, 1891) that sought regulation and protection for the work done by women and children. These regulations came as a result of the establishment of liberal governments in Spain after the conservative administration of Canovas del Castillo (1828–97). The Chair Act was one of the earliest social legislation passed by the Instituto de Reformas Sociales, established in 1903 and presided over by jurist Gumersindo Azcárate (1840–1917). Previous bills included the 1900 Regulation prohibiting women and children under ten years of age from working nights, and regulated maternity and lactation in the workplace. This was followed by a decree in 1908 which raised the minimum working age to sixteen, and defined which jobs (such as working with explosives) were risky for women to perform. The Instituto closed in 1924 as dictator General Miguel Primo de Rivera took office, and the Chair Act was nullified in 1944.

THE CHAIR ACT 1912.

Interior Ministry

Act

Don Alfonso XIII, King of Spain by the grace of God and the Constitution. To all who see and understand this Act, let it be known that the courts have decreed and sanctioned the following:

Art. 1. In warehouses, shops, offices, and in general throughout non-manufacturing establishments of whatever kind, where items or objects are sold or dispensed to the public or any related service is provided by female employees, and in neighboring premises, it will be mandatory for the owner or his representative or private company to have a seat available for each of those women. Each seat should be assigned exclusively to an employee, will be in the place where they carry out their occupation so it can be of use, and in addition to those that may be available to the public.

Neighboring premises, subject therefore to the obligation of the Act, are all those that, though separated from the place where the sale or the service takes place, are connected to it, whether in the same or a different store.

This act also extends to the fairs, markets, passageways, outdoor permanent exhibits or traveling industries, whether they are connected to another establishment.

Any employee may utilize her seat, if she is not occupied and even when she is, as long as the nature of her occupation allows it.

Art. 2. The enforcement of this Act shall be subject to the Labor Institute of Social Reforms, and in accordance with the provisions governing its function. (...)

Art. 4. At least one copy of this Act shall be placed visibly in the establishment or establishments where it is to be applied.

Questions for discussion

1. In general, regulation comes because of studies on the status of a certain sector of the population. The implementation of the Chair Act (*Ley de la Silla*) is a result of the high number of women that were employed in the service sector in Spain by the turn of the twentieth century. How do you think women employed in the service sector would have perceived this legislation? Would a female-headed business agree to uphold the mandates of the law?

2. Is this legislation about the protection or about the exclusion of women from the labor market?

3. Reflecting upon other laws regulating the work of women during this period and the development of Spain's and Europe's labor movement during this time, would you consider the *Instituto* a pro-feminist institution?

DOCUMENT 4
LABOR CHARTER, 1938 AND LAW OF POLITICAL AND LABOR RIGHTS OF WOMEN, 1961, *BOLETÍN OFICIAL DEL ESTADO* (OFFICIAL STATE BULLETIN)

In 1938, a year before the Civil War ended, the Francoist government issued the Labor Charter. Following Italy's fascist dictator Benito Mussolini's own labor reform, the Carta di Lavoro issued in 1927, the Labor Charter regulated Spain's labor relations, establishing vertical syndicalism or state-controlled unions, and outlining other work related issues such as working hours. With regard to women, the Labor Charter declared that women should be released from factory work, implying that the home would then be redefined as women's main sphere of influence. Women continued to work, though under the Labor Charter their working conditions worsened as they lost previous protection in the workplace. Over the years, and following Spain's opening to economic liberalization in the late 1950s and 1960s, more and more women entered the labor market and regained basic labor rights. The first law that slightly opened this route—although still under the regime's gendered premises—was the Ley de los derechos políticos y del trabajo de la mujer (Law of Political and Labor Rights for women) of 1961, which the single official party Falange Women's Section, sponsored and implemented.

LABOR JURISDICTION OF MARCH 20, 1938

Renewing the Catholic tradition of social justice and sense of humanity that informed the laws of our glorious past, the State assumes the task of securing for the Spanish people the following: Motherland, Bread, and Justice.

To achieve this—trying, moreover, to strengthen the unity, freedom and greatness of Spain—we turn to the social sphere willing to put wealth at the service of the Spanish people, subordinating the economy to the dignity of the human individuals, taking into account their material needs and the demands of their intellectual, moral, spiritual and religious lives.

... we declare:

I

1. Labor is man's participation in production by means of voluntarily exercising his intellectual and manual faculties, per his vocation, to achieve the decorum and ease of his own life and the development of the national economy.

2. Since it is essentially personal and human, labor cannot be reduced to a material concept of merchandize, or be subject to transactions incompatible with the personal dignity of those who work.

3. The right to work is a result of the duty imposed to man by God, so that he can fulfill his individual enterprises and bring prosperity and greatness of the country.

4. The State values and exalts labor, encourages expression of the creative spirit of man and, as such, it will protect labor with the force of the law, giving it the greatest considerations and making it compatible with the fulfillment of the other individual, family and social goals.

5. Labor, being a social duty, will be required inexcusably, in any of its forms, of all Spanish people who are not disabled estimating it as obligatory tribute to the Spanish national wealth.

6. Labor is one of the noblest attributes of hierarchy and honor, and it is a sufficient entitlement to require the assistance and protection of the State.

7. Service is the work that is carried out with heroism, selflessness and self-sacrifice, intending to contribute to the greater good that Spain represents.

8. All Spaniards have the right to work. The satisfaction of this right is a paramount mission of the State.

II

1. The State commits to exert constant and effective action in defense of the worker, his life and work. It shall conveniently limit the duration of the day so it is not excessive, and give the worker all sorts of defensive and humanitarian assurances. In particular, it shall prohibit night work for women and children; it shall regulate homework and free married women from the workshop and the factory.

2. The State shall maintain Sunday rest as sacred in the provision of work.

3. Without loss of pay and taking the technical needs of companies into account, the law will enforce religious and secular holidays declared by the State.

4. July 18, declared a national holiday to commemorate the Glorious Uprising, will also be considered Labor Exaltation Day.

5. Every worker shall be entitled to paid annual leave that will provide him a well-deserved rest, and the institutions that will ensure compliance with this provision will be organized.

6. The necessary institutions shall be created so that workers have the opportunity to enjoy all the benefits of the culture, the joy, the militia, health, and sports during their free time.

III

1. The remuneration of work shall be at least sufficient to provide a worker and his family with a moral and dignified life.

2. Child allowances shall be established by appropriate agencies.

3. The standard of living of workers will rise gradually and inflexibly to the extent permitted by the greater interest of the nation.

4. The State shall specify the minimum basis for the arrangements of labor, subject to which, relations between workers and firms will be established. The primary content of these relations will benefit not only labor and its remuneration, but also the arrangement of the elements of the company, based on justice, mutual loyalty and the subordination of economic values to human and social values.

5. Through the Union, the State will take care to know if all the economic conditions and the order in which the work is performed justly correspond to the appropriate working conditions.

6. The State shall ensure the security and continuity of labor.

7. The Company shall inform its staff on the progress of production to the extent necessary to enhance their sense of responsibility in it, in the terms established by law.

IV

Craftsmanship—inheritance of a glorious past of guilds—shall be promoted and protected effectively for being a complete projection of the human person in their work and for assuming a form of production equally disconnected from capitalist concentration and Marxist gregariousness.

V

1. The rules of labor in the agricultural industry shall comply with its special characteristics and seasonal variations imposed by nature.

2. The State shall especially take care of the technical education of the agricultural producer, enabling him to carry out all work required by each operating unit. (...)

VI

The State shall care for seafarers with the utmost attention, providing the appropriate measures to prevent the depreciation of the goods and to facilitate access to the ownership of the necessary elements for the performance of their profession.

VII

A new Labor Magistrate shall be created, subject to the principle that this function of justice corresponds to the State. (...)

IX

1. Credit shall be arranged in a way that, in addition to meeting its mandate to develop national wealth, it will help create and sustain the small farming, fishing, industrial, and commercial wealth.

2. Honesty and trust, based on competition and at work, shall constitute effective guarantees for credit grants.

3. The State shall relentlessly punish all forms of usury. (...)

XIII

1. The Spaniards, inasmuch they participate in work and production, form the Union Organization.

2. The Union Organization is formed by a group of industrial, agricultural, and services unions, organized by types of activities at the territorial and national level that includes all the branches of production. (...)

XIV

The State shall dictate the appropriate measures to protect domestic labor in our territory and through labor treaties with other world powers, and it shall protect the professional situation of Spanish workers residing abroad.

XV

On the date this Charter is enacted, Spain is committed to a heroic military task, which saves the values of the spirit and culture of the world at the cost of losing much of her material wealth. Domestic production should respond selflessly with all its elements to the generosity of young Spanish combatants and to Spain itself. Therefore, in this Charter of rights and duties, we consign as the most urgent and unavoidable, those elements of production that would contribute with equity and determination to rebuild Spain and the foundations of its power.

XVI

The State commits to provide young combatants with labor, honor or command positions, to which they are entitled as Spaniards and as heroes.

LAW OF POLITICAL AND LABOR RIGHTS OF WOMEN, JULY 23, 1961

The principle of non-discrimination on grounds of sex or condition in the entitlement and exercise by Spaniards of political, professional, and labor rights is categorically recognized by the Spain's Labor Charter: Article one states that "all Spaniards shall be able to act in public office and functions per their merit and ability" and Article twenty-four states that "all Spaniards have the right to work and the duty to engage in some socially useful activity." This Law does nothing more than develop and effectively implement such principles, removing restrictions and discrimination based on sociological situations of the past, which do not align with either the training or the capacity of the Spanish woman or her evident promotion to positions and tasks of work and responsibility.

(. . .) the law stipulates, obviously referring only to married women, that the limitations of rights, once more confirmed in the reformed Civil Code of nineteen fifty-eight, that marriage requires a guidance and authority which nature, religion and history attribute to the husband. The announcement made by the Labor Charter stating that married women would be liberated "from workshops and factories," continued to be a programmatic goal of the Spanish State. However, not even this rule put a halt on women laborers performing an increasing multiplicity of non-manual occupations. Such directives could not (and should not) have been implemented through discriminatory and prohibitive regulations which could cause more harm than good, but rather by raising the general income of men, which, in conjunction with other programs—notably the housing programs, to which the State dedicated many sleepless nights and efforts—would enable the head of household to provide a decent standard of living for his family. (. . .)

I Bequeath:

Art. 1. The law grants women equal rights to men to exercise all types of political and professional activities and work, with no more limitations than those established in this Act.

Art. 2.1 Women can participate in the election and be elected to the position of any public office. (. . .)

Art. 3.1. Under the same conditions as men, women can participate in job examinations and in any other systems used for the selection and provision of job positions of any public administrations. They shall also have access to all levels of education.

II Women shall be excluded from:

a) The Army, Navy and Air Force, unless a special expressed provision is granted . . .

b) Military institutions (...) involving the use of weapons for the performance of their duties.

c) The Administration of Justice in the positions of magistrates, judges, and prosecutors, except in juvenile and labor jurisdictions.

d) Staff certified by the Merchant Navy, with the exception of health personnel.

Art. 4. Women may enter into any kind of labor contracts. (...)
Labor regulations will recognize the principle of equal pay for work of equal value.

Art. 5. When, by law, marital authorization is required for exercising the rights expressed above, such request shall be stated explicitly.

Questions for discussion

1. The 1938 *Fuero del Trabajo* (Labor Charter) defined women as "liberated" from work. How do you think that women dedicated to housework perceived this legislation, as opposed to women who needed to work outside the home would perceive this legislation?

2. Work in the factory or outside the home became an important element in defining a woman's lack of moral standards during Franco's Spain. Did the dictatorship's labor legislation improve or worsen women's place in the labor market?

3. Women did not abruptly stop working after Franco took office in 1939. What sort of labor would women be likely to uphold under the regime's labor regulation?

4. By the late 1950s it was clear that women were necessary to the country's economy in a variety of sectors. Do you think that the *Sección Femenina*'s support of women's training and introduction to the labor force can be considered a feminist move?

DOCUMENT 5
MATESA SCANDAL, 1969

The MATESA financial scandal became public in 1969 near the end of Francisco Franco's dictatorship. This was a time when different factions within the government had emerged and the influence of the religious group Opus Dei was declining. MATESA, or Maquinaria Textil del Norte de España, S.A., was a manufacturing company that produced textile looms. To boost national innovation and production, the Francoist regime had created the Banco de Crédito Oficial (Official Credit Bank), which in this case was financing MATESA to export its looms and also to sell its patents abroad. The scandal erupted when the company came under investigation as it was unclear whether machines and patents were actually being sold; all the while the company was receiving loans from the government to do so. The scandal was a turning point in Spain's credit and financial system, and in 1971, shortly after its inadequacies and failings were clear, the government implemented the Law on the Organization and Regulation of Official Credit.

MATESA SCANDAL

Diario de Avisos. Friday August 1, 1969

Council of Ministers
Arrest and detention of chief executives of "MATESA" (. . .)
The government has been fully informed by the Ministers of Finance and Trade, about the situation of the company "Textile Machinery of Northern Spain [MATESA, by its acronym in Spanish]", said to reporters Mr Manuel Fraga Iribarne, the Minister of Information and Tourism, when he welcomed them today at 6 pm in his apartment located in La Coruña, to expand on the comments made by the Council of Ministers in a meeting held this morning at the Pazo de Meirás under the chairmanship of the Head of State.

Mainly engaged in the export of a specific model of looms—said Mr. Fraga Iribarne—MATESA has been using the official credit modality, related to export operations through the Industrial Credit Bank, in the manner and conditions that are common to the export activities per the applicable law. Although they have met their respective payment maturities of principal and the interest loans granted to the administration, there was knowledge of possible irregularities in MATESA's export activity regarding Spanish legislation on currency issues. According to the investigations carried out so far in Spain and abroad, part of the exports appear to be correct; however, it turns out that other machines have been sent to manufacturing firms linked to MATESA, and that others are on consignment or deposited abroad where there are indications that actual sales of such machines have not been effected, despite figures declared as firm sales both for the purposes of tax relief and export credit. "Regardless of what has been disclosed previously" the Minister of Information and Tourism continued to say "it would appear that pre-financing checks, whose present balance amounts to 5.539 million pesetas, have not been applied to manufacturing costs but have been misused for the acquisition of foreign stocks and shares in companies, partnerships and trade bodies mainly related to the textile industry."

Because of the above facts, the special financial crimes court ordered the arrest and detention of the company's CEOs, one of whom is at home under surveillance, recovering from a recent surgery. Pending the physician's authorization for his transfer to prison (. . .)

Questions for discussion

1. What does the publication and investigation of the MATESA scandal say about the stability and public legitimation of the Franco's regime in the late 1960s? Would censorship have allowed such a case to become public in the first decade of the dictatorship?

2. Although, for Spain to become part of the European Union in the 1980s, it was necessary to introduce new financial regulation, Spain's financial system is still based on the dictatorship's doings. What conclusions can we draw about the country's transition to democracy based on the continuation of both legislation and legislators in power after 1975?

3. MATESA's president, Juan Vilá Reyes (1925–2007), was sent to prison (reduced sentence) and fined in 1975, as well as some members of his family who were also involved in the company and in the financial scandal. He later continued to be a business owner. Consider and debate on the continuities that Spain presents from dictatorship to democracy.

DOCUMENT 6
SAMPLE OF WORKERS' SALARIES BY PROVINCES, 1973[3]

Provinces	1955	1960	1971
Alava	15,999	20,204	101,718
Albacete	6,525	11,083	47,189
Alicante	9,569	15,613	64,986
Almería	5,998	9,575	43,323
Badajoz	6,361	12,021	43,845
Baleares	12,159	19,276	94,300
Barcelona	17,568	27,564	97,347
Burgos	10,715	14,525	69,302
Cadiz	10,507	13,919	54,875
Cordova	8,000	13,907	51,017
Coruña (La)	8,713	13,607	54,215
Gerona	12,064	20,716	87,248
Guadalajara	8,795	12,842	63,967
Guipuzcoa	24,777	31,270	104,111
Huesca	9,322	18,512	73,960
Leon	9,359	13,592	58,186
Madrid	18,020	27,350	97,848
Oviedo	13,309	20,933	70,194
S.C. Tenerife	8,160	14,098	53,568
Valencia	13,201	23,759	68,817

Questions for discussion

1. Analyze the per capita income of Spain's provinces between 1955 and 1971 as well as Spain's demographics. Where is the population concentrated? What conclusions can we draw from such analysis?

2. Analyze Spain's provinces income per capita between 1955 and 1971 and Spain's industrial and agricultural distribution. What conclusions can we draw from such analysis?

3. Based on this table, where do you think internal migration was most prominent between 1955 and 1971?

MODULE 3
FEMINISMS

ABSTRACT

Different trends of feminist thought have analyzed the genesis and history of women's oppression, inferior social status and overall subordination to men. The debate over the nature and capabilities of women and their role in society was especially heated during the Enlightenment, a period that redefined the role of the modern woman. Although the goal for upper-class women was still marriage and motherhood, the higher status that they were given throughout the eighteenth century as wives and mothers was accompanied by higher expectations of women's education and a proliferation of conduct literature that prescribed women's contributions to the domestic sphere. *A Discourse About Women's Physical and Moral Education* (1790), by Josefa Amar y Borbón is a good example of this type of writings and is not very different from those of other European women writers of her time. Concepción Arenal's *Women of the Future* (1861) also deals with women's disadvantaged legal and social position and in the excerpt included here; she tries to prove that women's moral superiority. As is also the case with Amar y Borbón, Arenal's approach to some women's issues can nowadays be considered classist and, at times, more "feminine" than "feminist," but still essential reading when dealing with Spanish history of feminism. In the third document, Carmen de Burgos collects opinions on divorce, a topic that was the object of much debate at the beginning of the twentieth century in Spain. Carmen de Burgos' bold approach reappears in Hildegard Rodríguez's writings, many of which propose drastic sexual reform in the Spanish society of the 1930s. Lidia Falcón's radical feminism, and her denunciation of sexism, women's oppression, subjugation, and subordination is apparent in the excerpt selected from one of her most influential works, *The Feminist Reason* (1981), which served as the foundation for the feminist parties created in democratic Spain during the 1980s and 1990s. The last document shows the increasing social and political attention that gender violence has been receiving in Spain in the last three decades.

DOCUMENT 1

JOSEFA AMAR Y BORBÓN. *DISCURSO SOBRE LA EDUCACIÓN FÍSICA Y MORAL DE LAS MUJERES* (A DISCOURSE ABOUT WOMEN'S PHYSICAL AND MORAL EDUCATION, 1790)[1]

Josefa Amar y Borbón (1749–1883) is known as the most learned woman of the Spanish Enlightenment and she is also considered a pioneer in the establishment of the groundwork that later made possible the feminist movement. Her father was the court physician of King Ferdinand VI, which gave her access to the royal preceptors and libraries. In Madrid, she received an exquisite liberal, lay education, and throughout her life she shifted away from religion and the excessive involvement of the Catholic Church in education. She learned several languages (Latin, Greek, French, Italian, and English), and then became a translator, a writer, and an advocate for women's access to education and their participation in public life. In 1782, she was admitted to the men-only Economic Society of Aragón and in 1786, she published the essay "*Discurso en defensa del talento de las mujeres y su aptitud para el gobierno, y otros cargos en que se emplean los hombres*" (On the Defense of Women's Talent and their Aptitude for Government and Other Jobs Where Men are Employed). Her intellectual expertise in the humanities as well as the sciences, her encyclopedic knowledge about a wide variety of topics, and her involvement in public affairs, were attuned with the parameters of the universal Europeanism of the time and made her the epitome of an Enlightenment woman.

Her book *Discurso sobre la educación física y moral de las mujeres* (1790) (A Discourse About Women's Physical and Moral Education) follows the trend of the many eighteenth-century manner manuals, which prescribed on personal decorum, family conduct, and private and public health, while introducing the ideology that debunked the Old Regime. The passage that follows is a good example of the shortcomings inherent to Amar y Borbón's otherwise bold proposal on women's education. Her reformist proposals and views on femininity were advanced without breaking her close allegiance to the hegemonic upper class she belonged to and the values that this emergent bourgeoisie safeguarded.

DISCURSO SOBRE LA EDUCACIÓN FÍSICA Y MORAL DE LAS MUJERES (A DISCOURSE ABOUT WOMEN'S PHYSICAL AND MORAL EDUCATION, 1790)

Prologue

Education has always rightly been considered the most serious and important issue. Public and private happiness depend on it: if all individuals were discreet, well-informed, judicious, and moderated; if each family was orderly, united, and frugal, the Estate, which is formed by the bigger or smaller gathering of individuals and families, would necessarily benefit. Thus, the better the education is, the bigger number of happy people there will be, and the bigger the advantages that the Republic will enjoy. On the contrary, if it is bad, errors and disorder will be perpetuated, and disseminated by the imitation and the power of the first ideas received during childhood. It is not by chance that the Supreme Creator has determined that parents and teachers control the life, the health care, and the education of children, so that in this manner they can inspire them just and simple maxims so that children learn early to obey and respect the person that guides them. (…)

Women's education is usually considered a matter of little consequence. The Estate, the parents, and what is more, even women, look with indifference to learn one subject or another, or not learning anything at all. Who could explain the cause of this universal neglect? Saying that it is promoted by men so that women remain in ignorance, and in this way they can subdue them more freely, is a very simple-minded thought that vanishes easily, if we take into account that from the beginning of times there have been several wise men who have written accolades about women's ingenuity and have created catalogues, listing the most illustrious women in all subjects.[2] Let's be frank. In what way can men benefit from women's ignorance? When it comes to marriage, there will be no harmony between a well-educated man and a foolish woman. The institution of marriage presupposes the existence of two persons who will have to live forever in mutual society and union: to this end, it is necessary the communication of ideas, as well as that of interests; otherwise, marriages will never be united and peaceful. If we talk about equal treatment and rational society, knowledge will make people's behavior agreeable and useful. Therefore, it is imperative to find somewhere else the origin for this preoccupation, and it is in the education given to women.

Women are subject, just like men, to the obligations that are common to all individuals, such as the practice of religion and the observance of the civil laws of the country where they reside. Apart from these, they have the obligations pertaining to the Estate they embrace, and the circumstances in which they find themselves; that is, there is no difference between the sexes about this topic; therefore, they both need a competent instruction so that they can achieve the highest level of performance. The obligations of marriage are enormous and its influence gives a great deal of impulse to the advancement or the disruption of society in general. The order or disorder of private families transcends and is communicated to the public happiness and peacefulness. In these private families, women have their personal employment, which is the management and administration of the home, the care and upbringing of their children, and, above all, the intimate and perfect union with their husbands. The most common refrain is that women dominate and govern men as they see fit. That is the truth; therefore, this influence and power should be more useful to both; because now it is only based on personal beauty, and this ends soon, and even if it was permanent, there is no advantage in giving preference to exterior merits.

If the education of women is useful to the Estate, due to the reasons exposed above, it would also be no less useful to them. Since they are forced to base their respect in adornment and attractiveness, they try in maintaining one and the other. What cares and preoccupations do they have to undergo to conserve beauty, if they have it, or simulate it when nature has denied this benefit, as it occurs to most? It is true that beauty is an esteemed gift: there is no other power more absolute than beauty; in an instant, it possesses hearts and leads to many extremes, which does not happen with other gifts, whose influence is slower and quieter. However, beauty is a gratuitous gift, in which our own industry has little to do. Composure and artifice can achieve something, but natural defects cannot be entirely erased; and even if all women were beautiful, nothing would be achieved unless the privilege of making this gift permanent can be attained. In the actual state of things, there is nothing more fragile and perishable than beauty: smallpox, an illness, a fall and many other accidents destroy it easily; and even if there is no other enemy but time, it would be enough to diminish its value. How different the two periods of a woman's life are: when she is beautiful and then, after several years, when beauty is there no more! Those who have lived both periods can depict vehemently the misfortune the second one comes with; and it is a misfortune indeed, if no other merit that accompanies and survives beauty was acquired.

Despite all these frequent disappointments, almost all women care about good appearances first, and look at the rest of the gifts with indifference. This can be attributed in part to education; since childhood they are taught nothing but the art of adornment, and they see their mothers and friends dedicated to it as their first goal of their lives. The praise that they receive is commonly focused on being beautiful and lace-covered. That is why they study the art of adornment, and even though it has its difficulties in the right election and placement of accessories, many of them master it. It is true that women observe each other with great care, they imitate and stimulate each other, and the most trivial topic of the conversations they hold when they visit each other is around the things that contribute to the refinement and accomplishment of good taste. Nevertheless, there are some women who cannot excel in this art, due to the lack of desire or taste, or the ability to know how to choose what is more suitable to them; and, above all, because it depends on other people's fancy, and if they do not praise a Lady's composure, she becomes resentful after having wasted a few hours on it.

Since personal beauty is not the only gift that contributes to true happiness—either because not all women have it or can achieve it, or because when they do, its brightness and duration is fleeting, and when it is lost it leaves a painful void—it is essential to acquire other more solid and permanent gifts that accompany women in all ages, and that are not only advisable for the coexistence among people, but also useful to the person who has them; ultimately, these would be gifts that can be acquired through one's own industry. These gifts are those related to intelligence, which does not wither or gets old. Women anxiously desire compliments and worship, and it is true that they can get both while they are young, especially if they are good-looking; but if the latter disappears, what happens? What does this kind of farce that they perform end up when the queens, almost goddesses, find themselves without an entourage? It is necessary to have a great deal of self-control to tolerate this dethronement, when those who were seemingly obsequious before, become indifferent later. This comedy is sustained by youth and by exterior merit, but when these conclude, the illusion ends. As far as adornments are concerned, it is obvious that it is ridiculous and even impossible to maintain them the whole life; since what looks fine in a young woman, is ugly and laughable in an old lady. (. . .)

Despite all that has been said about women's aptitude to learn, it would not be appropriate to ask that all, indiscriminately, dedicate themselves to study as if they had to follow a profession or a career. This necessarily brings disorder, since it would be necessary that women attend college with men, which would cause more harm than good, or that there would be separate universities. It is advisable to have different occupations and social classes, in the same way that some men dedicate themselves to the letters and others to the arms, some to agriculture and some to various occupations and arts that are required by the general society; if such a variety did not exist, the need that they have for each other would not exist. For the same reason, there are certain occupations that traditionally correspond to women, such as needlework and weaving, that men could not do without neglecting their respective obligations. Women also have to know the domestic management and government, since they spend more hours at home and they can know and arrange the servants better. If this order was to be overturned so that women could spend the whole day studying, it would be necessary that men would take care of the house, and if the custom of them getting employment were to be changed, they would be useless for both purposes. Let's not construct an eccentric plan: let's try instead to rectify the one that is in place. To this end, it will be necessary that women cultivate their intellect without leaving their obligations aside; firstly, because it can contribute to make the yoke of marriage softer and more agreeable; secondly, because women should fully undertake their role as mothers; thirdly, because of the usefulness and advantage that results from learning, whatever age in life they are at. If education does not focus on these points, there will never be an overall benefit.

It seems that an education system should include all social classes, but the execution of such a thing would be impossible, if one understands that everything is relative is this world. It is true that the essential obligations pertain to all types of people without distinction, but not the same type of instruction is required to fulfill them. Therefore, we will not talk about those lower-class women, since it is enough for them to do by themselves the mechanical house chores. Most likely, their fate will be to join equally rough men for whom certain charm is not necessary. In this kind of marriage, happiness is achieved if the husband is hard-working and the wife helps as much as her strength permits. Not everybody looks at happiness in the same way and that makes the number of unhappy people less numerous. The wise distributor of gifts and talents has given more simple ideas to some people, so that they can easily achieve their desires and necessities, while others with more sensitivity and energy find bitterness in the variety of desires.

Therefore, enlightenment and cultivation of knowledge can be very useful to the type of women who, commonly speaking, will marry learned and well-educated men, so that perpetual harmony and union are strengthened. It is true that these gifts are not always a priority when getting married; we see that many marry when they fall in love with a woman's look, or with other personal grace; but it is also true that this personal charm disappears soon and, after they are together at all times, the graces wither in a very short period of time and they offer little variety; when men get used to them, they get tired, and there is a great risk that they would look with indifference precisely that which was vehemently desired before. *Sit formosa aliis uxor, tibi sit bona.* This is the most infallible rule. If the cases of people who profoundly loved each other before getting married, but then hate each other as fast as they fall in love, were not known, I would go more in depth about this matter; but nobody ignores this situation. The main reason is that the feelings are not based in solid merit. The most secure foundation to establish mutual affection is trust and the communication of ideas. A man who is the whole day occupied in business, many of them unpleasant, has the home and the family as the center of his repose and the liberation of the apprehensions that come with the drudgery and chores of a hard profession. This repose and relief will be complete if he has a peaceful and discreet wife in whom he can confide his secrets and with whom he can hold a rational conversation. On the contrary, if the wife is foolish and can only talk about adornment, she would cause him annoyance and resentment. It is not surprising to see the unfortunate consequences that such circumstances produce.

The education and upbringing of children belong equally to fathers and mothers. However, since nature places humans in the mother's womb for an amount of time, and provides women the means to feed them in the first months, it seems that in certain ways they are more bound to their protection and care than men. There is still another reason, which is that they spend more time at home; and having them almost all the time under their supervision, they can know and discipline them better. There is no doubt that this is the foundation of the common belief that the mother is the source of the children's vices; and truly, many of them, due to their complete negligence or to imprudent decisions, do not foster good education, and they might hinder the one that some fathers or teachers want to give. Other mothers show their preference for this child or the other, and they do not allow any punishment or reprimand, not realizing that true love means to try by all means to make children good and forgetting that parents have the obligation of taking care of all kids equally.

But it is time to deal with the two essential parts—physical and moral—that good education entails. The former, because it is linked to the strength of the body and its functions, which is so important in the course of life. The latter, because it is focused on arranging knowledge and customs, which is the only way to acquire a constant and true happiness. Who could have Thucydides, Demosthenes, or Cicero's eloquence to persuade women to dedicate their talents to this end. Those that would achieve it, would not provide the human kind less service that the one these wise men provided to their republics.

Questions for discussion

1. What is the intended reader of Amar y Borbón's writings? In what way are Amar y Borbón's ideas typical of the Enlightenment period?

2. Why does Amar y Borbón think it is important for a woman to have an education? What are the arguments that Amar y Borbón puts forward to show that men cannot benefit from women's lack of education?

3. What are the reasons why, per Amar y Borbón, not all women need to have the same kind of education? What are the dangers that Amar y Borbón foresees if all women decided to study? In what way does class play a role in women's education today in Spanish society, compared to the Enlightenment period?

4. In 1790, Amar y Borbón laments how women are at a disadvantage since they have been taught to take care of their appearances and not their education. In the same year, Catherine Macaulay presents similar views in *Letters on Education*. Two hundred years later, Naomi Wolf states the following in *The Beauty Myth* (1990): "The more legal and material hindrances women have broken through, the more strictly and heavily and cruelly images of female beauty have come to weigh upon us. (...) More women have more money and power and scope and legal recognition than we have ever had before; but in terms of how we feel about ourselves physically, we may actually be worse off than our unliberated grandmothers" (10). Give your opinion about Wolf's statement. Do you think women have liberated themselves from this a cultural fixation in the Western world about female beauty?

DOCUMENT 2
CONCEPCIÓN ARENAL, *LA MUJER DEL PORVENIR* (WOMEN OF THE FUTURE, 1861)[3]

Concepción Arenal Ponte (1820–93) is considered by many the first Spanish feminist. She was the first woman to attend university in Spain—dressed as a man since women were not welcomed in the classrooms—and the first one to get a degree in criminal law. A lawyer and a writer, she excelled as an activist and a social reformer. Ideologically, she sympathized with liberal Catholicism, utopic socialism, Krausism, and even anarchism. Although some historians have characterized Concepción Arenal as a conservative woman, most associate her with the progressive values of the liberal revolution that fought against the privileges and structures of the previous regime. It could not have been other way, especially after her father was imprisoned due to his opposition to Ferdinand VII's absolutism.

Although she remains a controversial and enigmatic figure, she has been recognized as a crusader for the feminist cause, promoting women's education and fighting for their emancipation, while exposing with great subtleness the contradictions inherent to social and gender issues. For example, she disapproved the fact that women had the same criminal responsibilities as men but they did not have the same civil rights. She also deplored that women could get degrees in law and medicine, but they could not become judges or doctors.

Her essays reveal a profound knowledge of human psychology, history, and law, as well as a sensibility to moral issues and human suffering. *La mujer del porvenir* (1861) (Women of the Future) can be considered her first feminist book. Here she challenges the well-established ideas about the physical inferiority of women and in the selected passage, she claims their moral superiority, arguing that women are more patient, compassionate, and sensitive than men.

CONCEPCIÓN ARENAL, *LA MUJER DEL PORVENIR* (WOMEN OF THE FUTURE, 1861)

Chapter III

Women's Moral Inferiority

There are some authors—we will do them a favor by not mentioning their names—that uphold the moral inferiority of women. Some laws cannot be understood unless they are a consequence of this opinion, which is also associated to some behaviors—only a few and ready to disappear. It can be acknowledged that this erroneous idea is almost vanishing, is dying.

What can be understood by moral superiority? If we compare two free and responsible individuals, it is morally superior to the other the one that is better and more virtuous, the one that has less bad inclinations and faces them with more energy, the one that does more good and less bad to his fellow man; putting it briefly: the one that is *better*. Are men better than women? Let's explore it.

Goodness is sensitivity, compassion, and patience. Are men as sensitive, as compassionate, and as patient as women? We suppose that no one will be headstrong enough to answer this question affirmatively; but in case there were, and considering that there are strange individuals, we will address some obvious facts so that, if someone does not see them, at least he can touch them.

Women's patience, a virtue that they exercise frequently, is apparent in all live situations. As a child, a girl starts helping her mother to take care of her younger siblings, and she gets involved in intricate tasks and in painstaking labor, which she accepts without complaint, but such tasks would be hard to impose on any boy. As a mother, a woman has immeasurable patience with her children, something a man would be not be remotely capable of. Although we do not think that all men are tyrants, knowing that, on the contrary, there are many, a lot, who are very good, and that most of them are better than could be expected, considering the laws, the opinions and the inferiority of women's intellectual estate, we believe that, generally speaking, peace among spouses requires more patience on the side of the wife, who, with few exceptions, is the most patient one.

Since women have less strength, it is providential that they are more patient; otherwise they would die in a fight that would be easily provoked but impossible to keep.

Women's higher sensitivity is perceived clearly, even without observing it; they are more affected and disturbed by everything than men. Women are more scared, excited, and enthusiastic and they predict things before men do. Their cry is the first one to be heard, their tears are the first ones to appear; pains hurt more and when men shiver, they shake. Physiologist says that they are more *irritable*, and people affirm that they are *weaker*; but they all agree, because it is apparent to all, that women are more *sensitive*.

Who takes care of the abandoned child, of the helpless sick person, and the decrepit old person? Who finds excuses for all the foolishness of the wretched souls? Who cannot witness so many things without crying? Who grieves *with* those who suffer and is *compassionate*? When do men sadden like women and when do they try to find consolation for the ailments of others? In the public venues and at home, at the hospital and at the orphanage, wherever there is pain, women are more compassionate than men.

Since women are more patient, more sensitive, and more compassionate than men, can we conclude that they are *better*?

And if women are the first ones to act when it comes to comfort the sorrowful, are they also in the same position when it comes to cause misfortune, to cause harm? Do they infringe God's commands and human laws? Do they respect honor, life and private property in the same way men do? Here the numbers speak for themselves.

Women are more emotional, less educated, driven to terrible circumstances due to public opinion some times, and oppressed by brutal force other times; they are reduced to poverty by a society that closes the access to the means of earning their livelihoods, and they have to listen to the horrible screaming of their hungry children because they do not have any bread to offer them; they suffer the shameful slap of public scorn when they are weak; they are exposed to boredom due to lack of a rational and useful occupation. Considering all the above, women should abandon themselves to desperation more frequently than men and commit suicide more than men. However, this is not what happens; the weak individuals endure with more strength a life of suffering; they fight until they fall, wounded by the hand of the omnipotent God, and not by their own guilty one. The rates vary from one country to the next; but in all of them there are always less women who commit suicide than men.

Some would say that this is a sign of cowardice, as if suicide was to be considered a courageous act, and as if women did not know how to face death when duty or charity commands it, as if they backed off in dangerous situations, cataclysms, and plagues.

The same causes that should push to commit suicide more women than men, should also bring more women to jails. They are poorer, less appreciated, and they have a worse education; therefore, they should be more prone to fall into the temptation of committing crimes and pay a higher tribute to prison and the gallows. It does not happen that way. In no country in the world can be compared women's criminality to men's, neither in number nor in the seriousness of offences. In the United States, where women are better educated and they have better opportunities at earning an honest living, the number of criminal women is so small, that when the penitentiary system was established, the reformers thought that women jails were not needed. In Spain, the rates of criminality is seven men for each woman, and while among men one fourth of the crimes are committed against persons, among women is only one out of thirteen.

Women see themselves in bad conditions, they find a lot of difficulties to earn a livelihood, they lack education and respect; still, in general, most of them end up in welfare homes and less in prison. Therefore, what is better for society and what is less bad? Can we tell what is best?

By observing the situation with attention and impartiality, we cannot ignore women's moral superiority. Women's passions are less violent and the instincts that lead to crime are less strong. Their desire to please, although when twisted by an absurd education can lead them frequently to ridiculous frivolities, makes them very sensitive to reprobation and, in many occasions, it serves as a constraint. Their passions are controlled by religious feelings that are stronger in them than in men. The fear of God restrains them, His love elevates and purifies them, and their hope in Him gives them strength and resignation; the *pious* sex has in piety one more element to walk with confidence along the path of virtue and to stand up after falling.

Loving parents, who see with sadness the birth of a daughter because they anticipate for her more sorrow, should calm down, because this physically weak creature, subject to so much pain, will have the endurance that resignation allows and the consolation that hope brings. Her higher sensitivity, source of many sorrows, will also bring a lot of joy;

she will be less attracted to evil passions and amid the hard strife with the world, she will find it easier to have peace in her soul. Even when she appears to be a victim, she is not always so, because she finds more joy in abnegation than in egoism. If she walks along the path of sorrow more frequently, she will not come across guilt so often. Her eyes will shed tears, but her hands almost never will spill blood. Do not approach the newborn girl with contempt or with fear; give her a welcoming kiss, saying: "Dear daughter, being a woman you might happen to be less fortunate, but you will also be more virtuous."

Questions for discussion

1. Who is the audience for whom this document is written?

2. What are the virtues that Concepción Arenal praises in women? Are they innate, according to Arenal? What is the role played by traditional society, religion, and the law?

3. Modern feminist trends would question the biological essentialism that underlies Arenal's essays. Identify what these issues are and express your opinion about them.

4. How would Arenal's views about the moral superiority of women be received by contemporary feminist movements?

DOCUMENT 3
CARMEN DE BURGOS, *EL DIVORCIO EN ESPAÑA* (DIVORCE IN SPAIN 1904)

Carmen de Burgos y Seguí (1867?–1932), also known as Colombine (a pen name she used in her writings) and by the nickname of "La Dama Roja" (the Red Dame) was a progressive teacher, a writer, a translator, a world traveler, and the first Spanish woman newspaper reporter who managed to support herself with her writings. During her life, she published hundreds of articles and *novellas*, as well as two books of interviews. In her personal life, she courageously defied social conventions and, as a well-known public figure, she tirelessly championed social causes (pacifism, anticlericalism, ideological stagnation), criticized government corruption, and defended women's rights, especially the right to vote. Carmen de Burgos was a strong and dauntless woman, an extraordinary human being who displayed and defended a proactive female identity that was very much in consonance with the prototype of the New Woman that was appearing in the turn-of-the-century European society. The audacious choices that she made in her personal life, her political and social stances, and the transgressive topics (such as transvestism and female homosexuality) that she included in some of her *novellas* make Carmen de Burgos one of the most thought-provoking women in twentieth-century Spain.

Although very close in thought to end-of-the-century *generationist* male writers, she was never associated with the so-called "Generation of 98." However, in her writings it is apparent the connection that exists between *regeneracionista* arguments defended by liberal and Krausista intellectuals and her activist involvement in favor of the education of women and their achievement of equal legal rights. The texts that follow should be read in the context of the controversial campaign that Carmen de Burgos organized in 1904 to fight for the legalization of divorce. The Catholic Church tried to sabotage the publication of the results of the survey that de Burgos was carrying out. Being aware of the importance of making all testimonies public, she decided to publish them in *El divorcio en España*, the book that made her popular and gave her a place in Madrid's intellectual arena.

EL DIVORCIO EN ESPAÑA (DIVORCE IN SPAIN)

Colombine:

My distinguished Madam: You kindly request my opinion about divorce. I am a staunch supporter of this social reform. Do I believe that the cases of adultery in Spain are so many that divorce becomes necessary? No, I do not think so. In fact, if a statistic about adultery in Spain could be done, I am sure that the number of infidelities, compared to other countries in Europe, would be insignificant. What is this a sign of? Morality? No. It is lack of life, lack of passion. Spain is—no matter what they say—the coldest and less passionate country in Europe. There is the legend, it is true, that Spanish men are terrible while Spanish women are ardent and with a volcanic heart; we wish they were!

Although it is sad to admit, it is necessary to confess that Spaniards are a feeble and weak people, cruel and lacking strong passions. The blood of the pompous Semitic individual, intelligent and cold, runs in the veins of almost all Spaniards. Like the Moors, Spanish men have very few relationships, and women from provincial cities, do not have them at all.

In Spain, men and women live as if they belonged to different species; they talk through a thick veil of considerations and formulas. Men insist that they cannot talk with women because their conversation revolves exclusively around clothes; but I have heard some young women say that they cannot talk to men because they are stupid. I do not know who is right; the fact is that this lack of communication among the sexes, together with the lack of passion, translates into very little spirited excitement between men and women, whether they are married or single.

Consequently, there are few cases of adultery, and because of these few cases, divorce is not very useful in practice. Furthermore, there is something else. If divorce were to be established in Spain for cases of adultery, it would have the same ending than the civil marriage: it would be ruined as a lifeless institution, as an instrument without a use, as a microscope in the hands of a savage.

If I do not believe that divorce will have a practical result. Why am I a supporter? I am a supporter because I believe that anything that helps to break this scab of laws and precepts, customs, intangible and immutable dogmas that do not let us live, seems good to me. I am a supporter because I believe that we must affirm that everything is revocable, that nothing is definitive, that everything can be transformed and become better.

This evolutionary idea confronts the Catholic sentiment of the immutable, the doctrinarian and dogmatic, that among Spaniards is prevalent in those that call themselves progressive and those that considered themselves reactionary, both in Salmerón and in Nocedal, both in Unamuno and in Father Coloma.

We are tied to so many laws, so many precepts, so many orders; we are already so stagnated by the splints of the Code, the morality, the society, and appearances, that even a respite, or one less tie, is considered progress.

Nowadays, bringing the debate of divorce to the forefront could be beneficial. The debate and the scandal (…) The mere exposition of the problem would bring protests from the corners of all the Spanish sacristies, from all the mystical and mundane congregations, from the theater boxes, from the stages, and from the brothels.

To shock is already something. When morality is absurd, scandal can be a form o good morality. And I will not continue so that my letter is not endless.

Faithfully yours,
Pío Baroja

———

When marriage does not work, it is a constant torture that can be avoided with divorce; but that measure, always extreme, can only be taken by those who do not have children, since they should never be aware of the discord that exists among parents. If they do not love each other as husband and wife, they can become good friends and come to an agreement about the course that their children would take.

If she performs her duties, a mother will not have time to get bored; and the father, after business and entertainment, will come home tired, but with the fondling of his little ones, he will come back with pleasure.

The Viscountess of Barrantes

———

Dear Colombine,

I am a staunch supporter of divorce, since I believe in love and not in marriage.

The priest's blessing, the judge's sentence, and social conventions are human inventions that love laughs at. Love is imagined in all mythologies as an eternal and capricious ruler, as a whimsical and unpredictable god.

When love leaves forever, why insisting on keeping the knot of marriage between to individuals who hate or despise each other? It is like being prisoners chained together and having to do together the most gross necessities.

Without love, the association between a man and a woman should not exist, no matter how many blessings consecrate it or how many laws protect it.

Healthy and strong people, when they do not love each other, should say farewell, without sorrow or resentment, taking their own paths to start their lives afresh again.

Vicente Blasco Ibáñez

———

Nuns Getting a Divorce

A few days ago, we published a telegram from Rome, informing about the important reform that Pope Pius X intends to undertake in the religious orders.

In the future—he says—nobody should influence novices; only those with a proven vocation will profess their vows, and *such vows will not be everlasting; they can break the vow of cloister if they change their mind.*

The news has been received with indescribable joy by the religious and it demonstrates the cultivated spirit and the superior ideas of the present successor of Saint Peter.

Not all religious go to the cloister with a true vocation, the same not all women get married being in love.

Sometimes, an exaltation of the mystical feeling, the attraction of a quiet a mysterious life, disillusionment, sorrows, inexperience and even egoism, are factors that lead virgin girls to convents.

But years go by, many of those girls become women, the impression that worked on their souls disappears, and regret arrives. Why condemning a creature to always suffer the consequences of unforeseeable circumstances?

Nuns call Jesus their *Divine Husband* and they consider themselves as *God's Wifes*; the day that they make their vows they wear an orange blossom crown and they dress a bridal costume, while they swear faithfulness to the glorious spouse.

It could happen, and it happens, that an earthly love takes possession of those innocent hearts and that their lips whisper another name while praying to Christ.

Then, those spirits darkened by the cloister, those determinations weakened by fasting, exaggerations, and sometimes superstitions, feel the guilt, *they accuse themselves of loving*; they consider offense what is natural law, the most beautiful law in life.

Why forcing them to eternal martyrdom, why making them feel that their love is adultery and belittle the idea of God, giving Him as a wife that weak woman and a simple mortal as His rival.

These logical reasons have been disregarded, as if everything concerning religion should remain immutable.

From this error arise the type of crimes and offenses that are registered in the convents annals, and that go against religion itself.

Today, the supreme head of the Church is a cultivated priest, more acquiescent of human weakness as he becomes more severe and virtuous; he understands the deficiencies some institutions have maintained through the rules, that go against the organization of a superior society.

If the noble elderly man carries out his proposal, nuns will be able to go to the monastery and kneel in front of an altar while their hearts are pure; if regret comes, the doors of their convents are not those of a prison; they can go back to the world, get married, be mothers and worship the divinity while they meet the goals of their existence.

This can be called *the nuns' divorce,* since it is the end of the spiritual bond, that has been considered a mystical matrimony and has had the same force of indissolubility as real marriage.

But if divorce from the *perfect husband* is allowed, why should not be allowed to the wives of simple mortals? The death of children? This is a matter that should be resolved by the laws that guarantee their welfare.

It would be irreverent to try to penetrate in the Pope's thoughts regarding this issue, which is more sociological than religious, but I am almost sure that the person who opens the cloister in the name of morality, would not allow, in the name of the same morality, the torments, the deceit and the bad example introduced in homes by people who go from not loving each other to detest each other.

Questions for discussion

1. Who are the writers of these opinions? Do you recognize the names of some Spanish famous writers?

2. Point out the most convincing reasons that the writers give in favor and against divorce. Compare the history of divorce in Spain and in other European countries.

3. In her article about nuns' divorce Carmen de Burgos establishes bold comparisons that could be considered too irreverent or provocative by traditionalists. Do you think they are effective to make Catholic people accept divorce?

4. The first divorce law was passed in Spain in 1931 during the government of the Second Republic, but then it was revoked in 1939 and divorce was illegal in Spain until 1981. Find out the reasons of this setback. Does gender play a role in the issue of divorce?

DOCUMENT 4
CONSUELO BERGES, "REPUBLICAN WOMEN'S UNION, PATHWAYS," *CULTURA INTEGRAL FEMENINA*, FEMINIST MAGAZINE (1933–36)[4]

With the subtitle "magazine of social integration to achieve a common and complete education for women," it was launched in 1933 as the organ of most outspoken and active feminist movement from center right to the republican left. The main goal was to pursue women's emancipation through knowledge and culture. Although it was directed by a man, José Aubin Rieu-Vernet, this periodical was the work of the Republican intellectual feminist movement, middle-class professionals, lawyers, full professors, writers or journalists, some of them part of the masonic lodges who would be elected representatives to the parliament. Many of them would suffer the exile and oblivion with the advent of the Francoist dictatorship. The document reproduced here is an excerpt from the first issue. It features prestigious lawyer Clara Campoamor (1896–1972) who was head of the editorial board and president of the Republican Women's Union. She was a member of parliament who defended the right to women's suffrage during the constituent assembly for the Constitution of 1931.

This was a pacifist and anti-fascist magazine with an editorial board of only women. It dedicated an ample section to inform its readers of the different feminist groups in Spain whose objectives were to improve the social and economic conditions of Spanish women. This monthly publication was published nationally and reached 24,200 copies only in Madrid. Published every fifteenth of the month it was terminated on July 15, 1936, three days later the Spanish Civil War began and a long dark dictatorship that kept feminism suppressed for nearly forty years.[5]

REPUBLICAN WOMEN'S UNION[6]

Pathways

It is little more than a year ago, Clara Campoamor fought and won in the Constituent Cortes the battle for women's rights. It was an intense conflict, fast and brilliant. (...) Fate had placed Clara Campoamor as MP who prevailed, pulsing the hypersensitive conscience of the Camera, with her resilient voice, conviction and convincing logic. (...) and Spanish women witness their political and civil liberation written in the Constitution.

Spanish women have not been aware yet of the enormous change in their favor, and neither have men. The true Spanish revolution (...) resides in the Constitution's articles that allow in the political arena a new force, unknown and possible full of surprises. Those surprises will be most likely different from the ones some fear and others anticipate.

How was Republican Women's Union born?

Clara Campoamor ended her role in the Cortes as the defender of the potential political value of Spanish women. (...) She needed women to be able to serve the Republic defending their rights and performing their duties. That is how the Republican Union of Women was born.

Clara Campoamor created a political organization for women (...), which meant the association of a few modest and determined women to start a journey. Hopefully some day Spain will be able to thank Clara Campoamor for her sense of responsibility and exemplary constructive effort. (...)

The organization's bylaws point out its goals:

1. Defence and protection of the legal, political and social rights of women.
2. Defence and protection of the child.
3. Citizens' political and civic education.
4. Women's preparation for the fulfilment of their civic duties both passive and active.
5. Dissemination and instruction of the international principles of fraternity, peoples' self-determination and pacifism.
6. Any other end analogous to these.

What do we pretend?

Last year in a political manifesto asking for support for our association, we proposed this to be a political think-tank where the different political forces could recruit well prepared affiliates. (...) Our association intends to be a transient space between the almost inexistent political representation of Spanish women in politics and their absolute and dedicated militant participation within the Republican parties. (...) Through lectures and workshops on political themes and general culture and also through the participation in the public arena in the parties' propaganda and technical assistance, Spanish women will be prepared and become familiar with their new civic duties. (...)

Likewise, we hope through the creation of the Youth branch of our organization to create a nascent political vigor among young women.

Questions for discussion

1. Write a brief biographical sketch of Clara Campoamor.

2. Women got the right to vote in the US and Britain after the First World War. How did the Spanish feminist movement compare to the United States and British feminisms?

3. What are the main concerns of the Republican Women's Union?

4. This text was published in the Magazine *Cultura Integral femenina* (1933–6). How important it is to have access to the press to disseminate the feminist ideals?

DOCUMENT 5
LIDIA FALCÓN, *LA RAZÓN FEMINISTA* (THE FEMINIST REASON 1981)[7]

Lidia Falcón (1935) has been one of the most polemical Spanish feminists of our times. Both her personal life and her work are a testimony of her profoundly radical feminist beliefs and her Marxist political stance. She grew up surrounded by strong women: her grandmother was an anarchist writer and a staunch political activist; her mother was a journalist who wrote numerous articles on women's issues, and her aunt, Carlota O'Neill, was a feminist dramatist. As a journalist and writer, she has dedicated all her life to defend women, discuss women's issues, and to make sure they are visible in the public arena. As a lawyer, she has fought for the rights of women, workers, and dissidents of Franco's regime and as a writer and a dramatist she has explored critically the many angles of patriarchal social structures with the view to dismantle a deep-rooted ideology that keeps women subjugated and treated as inferior citizens. The ultimate end of all Falcón's writings is to defend women's dignity, to promote a change in social structures, and to give women the opportunity to reject and imposed identity and substitute it with their own new-found individuality.

The Feminist Reason (1981) is Falcón's main theoretical work and her most influential writing, since it was taken by the feminist parties created in post-Franco Spain as the foundation for their ideological framework. Falcón draws on Marxist tenets to analyze the conditions of subjugation that women had to suffer throughout the history of humanity. For Falcón, the family serves as the main social unit for the exploitation of women. Women's role in society has always been underestimated and subordinated to men's, regardless of their social class. Falcón's main thesis is that men exploit women's sexuality and get economic and moral benefits from their reproductive powers. What follows is a summary of the thesis developed in the book, included in the introduction.

THE FEMINIST REASON

Introduction

The thesis of this work is that women belong to a social and economic class that has been exploited and oppressed by men, which consequently becomes an antagonist group for women. All the subjugations mentioned during the years by those who studied the topic explain with detail the continuous tortures, harassment, and humiliations that women suffered in the hands of men. And nothing else. It was as if the enormous amount of data that philosophers, politicians, historians, and anthropologists had was only good to sympathize with them and point to the bad situation that those who had been born women suffered. We lacked any scientific analysis and conclusions.

The so-called Marxists theoreticians from leftist political parties, philosophers, and professors applied mechanically to women's condition the Marxist declarations about class, the means of production, and the class struggle, and although they were faithful and orthodox Marxists, they become at the same time anti-Marxist. By equating the economic exploitation and social oppression of men and women—therefore completely negating reality—they refer to class struggle amalgamating all individuals, men and women who live in the same house and apparently share an economic condition. A few days ago, a leftist intellectual was irate when I stated that I could not use the term "laborer" to refer to the wife of a worker, if she only works in the house doing domestic chores, giving birth and taking care of children, because the explicit Marxist condition to be part of the proletariat is to give surplus value to the capital, when the worker's wife only provides services to her husband. The surprise and indignation were apparent in the vulgar and derogatory tone he used in his answer and they translated into statements that revealed his lack of economic background of the fundamental laws of capitalism. Political leaders and leftist ideologists, including women, usually react and reason in a similar way.

This misunderstanding about the female condition leads to the most important goal of the ruling classes: the lack of union among women and the loss of feminist objectives. The fighting and well-meaning decided a long time ago—so long ago that we find in Lenin his most authoritative ideologist—that the "bourgeois" women have antagonist contradictions with the proletarian woman and, as a consequence, they do not have anything in common with the revolutionary movement. It cannot be forgotten that for a long time the terms "feminism" and "bourgeois" were considered synonyms. Therefore, if the proletariat is the only class that can lead and make the revolution happen, the women who want to fight for social change should sign up in proletarian parties and fight within them to end up all their misery, in the sublime and perfect paradisiac ending of the socialist revolution.

As I already mentioned before, the bedside reading for the supporters of this simple theory—which is more than a theory—is *The Origin of the Family, Private Property and the Estate*, by Frederic Engels. He dedicates a chapter to the feminine condition, where he affirms that the origin of female submission derives from the invention of the private property in the beginning of civilization.

Today, almost a century after the publication of the little masterwork published by Marx's disciple, we know a few other things that force us to a correction of Engels' proposal and such corrections he would quickly and gladly acknowledge, had he lived in our days.

Nowadays, anthropological fieldwork, history, and archeology has shown us how the so-called natural peoples live, where private property, and in many cases the biological and physiological process of fecundation are unknown. In those communities, contrary to the statements of Engels and his followers, it is apparent the systematic exploitation that women are subject to, the enormous surplus labor that men extract from them, the way they are humiliated, raped, punished and assassinated, always considered as inferior human beings, placed in slave "status." There is no honest anthropologist who has found a trace of those utopic societies described by Engels, where equality, fraternity, and solidarity were practiced gently and generously with the women who, in his opinion, held economic, social, and political power. All the data that we have shows quite a different scenario, whether it is among the Indians in North or South America, the tribes in Central Africa or the Polynesian and Melanesian peoples. In all these societies, women are nothing but workers who receive no consideration and no retribution; they are condemned to be sold as wives to the husbands' harem so that they work for them, serve them, give birth to children, finally dying in old age while being despised. Female infanticide is practiced, and women do not take part in economic, social or political matters.

Therefore, the inventors of private property and monogamy are not the only ones responsible for women's fate. From the natural peoples who do not know writing or the process of fecundation and own the land communally, to the ancient peoples who, in all latitudes, have practices polygamy, a woman is the slave or servant for the father, the husband, the brothers, and later the sons. She is a pariah, the slave or the servant "nunca manumitido" (never freed), because a woman can never buy her liberty, which differentiates her from the slave.

By looking at all this data, it was necessary to propose a question that has not yet been answered, why? Why men—not only a specific social class, since not only princes exert exploitation and oppression—from all places and times have subjugated women with so viciously throughout the centuries? We must find the only answer in the material causes that differentiate men and women: the different role that they have in procreation. A woman can create, day by day a new human being inside herself and then give birth, and the man who has put the seed inside her cannot know categorically where the new human being was conceived and by whom. And this antagonism, "the first division of labor between men and women in procreation," arises with the first man who is aware of the advantages of possessing a child, a new labor force, servant and merchandise at once, and to get it he realizes that he has to dominate women.

The name of exploitations

"Men *do not therefore* bring the products of *their labor into* relation with *each* other as *values* because they see these objects merely as the material integuments of homogeneous human labor. The reverse is true: by equating their different products to each other in exchange as values, they equate their different kinds of labor as human labor. They do this without being aware of it. *Value*, therefore, *does not have* its description branded on its forehead; it rather transforms every *product* of labor into a *social hieroglyphic*. Later, men try to decipher the hieroglyphic, to get behind the secret of their own social product: for the characteristic, which objects of utility have of being values is as much men's social product as is their language."[8]

Value does not have its description branded on its forehead, and for several hundred years, ideologists try to decipher the hieroglyphic of the true value of the work done by women. But the point of departure has never been to analyze the role of women in society, her place in production and the production relationships with men.

Women have always had the capacity to reproduce human beings. They are the only ones who reproduce themselves. Women are the only ones who make one more human being. This human being is the first good appreciated by men, since it guarantees the conservation of the species, the production of assets, and the social satisfactions. It is the product that men appreciate more than anything else, after themselves.

Sex defines women for the procreation of children and men make this reproductive capacity their own by dominating their sexuality, by getting the pleasure that they believe they have the undeniable right to, and this appropriation allows them to relegate women to the most monotonous, routine, harder and worst paid production tasks. The exploitation that all women suffer qualify and define them as a class that is oppressed and exploited by men, who are their antagonist enemy.

Sexuality, reproduction, and the production of the consumer goods necessary for the survival of the family, are the three exploitations that women have been suffering quietly for millions of years. Only now, barely a century ago, women have started to be uneasy about their submissive status, by their disguised slavery, by their "providential destiny." From this uneasiness, the focus of their rebelliousness starts and they will soon become a fire of revolutions. But to achieve perfection in the strategy and in the revolutionary practice, necessary to all classes to achieve victory, it is necessary to know the meaning of our work and our social relationships, It is important to name our miseries, to know the meaning of the economic laws that rule our slavery, and to be able to understand why men behave like tyrants or like poets with women. Ultimately, we need to go from the utopic feminism of lamenting for the eternal female suffering and the senseless whimsical solutions, to the scientific feminism that unveils the laws of the value of female production, of reproduction and domestic work, and the laws of the production relations with exploiting men within the frame of the domestic mode or production.

This book is the beginning of this research that moves through the stony paths of scientific feminism. A detailed analysis of the themes that I have outlined in this introduction is found in the text that follows. Read it.

Questions for discussion

1. Why is social class an important component when dealing with gender issues?

2. Lidia Falcón adheres to the Marxist feminist movements that were prevalent in the Western world in the 1980s. According to her, women's liberation has to come hand in hand with a complete restructuration of the capitalist economy. Do capitalism and private property affect women in a different way to men? Do you think that domestic work of stay-home wives and mothers should be compensated? Elaborate your answer by giving examples of your own country.

3. Sexuality, reproduction, and domestic work are, according to Falcón, the three areas where women have been exploited the most. Summarize Falcon's ideas on this issue.

4. How does the content of this document affect the political and social opportunities of Spanish women in the last couple of decades? Is there any value in reading this document today?

5. In "The Traffic in Women. Notes on the Political Economy of Sex," Gale Rubin suggests that sexism might be "a by-product of capitalism's relentless appetite for profit." Explain this statement considering Lidia Falcón's text.

DOCUMENT 6

LEY ORGÁNICA 1/2004, DE 28 DE DICIEMBRE, DE MEDIDAS DE PROTECCIÓN INTEGRAL CONTRA LA VIOLENCIA DE GÉNERO (LIVG) (ORGANIC LAW 1/2004 OF DECEMBER 28 ON INTEGRATED PROTECTION MEASURES AGAINST GENDER VIOLENCE)

Since the end of Franco's dictatorship in 1975, Spain underwent important legal and social changes that have transformed its reputation from being an ultra-religious, conservative, and male-dominated country to a modern, liberal society. Although legislation about divorce, abortion, and gay marriage has been approved in the last four decades and the salary gap is slowly closing, gender inequality persists. Gender violence is a proof that sexist attitudes remain deeply-rooted in Spanish society. In 1997, the Instituto de la Mujer (Women's Institute) elaborated the Comprehensive Plan to Combat Domestic Violence, and in 2004 the Socialist government of José Luis Rodríguez Zapatero passed a ground-breaking law whose goal was to eradicate domestic violence. As you can see in the text below, this law encourages women to denounce their aggressors and facilitates the process of seeking protection orders and legal redress. It also fosters education based on respect and tolerance and provides social resources to provide care and protection for victims.

However, legal measures do not change individual and social attitudes overnight. According to the Survey on Violence published in November 2015, only nine of the forty-eight women killed in 2015 filed a police complaint, since most women are afraid or ashamed of the abuse that they suffer at the hands of their partners, or consider that it is not serious enough to warrant reporting it to the authorities. The survey also revealed that sixty-five percent of the victims were unemployed, and eighty-one percent believe that being financially independent was crucial to deal with abuse. Although this law has had many detractors, it has been an important step to address an issue that is still unresolved worldwide.

LEY ORGÁNICA 1/2004, DE 28 DE DICIEMBRE, DE MEDIDAS DE PROTECCIÓN INTEGRAL CONTRA LA VIOLENCIA DE GÉNERO (LIVG) (ORGANIC LAW 1/2004 OF DECEMBER 28 ON INTEGRATED PROTECTION MEASURES AGAINST GENDER VIOLENCE)

I

Gender violence is not a problem affecting the private sphere. On the contrary, it manifests itself as the most brutal symbol of inequality in our society. It is a violence that is directed against women by virtue of being women, considered by their aggressors devoid of the minimum rights of freedom, respect, and decision making.

Our Constitution incorporates in Article 15 everybody's right to physical and moral integrity, not allowing in any case neither torture nor inhuman or degrading treatment and punishment. Our Constitution adds that these rights are binding on all public authorities and its exercise can only be regulated by law.

In 1995, the United Nations Fourth World Conference recognized that violence against women is an obstacle to achieving the goals of equality, development and peace, and it violates and impairs the enjoyment of human rights and fundamental freedoms. Besides, UN broadly defines it as a manifestation of the historically unequal power relations between women and men. There is now even a technical definition of the battered woman syndrome which derives from "the aggressions suffered by women as a result of the sociocultural constraints acting on both males and females, which put them in a position of subordination to men and which are expressed in the three core areas of relationship of the person: abuse within intimate relationships, sexual aggression in social life and harassment in the workplace."

In the Spanish reality, attacks on women have a special impact, and there is now greater awareness of them than in the past, thanks largely to the efforts of women's organizations in their fight against all forms of gender violence. It is no longer an "invisible crime," but one that produces a collective rejection and a clear social alarm.

II

Governments cannot be oblivious to gender violence, which is one of the most flagrant violations of fundamental rights such as freedom, equality, life, safety and non-discrimination enshrined in our Constitution. Those same authorities have, in accordance with Article 9.2 of the Constitution, the obligation to take positive action to make these rights real and effective, removing obstacles that prevent or hinder their fulfillment.

In recent years, there has been legislative progress in combating gender violence under Spanish law: the Organic Law 11/2003 (September, 29) Concrete Measures on Public Safety, Domestic Violence and the Social Integration of Foreigners; Organic Law 15/2003 (November, 25), amending the Organic Law 10/1995 (November, 23) of the

Penal Code; or Law 27/2003 (July 31), regulating the Order for the Protection of Victims of Domestic Violence; in addition to laws passed by various Autonomous Communities within their jurisdictions. All of them have affected various civil, criminal, social or educational areas through their respective regulations.

The Law aims to address the recommendations of international organizations by providing a global response to the violence inflicted upon women. In this regard we can cite the Convention on the Elimination of All Forms of Discrimination on Women in 1979; the United Nations Declaration on the Elimination of Violence against Women, proclaimed in December 1993 by the General Assembly; Resolutions of the last International Conference on Women held in Beijing in September 1995; Resolution WHA49.25 of the World Health Assembly declaring violence a priority public health problem proclaimed in 1996 by WHO; the European Parliament report of July 1997; the UN Resolution of the Commission on Human Rights, 1997; and the Declaration of 1999 as the European Year for Combating Violence Against Women, among others. Most recently, Decision No 803/2004/CE by the European Parliament—approved the creation of a community action program (2004–8) to prevent and combat violence against children, young people and women and to protect victims and groups at risk (Daphne II program)—has set the position and strategy of the representatives of the citizens of the European Union in this regard.

The scope of the Law covers not only issues regarding preventive, educational, social, and overall care of the victims, but also civil legislation that affects the family or living companions where mainly attacks occur, as well as the principle of subsidiarity in public administrations. It also addresses upfront the punitive response that all the manifestations of violence that this law regulates should receive.

Gender violence is approached by the Law in an integrated and multidisciplinary way, starting with the process of socialization and education.

The conquest of equality and respect for human dignity and people's freedom must be a priority at all levels of socialization.

The Act provides measures for awareness and intervention in the educational field. It strengthens, with particular reference to the field of advertising, an image that respects the equality and dignity of women. It supports victims through the recognition of rights such as information, legal assistance and other social protection and economic support. Thus it provides an integrated legal response that encompasses both procedural rules, creating new instances, as well adequate training for policemen, health workers, and legal operators that are responsible for obtaining evidence and for the enforcement of the law.

Awareness and intervention measures are also established in the health sector to optimize early detection and physical and psychological care of the victims, in coordination with other support measures.

Situations of violence against women also affect children who live within the family circle and who are direct or indirect victims of gender violence. The Act provides protection of the rights of minors, and it also ensures effective protection measures taken with regard to women.

III

The Act is structured as follows: a preliminary title, five titles, twenty additional provisions, two transitional provisions, one derogatory provision, and seven final provisions.

The preliminary title includes the general provisions of the Act that relate to its purpose and guiding principles.

Title I establishes measures of awareness, prevention and detection, as well as intervention in different areas. In the educational system, obligations for transmitting values of respect for the dignity of women and equality between men and women are specified. The fundamental goal of education is to provide comprehensive training that enables individuals to shape their own identity and build a conception of reality that integrates both knowledge and an ethical evaluation of it.

Secondary education curricular content incorporates education on equality between men and women and against gender violence, and all school councils will have a new member in charge of encouraging educational measures in favor of equality and against violence on women.

In the advertising field, the dignity of women and their right to non-stereotyped or discriminatory images, whether they are exhibited privately or in the public media, should be respected. On the other hand, this Act modifies the actions of cessation or rectification of advertising, legitimizing institutions and associations that work for the equality between men and women.

In the health field, early detection and care support to victims are contemplated, and sanitary protocols are established for the attacks arising from gender violence; such protocols will be submitted to the relevant courts in order to expedite the judicial process. Also, a commission will be created within the Interterritorial Council of the National Health System to provide technical support, and to coordinate and evaluate the health measures established by this Act.

In Title II, concerning the rights of women who have been victims of violence, Chapter I guarantees the right of access to information and integrated welfare through services of permanent, urgent and specialized attention that will be provided by specialists and multidisciplinary professionals. In order to contribute to the implementation of these services, a Fund that can be accessed by the Autonomous Communities will be established, according to objective criteria to be determined in the respective Sector Conference.

Also, the Act recognizes the right to free legal aid, in order to ensure that the victims with insufficient resources enter the litigation with legal aid for all processes and procedures related to gender violence in which they are involved, receiving the same legal assistance in all processes. This measure is extended to affected parties, in the case of death of the victim.

Protective measures in the social field are also established, modifying the Royal Decree 1/1995 of March 24, which approves the revised text of the Workers Statute, justifying work-related absences of the victims of gender violence, allowing them geographical mobility, job security, and the termination of the contract.

In the same sense, the Act contemplates measures of support for female public servants who suffer gender violence, amending the relevant provisions of Act 30/1984 of August 2, on Measures for the Reform of Public Administration.

Economic support measures are likewise regulated by modifying the Royal Legislative Decree 1/1994 of June 20, approving the revised text of the General Social Security Act, so that victims of gender violence generate the right to legal unemployment compensation when they resolve or voluntarily suspend their employment contract.

To ensure that victims of gender violence lacking economic resources receive social aid—in those cases where it is deemed that the victims because of their age, lack of specialized training and social circumstances will not substantially improve their employability—they can join a specific action program that will promote their reintegration in the labor market. This aid, which shall be adjusted in relation to age and family responsibilities of the victims will provide minimum subsistence resources to enable them to become independent from their aggressors; such aid will be compatible with those stipulated by the Law 35/1995 of December 11 on Aid and Assistance to Victims of Violent Crimes and Crimes Against Sexual Freedom.

Questions for discussion

1. Research shows that most Spanish women are more vulnerable to becoming victims of gender violence and also less capable of abandoning toxic relationships. What are some of the reasons that explain this situation?

2. Gender violence includes physical, sexual, emotional, and psychological abuse. Are all of them equally important? Why is psychological abuse sometimes not considered an aggressive behavior?

3. The Spanish economic crisis that started in 2008 and the austerity measures taken as a result have forced the Spanish government to reduce drastically funding for some of the programs described in the above text. Some believe that only the victims should receive the scarce funds available, while others think that in order to eradicate the problem, aggressors should continue receiving therapy so that they can be reinserted into society. What do you think about this issue? When funds are limited, should they be directed to help the perpetrators or the victims? Can the perpetrators be also considered victims of a culture that associates masculinity with violent behaviors?

4. More than ten years after the approval of this law, sexist stereotypes and different forms of aggressive behavior persists in Spain and every year many women die at the hands of their partners. What in your opinion can be done to end this situation? Are the gender violence statistics in Spain similar to the ones in your own country?

MODULE 4
EVERYDAY LIFE AND MATERIAL CULTURE

ABSTRACT

In this module, we examine everyday life and material culture as reflected in the press, photography, and graphic novels. The cultural historian should never neglect the special role played by visual sources, especially in the digital age. Visual literacy is a crucial piece in the communication process within a multilingual global economy.

Historian Peter Burke reminds us of the "invisibility of the visual" in traditional historical narratives. The use of illustrations in history books has always been a secondary preoccupation of the professional historian. In the last three decades, however, the relevance of the visual document to the construction of the story has become more apparent. Burke points out a genealogy of cultural historians like Jacob Burckhardt (1818–97), Johan Huizinga (1872–1945), Aby Warburg (1866–1929), and Gilberto Freyre (1900–87), who inaugurate what American critic William Mitchell called "pictorial turn," and received a further impetus in the 1960s as historians recognized the value of images as tools to reconstruct a history from below.[1]

DOCUMENT 1
SINGER SEWING MACHINE ADVERTISEMENT (c. 1910)[2]

By the beginning of the twentieth century, the sewing machine became one of the most used appliances in Spanish households. Singer was a popular brand, an international company based in the United States that had expanded globally beginning in the 1860s. The first sewing machines arrived in Spain in the 1860s, and by the 1890s Singer had a well-established retail organization, reaching every city and rural area in the Iberian Peninsula. The sewing machine, an expensive appliance even for middle-class families, was a symbol of modernization in Spain. As the advertisement demonstrates, the sewing machine would modernize women's home duties while upholding middle-class domesticity ideals. But the sewing machine revolutionized lower income households as well. Singer offered its machines on credit. Although the sewing machine also meant more sweatshops with miserable working conditions for women, for many dressmakers and seamstresses the sewing machine became an important piece of property with which to make their homes a business. Hundreds of women were also employed in the Singer offices and shops, selling and adapting the sewing machine to local consumer preferences and uses. The sewing machine was widely used in Spain until the 1980s when cheaper ready-to-wear clothing began to be widely available.

Figure 3. Singer Sewing Machine Advertisement (c. 1910).

Questions for discussion

1. Based on the diverse sewing activities that may be performed inside the home, for which do you think the sewing machine was mostly used?

2. The Singer Sewing Machine Company sold millions of sewing machines around the world. High sales in Spain surprised the managers of the company because the country's industrial development was slow and its consumers' income level was low.

   How does the case of Spain, in view of cultural practices, change our perspective on the country's place in the global economy at the turn of the twentieth century when studying the economy at large?

3. Think about embroidery; is this an activity for which you would have expected the sewing machine to be widely used?

4. Looking at the advertisement, discuss how an industrial appliance could have become such a cultural symbol of domesticity and private life.

DOCUMENT 2
BLANCO Y NEGRO, COVER (MAGAZINE WHITE AND BLACK, 1936)

Blanco y Negro, founded in 1891 by Spanish journalist and impresario Torcuato Luca de Tena (1861–1929), was the first illustrated magazine in the country to utilize color and couché paper. The format and content followed the German magazine *Fliegende Blätter*.[3] The significance of the artistic element in the periodical cannot be underestimated. Members of the literary Generation of '98 like Azorín, Maeztu, Emilia Pardo Bazán, Manuel Machado, Juan Ramón Jiménez, and Blasco Ibáñez contributed to the journal, which had a circulation of 80,000 copies at the turn of the twentieth century. The *Blanco y Negro* format included brief chronicles, short stories, and poetry, along with magnificent illustrations. The goal was to entertain and provide information about the cultural life of the urban modern society at the turn of the twentieth century: sporting events, theater openings, and cultural gatherings were on display in a happy balance between images and words. The image took over the pages, appealing both to men and women, as the magazine featured coverage of fashion and bullfighting, celebrities from the entertainment industry, and the plastic arts. The printing press was located in Madrid on the fashionable Serrano Street in the upper middle-class Salamanca district. The production of this successful publication also led to the publication of the newspaper *ABC*. The daily's main characteristics reflected conservative politics: defense of the monarchy, Spain's unity, Catholicism and respect for the Armed Forces, free trade, excellence in journalism, and commitment to graphic reporting. The magazine *Blanco y Negro* experienced several periods of publication: from 1891–1939 it was an independent weekly confiscated by the Republican government during the Civil War. In 1957 it reopened and ran until 1988 as an independent publication. The third period lasted until 2002, after which it appeared as a Sunday supplement of the *ABC* newspaper. Today it continues as a weekly supplement with a different name, *ABCD Las Artes y las Letras*. The illustration included here is a cover from 1936.

Figure 4. *Blanco y Negro*, cover 1936.

Questions for discussion

1. Describe the image and compare it with the cover of *National Geographic* included in this Module. In your opinion, which image represents modernity?

2. Compare the illustration and the history of *Blanco y Negro* with other international journals such as: *Harper's Magazine*, *The New Yorker*, and *Punch*.

3. These publications covered topics that reflected the emergence of consumption and sought the readership of new urban middle classes. Compare the expansion of these publications at the turn of the twentieth century with the explosion of digital blogs and other social media at the turn of the twenty-first century.

4. How does visual language construct social roles along gender and racial lines? How have the messages changed over time?

DOCUMENT 3
RICARD TERRÉ, *HOLY WEEK*, 1957[4]

Catalan photographer Ricard Terré (1928–2009) captured this image in 1957 in Barcelona during Holy Week, in which a long line of women marched in the traditional street processions following figures representing the Way of the Cross. The penitent women are completely covered in black opaque veils, marching in mourning and carrying long candles. Considered one of the most important photographers along with Joan Colom, Xavier Miserachs, and Ramón Masats adhering to the reportage and realist style of the so-called Agrupación Fotográfica de Cataluña (Catalonia's Photographic Group), Terré captures universal moments in time, full of poetic meaning. Art critic Laura Terré states that: "Like poets, he [Ricard Terré] utilizes images not like representations of reality, but rather as similes, metaphors of another innermost world. They are not just representations of the personal world of the photographer—and that is where their strength resides—but rather they are in harmony with the soul that enlivens the surrounding reality."[5] Therefore, Terré's images capture the historical invisible and universal moments that a keen historian's eye may benefit from in constructing insightful appraisals of the human condition.

Ricard Terré joined the group AFAL (Agrupación Fotográfica Almeriense, 1956–63), an artistic initiative that also involved cinematography and resulted in the internationalization of Spanish photographers.

This image captures the National Catholic ideology that served the Francoist dictatorship (1939–75) as it reentered the international political arena in the context of the Cold War. In 1953, Spain signed two important international treaties: first, the Pact of Madrid, with the United States, that would start the economic aid and the transition from autarky to consumerism in Spain, as well as the establishment of American military bases in Spain. The second treaty was the Concordat with the Vatican that would solidify the preeminent role of the Catholic Church in Spain.

Figure 5. Ricard Terré, *Holy Week* 1957.

Questions for discussion

1. Holy Week in Spain during the Francoist period represented the ultimate public expression of the National Catholicism ideology of the regime. What possible political purpose did these public mass processions serve during the transition from autarky to consumerism?

2. Describe the scene represented in the image. Is there any contemporary representation of women that come to mind?

3. How is death ever-present in the picture? What sentiment is the photographer conveying about everyday life under Francoism?

4. What can we infer from the full coverage of the body (female or male) and about the religious character of the people?

DOCUMENT 4
PARACUELLOS, COMIC BY CARLOS GIMÉNEZ 1975

Carlos Giménez was born in Madrid in 1941.[6] His father died the following year, leaving behind a widow and three children. Tragedy followed the family as his mother fell prey to tuberculosis a few years later. The youngest of three, Carlos and his middle brother were placed in two different orphanages, while the oldest child went to live with relatives. This scenario was not unusual in the "years of hunger," as the 1940s were called. Ration booklets were in circulation until 1952, and many of the children of the poor entered the welfare system through the Falangist agency Auxilio Social (Social Help). Mercedes Sanz Bachiller created this organization. She was the widow of Onésimo Redondo, one of the founders of the pseudo-fascist political organization JONS (Committees of the Nationalist Syndicalist Offensive). In 1937, JONS unified with Falange Española Tradicionalista (Traditionalist Spanish Phalanx), founded by José Antonio Primo de Rivera, which resulted in the single party FET de las JONS with Francisco Franco as sole leader and dictator.

Auxilio Social was originally called Auxilio de Invierno (Winter Help) because it had been created during the Spanish Civil War (1936–9) in the image of its Nazi counterpart Winter-Hilfe. Following the premise of what psychiatrist Antonio Vallejo Nágera proposed in his work *Eugenesia de la Hispanidad* (Hispanic Eugenics, 1936), the offspring of the vanquished in the war were to be indoctrinated into the fascist and ultra-Catholic values of the New Spain. Many of these children came from the female prisons where the inmates who gave birth would never see their babies again. There were also children whose families could not provide for them and were thus turned over to the state apparatus to be taken care of.

Paracuellos was one of the state orphanages where Carlos Giménez spent his childhood. He grew up to become one of the most respected cartoonists in recent Spanish history. *Paracuellos* is a series of comics that capture Giménez's poignant stories of being forced to grow up in church-run "orphanages," along with thousands of other "children of the defeated," in Franco's fascist Spain. As Will Eisner observes, "Carlos Giménez speaks with humor and sensitivity to the human condition. His work is international."[7]

Figures 6.1 and 6.2. *Paracuellos* comic by Carlos Giménez, 1975.

From left to right: Frame 1: This is Rudy; his father is in jail because he was a "Red" (Communist). Frame 2: This is "Zampa"; he does not have a father or mother, but he does have a brother in another school.
Frame 3: This is Antolín; he is an albino. It is said that he chews the cud and can see in the dark.
Frame 4: This is "Pirracas"; he eats flies, butterflies, and wasps, and he digs through vomit.
Frame 5: This is 'Huertetuna"; he wets his bed.[8]

Questions for discussion

1. The graphic novel medium has become a means to explore complex violent political events through the voice of children. How is the story told differently from the narrative of an adult?

2. Describe the characters on the first image. How does the artist represent them in relation to the children?

3. Compare this work with cartoonist Art Spiegelman's *Maus* and Marjane Satrapi's *Persepolis,* as well as with the film *Waltz with Bashir* by Ari Folman. What is their commentary on suffering and politics? Is there anything universal running through these artistic renditions of historical experiences?

4. Who is the audience for these works?

DOCUMENT 5
"THE CHANGING FACE OF OLD SPAIN,"
NATIONAL GEOGRAPHIC COVER, 1965

The 1960s were known as the "years of development" and the "miracle years." The misery of the 1940s was over, and initial autarky gave way to the consumer economy that American dollars brought. In 1965, the cover of *National Geographic* featured the image of a contorted flamenco dancer, and the issue included a detailed report of the modernization undergone in the decade since the Francoist regime and the United States signed the economic and military Pact of Madrid (1953). Tourism and emigration were the two major changes affecting the everyday lives of Spaniards. There was an important interior migration from the rural areas to the urban centers such as Madrid, Barcelona, and Bilbao in the early 1960s. Then, Spanish workers started to migrate to other European countries as well, with a guest worker contract that allowed them to enter the German or French labor forces. Although the remittances from these workers benefitted the Spanish economy, the displacement also had social consequences, as these families were separated, often with the father abroad by himself and the wife left behind in Spain to raise their children. The new social and moral behaviors the emigrants brought back to Spain, made them realize the great differences between the liberties in Spain and those abroad.

Tourists came to Spain by the millions. The slogan "Spain is different," coined by the Ministry of Information and Tourism under Manuel Fraga (1922–2012), attempted to capitalize on an old exotic otherness of the Iberian Peninsula, with bullfights, flamenco, and sunny beaches. It seems as if the image of the flamenco dancer in this *National Geographic* issue, for example, is "trying" to fit into the yellow frame of the western gaze. Dressed in her traditional attire, the dancer is frozen in a knotted pose that suggests Spain's tremendous efforts to enter the international political affairs of the West.

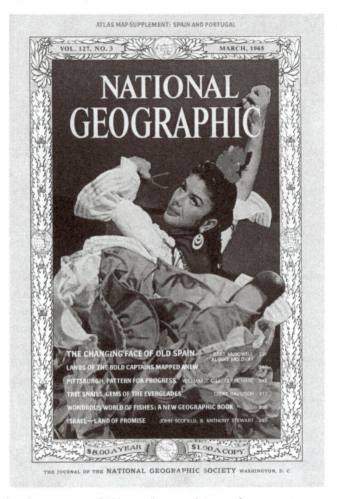

Figure 7. "The Changing Face of Old Spain," *National Geographic* cover, 1965.

Questions for discussion

1. What is distinctively Spanish about this image? What is modern?

2. What is the role of a publication like *National Geographic* from a cultural perspective? Does it help its readers understand other cultures better? Look for other covers of the same publication during the 1960s showing different regions of the world.

3. Why do you think *National Geographic* chose to portray the image of a woman? How have gender-specific images of a nation been used throughout history as a call to war or as a representation of a country?

4. How are tourist campaigns designed today? Are gender and sexuality part of the advertising?

DOCUMENT 6
ADVERTISEMENT FOR JABÓN LAGARTO, 1960s

Spain's economic boom in the 1960s was the result of the United States' economic loans after the signing of the Pact of Madrid in August 1953 between the two countries. The self-sufficient economic model of autarky dominated the 1940s, known as the "hunger years." The first Stabilization Plan of 1959 opened the door to planning, urbanization, emigration of Spaniards to other European countries, and the arrival of tourists in their millions to sunny Spain. A new consumer woman was to replace the productive model of homemaker of the past. Housework became a science, and cleanliness could be purchased and achieved to perfection. Advertising became the most important means of engaging the mass of consumers. The images included here belong to a Spanish company that produced soap and cleaning products. In 1910, a business owned by two Basque families—the Lizariturry and the Rezola families—contacted the German inventor Peter Krebitz and, with his patents, established in Spain one of the most modern soap factories in the continent at the time. Lagarto soap was introduced in 1914 in the city of San Sebastian. During the 1960s there was a broad selection of products available to the homemaker that included, not only soap, but also detergents specially formulated for the new washing machines and dishwashers in the market.

Figure 8. Advertisement for Jabón Lagarto, 1960s.

Questions for discussion

1. Who is the target population in this advertisement? Think not only about the gender, but also the socio-economic status.

2. Some of the words used in the ad are "atomized soap" or "controlled foam." What is the message they are trying to convey?

3. How do you know this is a 1960s ad? Describe the image and identify some characteristics that convey modernity.

MODULE 5
EDUCATION

ABSTRACT

This module gathers several documents that illustrate the significant role of education in the history of modern Spain. For centuries, the forces of tradition and order engaged the forces of change and modernization in the educational battlefield. Central to the construction of national and individual identities is the sense of belonging to the civil society emerging because of the Rousseaunian social contract. The Enlightenment's promise of progress is achieved through the shaping of good citizens, and the notion of public education becomes key to unlocking the common good. In the documents that follow we discuss how the promise of progress was a gendered specific one, enshrining separate spheres of competence for men and women, public for the former and domestic for the latter.

DOCUMENT 1
JUAN LUIS VIVES, FROM *THE EDUCATION OF A CHRISTIAN WOMAN* (1523)

Juan Luis Vives (1493–1540) is one of the most important humanists of his time, along with Thomas More (1478–1535) and Erasmus of Rotterdam (1466–1536). Vives was born in Valencia of Judeo-Converso origins and spent most of his life outside of the Iberian Peninsula. He studied at the University of Paris from 1506 to 1519 and was later appointed professor at the University of Leuven in the Netherlands, where he befriended Erasmus. When he published *The Education of a Christian Woman*, he was a doctor of law and lectured in philosophy at Corpus Christi College, Oxford. He was appointed tutor of Princess Mary, daughter of Henry VIII and Catherine of Aragon. He dedicated the manual presented here to Queen Catherine, who would be repudiated by Henry VIII to marry Anne Boleyn. *The Education of a Christian Woman* was translated to most European languages and became the cultural standard for female virtue and respectability. Centuries later, its emphasis on chastity and pious behavior would resonate with Victorian values, and it remains a key text to understanding gender stereotypes.

PREFACE TO THE BOOKS ON *THE EDUCATION OF A CHRISTIAN WOMAN* BY JUAN LUIS VIVES. ADDRESSED TO HER MOST SERENE MAJESTY, CATHERINE OF ARAGON, QUEEN OF ENGLAND, ETC.[1]

1. Moved by the holiness of your life and your ardent zeal for sacred studies, I have endeavored to write something for Your Majesty on the education of a Christian woman, a subject of paramount importance, but one that has not been treated hitherto by anyone among the great multitude and diversity of talented writers of the past. For what is so necessary as the spiritual formation of those who are our inseparable companions in every condition of life? Feelings of good will are strong among good persons but not lasting among the wicked. With good reason Aristotle says that those states that do not provide for the proper education of women deprive themselves of a great part of their prosperity. Obviously, there is nothing so troublesome as sharing one's life with a person of no principles. And if this can be said with good cause of states, more justly can it be said of the individual household. Moreover, when Xenophon and Aristotle transmitted rules for the management of domestic affairs, and Plato for the state, they made some observations pertaining to the duty of the woman. Tertullian, Cyprian, Jerome,

Ambrose, Augustine, and Fulgentius discussed the status of virgins and widows in such a way that they advocate a way of life rather than give instruction about it. They spent all their time singing the praises of chastity, a commendable undertaking in itself and one worthy of those minds and of the sanctity of that virtue, but they gave very few precepts or rules of life, thinking it preferable to exhort their reader to the best conduct and to point the way to the highest examples rather than give instructions about more lowly matters.

But leaving exhortation to them so that each may choose for herself a way of life based on their authority rather than on my opinion, I formulate practical rules for living. Thus, in the first book, I begin with the first stage of a woman's life and continue up with the state of matrimony; then in the second book, I make recommendations on how time is to be passed properly and happily with one's husband from marriage to widowhood; and in the last book, instruction is given concerning widowhood.

2. And since it could not be avoided, many things are said in the first book that pertain to wives and widows, many in the following that pertain to the unwed, and some things in the third book that pertain to all three. I say this so that the unmarried girl will not think that she has to read only the first book, or the married woman the second or the widow the third. I think every class of woman should read all of the books. Perhaps I have been briefer in my treatment than some would have wished, but anyone will consider carefully the reason for my decision, he will understand that it was not done without good reason. For in giving precepts, brevity should not be among the least considerations, lest through verbosity you overwhelm the minds of the readers rather than instruct them. And the precepts should be such than one can learn them easily and retain them in the memory. For we must not be ignorant of the laws by which we should live. The apostles—Peter, Paul, James, John, and Jude—who transmitted religious teachings to the world, that, besides being divine in origin, were also few and brief, revealed this to us by Christ and after him. And indeed who could observe those laws that are not even kept by those who have grown old with them? For that reason I have not extended the examples, of which I have given a great many; nor have I digressed into the commonplaces of virtues and vices, a very extensive topic on which to expatiate, and one that often presented itself throughout the work and almost invited elaboration. But I wished my book to stay within limits so it could be read without fatigue and even re-read.

3. In addition, although rules of conduct for men are numerous the moral formation of women can be imparted with very few precepts, since men are occupied both within the home and outside, in public and in private, and for that reason lengthy volumes are required to explain the norms to be observed in their varied duties. A woman's only care is chastity; therefore when this has been thoroughly elucidated, she may be considered to have received sufficient instruction. Wherefore even more hateful is the crime of those who seek to

corrupt this one good that women possess, as if you were set on extinguishing the sight left to a one-eyed person. There are those who write filthy and scurrilous poems, and what pretext that has even the semblance of honesty they can adduce for their intent I do not see, save that their minds, corrupted by wickedness and tainted with poison, can emit only poison, with which to destroy everything around them. They say they are lovers and I do not doubt it, for they too are blind and insane. It is as if you cannot gain the submission of your mistress without at the same time corrupting and defiling all other women along with her. To my mind no one was ever most justly exiled than Ovidius Naso, if indeed he was banished because of the Art of Love. Others have sung of lewd and disgraceful things, but this supreme craftsman reduced depravity to rules and precepts—can you imagine!—A master of unchastely and public corrupter of the morals of the state.

4. I have no doubt that to some I shall seem unduly harsh and severe, but if they were to read the minute particulars that sacred writers discuss and see how meticulously they examine every detail, and with what severity of language and tone they would judge me to be too mild and indulgent. But such is the nature of things that to the good the path of virtue seems very accessible and pleasant, while that of vice seems narrow and rough. For the wicked, neither the path they tread is pleasant, nor is the path of uprightness wide enough or open to them. This being the case, we must agree more with the good and believe that the wicked are more easily deceived in their judgment than the generality of good men. Pythagoras and others of his school, adopting the letter Y [upsilon] as their symbol, say after overcoming the first difficulties in the acquisition of virtue, the rest is easy. And Plato, concurring with Pythagoras, urges us to choose the best way of life, which habit will render most agreeable. Our Lord in the gospel called the path to the Kingdom of God narrow, not because it is so in very fact, but because few enter upon it, unless one were to think that his saying is false: "My yoke is easy and my burden light"; along with the promise that there is no one who leaves anything for his sake who will not have much greater thanks, even in his life. What is meant thereby but the pleasure and satisfaction that virtue brings with it.

5. Therefore, I know who will find my precepts too severe and rigid: young men, the inexperienced, the lascivious, and the depraved, who cannot bear the sight of a virtuous woman, who, like unbridled, well-fed horses, neigh at every mare. Likewise, my precepts will not appeal to stupid, vain, and foolish girls, who enjoy being looked at and courted and would like their vices to be approved by the multitudes of sinners, as if the consensus of the common crowd could change the way things are. It is nothing new that the wicked hate those that give good advice. Theophrastus gave many stern precepts about marriage and in so doing incited the wrath of the courtesans against him; and Leontion, the concubine of Metrodorus, rushed forward to spew out a senseless and shameless tract against a

man of such learning and eloquence. The deed was seen to be so scandalous that, as if to signify there was no hope left, it gave rise to the proverb: "to choose tree to hang yourself." Saint Jerome writes to Demetrias about something that happened to him in the following manner: "About thirty years ago I wrote a book on the preservation of virginity, in which it was necessary for me to lash out against vices and expose the snares of the devil for the instruction of the young girl whom I was counseling. The language gave offense to many since each one, interpreting what I was saying as directed against himself, did not accept my words as a friendly admonition but felt aversion toward me as one who was incriminating his actions." Thus, says Jerome. So, what kind of person will I offend with my pious admonitions? Those from whom if I were to please I would earn reprehension and blame.

6. On my side, I will have men of sobriety and common sense, chaste virgins, virtuous matrons, prudent widows—in a word, all those who are truly Christian at heart and not only in name, all of whom know and recognize that nothing can be more mild and moderate than the precepts of our faith, from which may Christ never allow us to divert our minds and our thoughts by even a hair breath. To holy women I have merely given gentle advice concerning their duties. Others, I have chastised, at times rather sharply, because I saw that teachings alone are of little benefit to those who resist one who guides them and must be dragged along almost against their will to their proper goal. Therefore, I have spoken rather plainly on occasion so that seeing the repulsiveness of their conduct as if it were depicted in a painting; they might feel ashamed and cease acting in a shameful manner. At the same time, good women might have reason to rejoice that they are far removed from these vices and might make all the more effort to distance themselves even further and to retreat into the innermost precincts of virtue. I have preferred, following the advice of Jerome, to run the risk of offending propriety rather than undermining my argument, without, however, lapsing into indecency, the worst thing a teacher of chastity could do. As a result, sometimes more things are to be understood than are expressed. Things that would not accord with accepted moral standards I have supported and sustained with the testimony of great authorities, lest they be nullified by the force of public opinion.

7. I dedicate this book to you, glorious Queen, just as a painter might represent your likeness with utmost skill. As you would see your physical likeness portrayed there, so in these books you will see the image of your mind, since you were both a virgin and a promised spouse and a widow and now wife (as please God, you may long continue), and since you have so conducted yourself in all these various states of life that whatever you did is a model of an exemplary life to others. But you prefer that virtues be praised rather than yourself. Although no one can praise female virtues without including you in that same praise, I shall nonetheless obey you, provided that you know that under the rubric of excellent and outstanding virtues other women similar to you may be mentioned by name,

but it is you always, even if tacitly, who are spoken of. For virtues cannot be extolled with praise without commending those who, though unnamed, excelled in those virtues. Your daughter Mary will read these recommendations and will produce them as the models herself on the example of your goodness and wisdom to be found within her own home. She will do this assuredly and, unless she alone belies all human expectations, must of necessity be virtuous and holy as the offspring of you and Henry VIII, such a noble and honored pair. Therefore, all women will have an example to follow in your life and actions, and, in this work dedicated to you, precepts and rules for the conduct of their lives. Both of these they will owe to your moral integrity, by which you have lived and through which I have been inspired to write. Farewell.

Bruges, 5 April 1523

Questions for discussion

1. Who is the audience for whom this document is written?

2. Explain the concepts of virginity, chastity, and moral integrity as described by the author.

3. What is the historical context in which the author writes? Explain the religious turmoil that ensued a few years later leading to the separation of the English Church under Henry VIII from the Catholic Church, as a result of his divorce from Catherine of Aragon and marriage to Anne Boleyn. According to Vives' view, how is "virtue" compromised during this political/religious crisis?

4. How does the content of this document affect the political and social opportunities of women in the centuries ahead? Is there any value in reading this document today?

DOCUMENT 2
GASPAR MELCHOR DE JOVELLANOS, FROM "GUIDELINES FOR THE CREATION OF A PLAN OF PUBLIC INSTRUCTION. SEVILLE, NOVEMBER 16, 1809"[2]

Gaspar Melchor de Jovellanos (1744–1811), philosopher, economist, and statesman, is considered the most important representative of the Spanish Enlightenment. His writings addressed political, economic, and philosophical issues and include: *Informe sobre la Ley Agraria, 1794* (Report on the Agrarian Law); *Memoria para el arreglo de la policía de los espectáculos y diversiones públicas, y sobre su origen en España, 1790* (Report on the Arrangement of Policing Spectacles and Public Diversions, and its Origin in Spain); *Memoria sobre la educación pública, 1801* (Report on Public Education); *Memorias histórico-artísticas de arquitectura,1804–1808* (Essays on Architecture); and *Memoria en defensa de la Junta Central, 1811* (Report in Defense of the Central Junta).

Jovellanos lived through the violent war ensuing the Napoleonic invasion of the Peninsula in 1808. What followed, were six years of the so-called Peninsular War in Anglo-Saxon historiography or the War for Independence (1808–14) in the Spanish historical account. Francisco de Goya portrayed the horrors of the conflict in his etchings "The Disasters of War" also referred to in this volume.

The country was left to self-governing juntas of citizens opposing the newly established monarchy of Joseph Bonaparte, Napoleon's brother. In 1809, as a member of the Supreme Junta in Seville, Jovellanos issued the "Guidelines for the Creation of a Plan of Public Instruction to the Junta of this Matter" reproduced in part here. In this document, Jovellanos proposes the implementation of public instruction as a matter of national common good and indispensable to achieving prosperity and the establishment of a civil society.

"GUIDELINES FOR THE CREATION OF A PLAN OF PUBLIC INSTRUCTION"

The objective of the Junta of Public Instruction will be to deliberate and propose all the means to improve, promote, and expand national instruction. All the report, memoranda, and excerpts will be submitted to the Cortes committee.

Based on these texts, and as a result of the Junta's members' reflection after their discussions, the committee will propose all the measures they deem most necessary to achieve such an important goal:

- In these deliberations the Junta will cover as many branches as necessary for the national education, considering the broader sense of their discussions.

  The ultimate goal will be the complete instruction of the State individuals regardless of class or profession in order to achieve their personal happiness, and contribute to the common good of the nation.

Whereas,

1. the means of communication;

2. the means of dissemination of the necessary instruction to achieve this grand objective. Taking into account the physical, intellectual and moral aptitudes of the citizens.

(…)

Being so important the education of girls, the instruction of the precious half of the Spanish nation must have as its main objective to prepare good and virtuous mothers. This matter is much more important when the objective is also to fuse this instruction with the decorum of their behavior; the improvement of domestic education resides precisely in the improvement of our customs. This first level of education has a well-known impact on the literacy, moral, and civic education of the youth. Therefore, the Junta will consider very seriously the means to establish throughout the reign:

1. free and public schools for poor girls, so that they learn to read, the principles of Religion, and the skills necessary to become good and modest mothers;

2. to establish schools for girls where those who come from rich families may pay to receive a more complete and thorough education.

Ecclesiastical sciences represent a very important branch of practical instruction that embraces Christian morality and religion as a higher goal. Although the development of the conciliar seminars and the curriculum is the responsibility of the Ecclesiastical Junta recently created, it is desirable that the public instruction junta also be a part of it so that all methods of education are uniform in the different parts of the realm. In this manner, so must be the methods utilized to pursue it, and so that national instructions might not be disturbed by diverse systems, methods, schools, and opinions, which have suffered public instruction and the progress of solid knowledge up until now. To accomplish this end, communication between the two juntas is necessary, and for this purpose the presidents of each one will procure the appointment of some individuals from both to convene and plan the methods and rulings of general instruction.

To agree on the foundations upon which the principles of methods and elementary doctrine of general education must rest, it is necessary that the junta determines the following guidelines:

1. It will take under consideration whether all the instruction from primary education and that of the study of speculative and practical sciences must be free for all citizens.

2. Whether it is convenient also that instruction is free for seminars and schools, so that everyone does not pay for anything more than their room and board in addition to any voluntary or extracurricular endeavors.

3. Whether it is convenient that in those towns where there is a university or institute, a subject of high reputation in his field may be allowed to teach a specific branch of such field and be paid by those who voluntarily may want to study it. If so, it will be necessary to provide a permit and oversee its instruction as well as determine the honorarium owed to the master by his pupils.

4. Whether it is convenient that the instruction of schools, universities, and institutes in the entire realm be imparted with the same method and materials, so that once the elementary doctrine has been unified, all capricious opinions be excluded, whose origins are not other than the works studied and the arbitrary judgment of the teachers in explaining their doctrines. This uniformity does not intend to be harmful for national scientific progress: First, because the elements selected for instruction must always be the best known at the time, always updated as other innovations appear; second, because scholars given always to cultivate and promote science will enjoy absolute freedom of opinion unless it goes against Religion and morality and against public peace.

5. To abbreviate the cycle of instruction and to avoid long and tedious memorizing study for the youth, it is convenient that the elementary works selected are brief and purely reduced to the scientific principles, with annotations succinctly illustrating those principles. In this way students will be able to read and meditate, without adornment, and leaving to their teachers' judgment the extension and development of the scientific study, for example, by pointing their pupils to the best works that, once completed, will deepen their knowledge.

6. Whether it is convenient that the works selected for elementary instruction may cover the general principles of each primal science, which will be more beneficial because the students will understand better the sciences derived from those primal ones; and, hence, instruction and education will extend to all fields of study resulting from the subdivision of the different sciences.

7. To this end, the Junta will consider that although this subdivision may be beneficial to promote and advance the transcendental study of the sciences, when scholars focus and study the various areas of their fields, it is also detrimental in elementary instruction to forget the need for unified principles that must guide it and upon all doctrine must rest.

8. And since all instruction must be in Castilian, the Junta will deliberate: 1. The means to translate, edit, or write the new elementary books selected, 2. Whether it will be necessary to translate or draft other more extensive works of the same sciences written on those principles, so that these materials may be an aid to the teachers' preparation.

9. It is convenient also to consider that it is not enough to attend school or institute to receive instruction. To benefit from it, it will be mandated that in all educational establishments students will not be admitted to a classroom without having passed a public exam proving his knowledge of the previous course. This maxim, faithfully observed, will offer young applied people stimulating encouragement to move ahead in their studies and to those who are lazy and distracted, a just punishment for their apathy.

(...)

The Junta, in view of these considerations presented for your deliberation, calls your attention to a topic of great importance and transcendence. Once they are considered and improved with their zeal and enlightenment, the Junta will propose to the Cortes all it deems necessary to direct, improve, and expand national instruction, considering it as the foundation for a most abundant fountain of public happiness. It is impossible to ignore that without physical education there will not be agile citizens, robust and strong; without political and moral instruction, it won't be possible to reform the laws that will guarantee these citizens safety, neither the character and customs which will make them happy and virtuous; and without practical sciences and useful skills they will not be able to perfect agriculture, industry, commerce, and other professions that will allow them to grow, protect, and profit. And finally, being also constant that a wiser nation is always, under equal circumstances, the most powerful, Spain, placed by God in the most favorable position, under a most benign sky, on a most fertile soil, owner of the riches and extensive provinces, and replete of the most ingenious and capable talents, can and must rise through wise laws and solid instruction to become the first nation on earth.

Seville, 16 November 1809
Gaspar de Jovellanos

Questions for discussion

1. To whom is Jovellanos addressing this document?
2. What are the bases for establishing public education? What are the anticipated outcomes and benefits for the nation?
3. Is the public education designed here by Jovellanos the same for men and women? How does religion inform the gender divide?
4. Are there any principles in this document that still inform our public education today?

DOCUMENT 3
LAW OF PUBLIC INSTRUCTION, KNOWN AS "MOYANO LAW," SEPTEMBER 9, 1857[3]

The Law of Public Instruction of September 9, 1857, also known as Ley Moyano after Claudio Moyano (1809–90), Minister of Development at the time, was a result of the consensus between progressive and moderate liberals. This legislation represented the final consolidation of the liberal educational system and the establishment of universal public education that included girls in the primary level. The model developed under this law remained unchanged for over a century and initially was unevenly implemented throughout the country due to lack of resources.

The main characteristics of this law are: mandatory and universal primary education; centralization of instruction; moderate tone regarding the most problematic issues such as the Catholic Church's role in education and the scientific content for the secondary education curriculum; legalization and establishment of private education, mainly Catholic in the primary and secondary levels of instruction; and finally, the inclusion of professional training and study as higher education.

LAW OF PUBLIC INSTRUCTION

Isabel II, by the grace of God and the Spanish Monarchy's Constitution, Queen of the Spains: To all who might see and understand this, be advised: that, using the authorization given to the Government by law of 17th of July of this year, I have resolved, in accordance with the advice of my Council of Ministers, that it will decree upon its publication in the Peninsula and adjacent Islands, the following:

LAW OF PUBLIC INSTRUCTION

FIRST SECTION: About the studies

FIRST TITLE: On Primary Instruction

Article 1st. Primary instruction is divided into elementary and superior

Art. 2nd. Elementary Primary instruction comprises:
  First: Christian doctrine and basic Sacred History appropriate for children
  Second: Reading
  Third: Writing

Fourth: Principles of Castilian grammar, with orthographical exercises

Fifth: Arithmetic Principles, with the legal system of measurements, weight, and currency

Sixth: Basic knowledge of agriculture, industry, and commerce, according to each location.

Art. 3rd. The instruction that does not cover all the subjects mentioned will be considered incomplete according to the articles 100, 102, 103, 181, and 189.

Art. 4th. In addition to a prudent expansion of those subjects mentioned in Article 2nd, upper level primary instruction will cover:

First: Principles of Geometry, Technical Drawing, and surveying

Second: Basic knowledge of Geography and History and in particular Spain

Third: Basic Knowledge of Physics and Natural History accommodating them to the most basic daily life needs.

Art. 5th. For girls receiving elementary and upper instruction, the studies mentioned in paragraph sixth of Article 2nd will be omitted, as well as the first and third paragraphs of Art. 4th, and replaced with:

First: Skills proper for their sex

Second: Elementary applied drawing of said skills

Third: Some knowledge of domestic cleanliness.

Art. 6th. Primary instruction will be imparted, with the appropriate modifications, to deaf and mute as well as blind individuals in special establishments in place today and in others to be created for this purpose, without going against article 108 of this law.

Art. 7th. Primary education is mandatory for all Spaniards. Parents and guardians will send their children to the public schools at the age of six until they turn nine unless they can provide this type of instruction at home or in another private venue.

Art. 8th. Those who do not comply with this obligation, having a school in their town or village or within a distance that the children may attend comfortably, will be penalized and forced by the Authorities and punished with a fee between 2 and 20 reals.

Art. 9th. Primary instruction will be free in the public schools to children whose parents or guardians cannot pay for it, having to submit a document issued to this effect by the parish priest and supervised by the mayor.

Art. 10th. The primary instruction studies are not limited to a fixed number of courses; the different lessons may last a year, shortening the times during the summer.

Art. 11th. The Government will facilitate the review by parish priests of the Christian morality and doctrine for the children of primary schools, at least once per week.

* * *

CHAPTER III: About Professional Instruction

Art. 61. The Professional Instruction refers to:
- Veterinary
- Commerce instructors
- Nautical instruction
- Master builders, quantity surveyors, surveyors
- Primary instruction teachers

Art. 68. The necessary studies to obtain the title of Teacher of primary instruction are:
- Catechism explaining of Christian doctrine
- Elements of sacred history
- Reading
- Calligraphy
- Castilian grammar with practical exercises of composition
- Arithmetic
- Basic geometry, technical drawing, and surveying
- Basic geography
- Compendium of history of Spain
- Basic agriculture
- Principles of pedagogy and teaching methods
- Practice in teaching

Art. 69. To be an upper level Primary Instruction Teacher:
- First, having studied subjects mentioned in the previous article
- Second, having acquired some knowledge of algebra, universal history, and the common phenomena in nature

Art. 70. To be a professor of a Normal School it is necessary to have studied:
- First, elements of rhetoric and poetics
- Second, a complete course of pedagogy pertaining to primary instruction with application to the teaching of mute and deaf as well as blind individuals
- Third, administrative law, as it relates to primary instruction

Art. 71. To be a Female Teacher of primary instruction it is required:
- First, to have studied the appropriate extension of Normal School for female teachers that covers the instruction of girls, elementary and upper level, depending on the level they pursue
- Second, to be educated in the principles and methods of teaching. Also, teachers from private institutions will be accepted, when they are able to certify two years of practice in some model school.

Art. 72. The regulations will determine the knowledge needed to acquire and practice the professions not mentioned in this title.

(...)

SECOND SECTION: About the Establishments of Instruction

FIRST TITLE: On Public Establishments

First Chapter: Schools of Primary Instruction

Art. 97. Schools of Public Instruction are those sustained fully or in part by public funds, charitable donations, or foundations. These schools will be under the authority of each town, which will include in their municipal budgets, as a mandatory expense, the amount necessary to sustain the schools; included in this budget are the contributions of the other sources mentioned above.

Every year, however, there will be earmarked in the national budget the amount of 1 million reals, at least, to assist those villages that cannot pay by themselves the cost of primary instruction. The Government will dictate, after consulting the Royal Council of Public Instruction, the appropriate measures to equally distribute the funds.

Art. 98. The rights of patronage will be respected by this law, except, obviously, the supreme right of the Government to inspect them.

Art. 99. The schools will be either elementary or upper level according to the subject mentioned in each grade of instruction.

Art. 100. Every village of 500 souls must have a public school for boys and another one, even if incomplete, for girls. The ones incomplete for boys will be only allowed in villages of smaller populations.

Art. 101. In villages with 2,000 souls there will be two complete schools for boys and another two for girls.

Those with 4,000 souls will have three; and so on, increasing a school per each sex per 2,000 inhabitants, and including in this the private schools, but always one third of them will be public schools.

Art. 102. Those villages with less than 500 inhabitants should unite with the ones close by to create a district where they can establish a complete public primary school, when the nature of the terrain allows the children to attend comfortably; under other circumstances, the village will create an incomplete school, and if this is not possible, it will create a temporary one.

Incomplete schools and the temporary ones will be staffed by adjuncts and temps, under the direction and supervision of the teacher at the closest complete school.

Art. 103. Only in the incomplete schools will the attendance of boys and girls together in the same location be allowed, but with appropriate separation.

Art. 104. In the capitals of provinces with 10,000 souls, one of the public schools will be upper level.

Town councils will be able to establish them in small villages with smaller populations as they see fit, without neglecting the elementary level.

Art. 105. The government will also make sure that in towns of 10,000 souls, there will be preschools.

Art. 106. Likewise, the government will foment the establishment of evening and Sunday schools for adults whose education has been neglected or who may want to expand their studies.

Art. 107. In towns of 10,000 souls there will be one of these classes, in addition to technical and decorative drawing, as well as applied mechanical arts.

Art. 108. The Government will also promote the instruction of deaf-mute and blind individuals, making sure that there is at least one school of this kind in each University district, and that in the public schools for boys as much attention as possible is paid to the education of these unfortunates.
(...)

Art. 180. In addition to the general requirements, the following is necessary to aspire to teach in public schools:
- First, be twenty years old
- Second, have the appropriate diploma

Art. 181. Those in charge of incomplete schools are exempt of this requirement, as well as the preschool teachers. They all will be able to practice with a certificate of aptitude and morality, issued by the local Junta and supervised by the province governor per the regulations.

Art. 182. The Rector of the university district will appoint the public school teachers whose salary is less than 4,000 reals, and for the female teachers who earn less than 3,000. It is up to the General Directorate of Public Instruction to fill the vacant positions of new teachers whose salaries will be less than 6,000, and for the female teachers no more than 5,000. Those of higher remuneration will be by Royal appointment.
(...)

Art. 191. Teachers of complete public elementary schools will enjoy: First, decent housing for him and his family; second, a fixed salary of 2,500 reals per year, at least in the villages with 500 to 1,000 souls: of 3,300 reals in the villages 1,000 to 3,000; of 4,400 reals in those 3,000 to 10,000; of 5,500 reals in those 10,000 to 20,000: of 6,600 reals in those 20,000 to 40,000; of 8,000 reals in those 40,000 and more; and of 9,000 reals in Madrid.

Art. 192. Male and female school teachers will receive a fixed salary, product of the fees paid by those children able to pay. The local Junta will determine their salaries with the approval of the province.

Art. 193. In the villages with fewer than 500 souls, after consulting the town council, the Governor will establish the salaries the town must pay the teacher, or the amount necessary to provide for the district established, per what is stated in Article 102.

Art. 194. Female teachers will receive a compensation that is a third less than the one established for the male teachers as stated in Art. 191.

Questions for discussion

1. What are the subjects delineated in the law to be part of the curriculum? Are they the same for girls as for boys?
2. What does it mean that girls need to be trained in "skills proper for their sex"?
3. How are schools funded per the law?
4. Describe the qualifications required for the teachers. Are male and female teachers paid the same?

DOCUMENT 4
SECONDARY EDUCATION LAW, 1953[4]

From 1953 until the end of the regime in 1975, the period known as *tardofranquismo*, National Catholicism became the doctrine instilled in Spaniards in the wake of the August 1953 economic aid and military Pact of Madrid with the United States, while Franco's regime was welcomed into the international political landscape of the Cold War. Franco, now perceived as a "benign dictator" and self-proclaimed sentinel of the West against Communism, led Spain into the United Nations in 1955.

The last two decades of the dictatorship witnessed unavoidable modernization, urbanization, and a massive arrival of tourists seeking an exotic sunshine-bathed country. The educational system experienced a series of reforms led by Minister Joaquin Ruiz Giménez like the reform of the Secondary Education Law in 1953 included here.

The reform of the secondary education in 1953 is one of a series of changes in the regime legal apparatus which facilitated the transition to the consumer economy. Gender relations were addressed in the reform of the Civil Code in 1958 and the Law of Political and Professional Rights of Women in 1961. In this context, the reading of the educational reform of 1953 sheds some light on how the regime prepared girls to perpetuate domestic values into the 1960s.

CHAPTER VII / CURRICULUM

Art. 74: The general plan for Secondary Education will be the rule for all the secondary schools, unless there is a decree that designs a special curriculum with an experimental character because it is in a protectorate territory or abroad or due to specific academic and professional goals.

Art. 75: Every special secondary studies plan will be approved by decree and previous agreement of the National Education Council, and it will be subject to revisions whenever the Ministry sees fit.

Art. 76: The Ministry, through its advisory agencies, will maintain the necessary monitoring of the general and special curricula so that their application is in accordance with the experience and progress of teaching techniques.

Art. 77: The Secondary Education provided in the female schools will be ruled by a special curriculum, which will have as mandatory subjects the teachings pertaining to the care of the home and to prepare them for the feminine professions.

Art. 78: Secondary Education is divided into two phases: basic and upper level.

Art. 79: The basic level of Secondary Education:
a) will consist of four courses
b) will be designed according to the pedagogical level of the students
c) will consist of the subjects necessary to achieve the minimum level of education to reach the ability to perform professions of medium level that require a diploma
d) only students who are ten years old will be able to start the first year of Secondary Education. Once completed, students will receive the diploma of basic Secondary Education

Art. 80: The subjects covered in the basic Secondary Education will be distributed throughout the four years of instruction and include the following:
Religion, Spanish Language and Literature, Mathematics, Geography and History, Physics, Chemistry, and Natural Science, Drawing, and a Foreign Language.

Art. 81: Upper level Secondary Education will:
a) last two years from the time the student turns fourteen years old
b) be designed according to the pedagogical level of the students
c) cover subjects of general culture common to all the students, although it will allow them to choose a professional focus—whether humanities or sciences—to provide them with specialized instruction. These choices will not limit their future academic decisions

Art 82: In accordance with the previous article, the common subjects will include:
Religion, Philosophical Foundations, Literature (Text analysis and Composition), Art and Cultural History, Natural, Mathematical, and Physical Sciences, and a modern foreign language.

Mandatory subjects within the vocational choices will include: Greek and Latin for those who choose humanities; and Mathematics and Physics for those who choose the sciences.

Art. 83: Those students in the upper level of Secondary Education who intend to attend the University, Special Engineering and Architecture Schools, and any other Higher Education Centers will complete a pre-university course in the High Schools designated for it.

All students will be trained in the reading and analysis of fundamental literary and philosophical texts, in the synthesis of lecturing and composition as well as in the practical use of the modern foreign languages studied. In addition, those students who specialize in Humanities will translate classic languages, and those who specialize in the Sciences will focus on Mathematics and Physics.

Art. 84: The general and specific curricula will regulate closely the fundamental, secondary, and complementary subjects to make sure they comply with the assessment and tests provided.

The Ministry will determine the yearly schedule of schools to accommodate the best psychological and physical development of students, the teaching performance of the professors, and the healthy relationship between students and their families.

The questionnaires will always follow these principles.

Art. 85: The instruction in the values of the national spirit, physical education, and, in the case of female students, their domestic training, will be fundamental, mandatory, and properly included in all the curricula, in the schedule, and in the exams for each grade.

The instruction of the national spirit will be implemented in the established courses. The Youth Front, Female Section of Falange Española Tradicionalista, and JONS (Traditionalist Spanish Phalanx of the Juntas of the National Syndicalist Offensive) as deemed appropriate will provided exams and final accreditation.

The National administrations of Youth Front and Female Section will be able to appoint the teaching personnel and the inspection of the instruction, following the prerogatives specified in this law.

These National administrations will be able to receive the support of the professors in the Secondary schools who are members of the SEPEM.[5]

Questions for discussion

1. How did the law intend to regulate female Secondary Education?

2. Explain how Article Eighty-five contributes to perpetuating a gender specific society. Are women and men expected to achieve equal educational goals?

3. How did the Youth Front and Women's Section participate in the indoctrination of Falangist principles? How did those principles relate to citizenship under the dictatorship?

4. According to the curriculum for girls, what would be their likely career choices once they obtained their diplomas?

DOCUMENT 5
CONSTITUTION 1931, ARTICLES 48–50 AND CONSTITUTION 1978, ARTICLE 27

The Constitution of 1978 would become the heir of the democratic values that failed with the enactment of the Second Republic Constitution of 1931. The most important task of the republican governments in the 1930s was to eradicate the almost seventy percent illiteracy rate that the country suffered. No doubt the republic would be remembered as "The Republic of Professors." Education remained central to the construction of the national identity, and in the newly democratic republic, this was key to forging good citizenship. The same aspirations informed the Constitution of 1978 in the immediate post-dictatorship era and laid the foundation for a democratic transition after forty years of Francoist indoctrination in the educational system.

The major difference between the two documents focuses on the tension between secularization and traditional Catholic values. The spirit of consensus was the main goal in the drafting of the 1978 Magna Carta. While the 1931 constitution sought to establish a ley public education, the 1978 text allowed for both public and private religious education.

CONSTITUTION OF 1931 ARTICLES 48–50[6]

Art. 48. The service to culture is an essential attribution of the State, implemented through educational institutions unified into a single system apparatus.

Primary education will be mandatory and free.

Instructors, teachers, and professors of the official educational system are public servants. Freedom of expression is recognized and guaranteed.

The Republic will legislate and facilitate access to all levels of education for those Spaniards in economic need so that they are not excluded, unless it is due to lack of aptitude or vocation.

Education will be secular, will make applied knowledge the basis of its methodology, and will be inspired by the ideals of human solidarity.

Churches will be given the right, subject to State supervision, to teach their respective doctrines in their private institutions.

Art. 49. The State will issue in exclusivity academic and professional diplomas, establishing to this end the tests and requisites necessary to obtain those credentials, even when those certificates are from Educational centers in autonomous regions. A law of public instruction will determine the age of schooling for each grade, the length of education, the content of the curriculum, and the conditions under which education is authorized in private institutions.

Art. 50. Autonomous regions may organize their instruction in the native languages, per the regulations of the statutes. The study of Castilian is mandatory, and this will be the language of instruction in the primary and secondary education centers in those autonomous regions. The State will be able to maintain teaching institutions in those regions in the language of the Republic.

The State will exercise the supreme inspection of the national territory to ensure compliance with the regulations contained in this article and the two previous ones.

The State will see to the expansion of the Spanish culture through the establishment of delegations and centers of learning abroad, especially in the Latin American countries.

CONSTITUTION OF 1978 ARTICLE 27[7]

Art. 27. Right to an Education

1. Everyone has the right to an education. Freedom of instruction is recognized.

2. The main objective of Education is the full development of the human character with respect to the democratic principles of coexistence and to the fundamental rights and liberties.

3. Public institutions guarantee and assist parents so that their children may receive the religious and moral instruction in accordance with their own convictions.

4. Basic Education is mandatory and free.

5. Public institutions guarantee the right of everyone to an education, through a general curriculum, with effective participation of all the stakeholders and the creation of centers of learning.

6. The right of individuals and institutions to create centers of education is recognized, within the boundaries of the constitutional principles.

7. Teachers and parents as well as pupils will take part in the administration and control of the centers sustained by public funds, per the terms established by law.

8. Public powers will inspect and accredit the educational system to guarantee compliance with the law.

9. Public powers will help those educational institutions that comply with the requirements of the law.

10. Autonomy of the Universities is recognized within the terms established by law.

Questions for discussion

1. Explain the following statement from the Constitution of 1931: "Education will be secular, will make applied knowledge the basis of its methodology, and will be inspired by the ideals of human solidarity."

2. The Constitution of 1978 proclaims, "The main objective of Education is the full development of the human character with respect to the democratic principles of coexistence and to the fundamental rights and liberties." Explain this statement.

3. How does the Constitution of 1931 propose to expand Spanish culture beyond Spain?

4. How do these two constitutions define public education?

DOCUMENT 6
ORGANIC LAW OF EDUCATION, 2006

Educational reform remains central to the bolstering of democratic values in Spanish society. The Organic Law of Education was enacted twenty years after the entrance of Spain in the European Community. Since 1970, education has undergone many changes as demonstrated by the seven laws enacted since then. Three laws have molded education in the country. The Law of 1970 issued at the end of the Francoist regime remained in place until 1990, when the so-called LOGSE (*Ley Orgánica General del Sistema Educativo*, or General Organic Law of the Educational System) introduced mandatory schooling until the age of sixteen. In 2006, the Organic Law of Education (LOE, *Ley Orgánica de Educación*) was ushered in by the socialist government of José Luis Rodríguez Zapatero. One of the most controversial elements introduced by this law was the option to make religion an elective rather than a compulsory class. The law also included a new mandatory class in Citizenship instruction and Human Rights, and a reduction in the number of teaching hours in Language and Literature.

In 2013, the Popular Party in office enacted the Organic Law for the improvement of Educational Quality, or LOMCE (*Ley Orgánica para la Mejora de la Calidad Educativa*), known as the Wert Law after the minister in office. This law was a reform of the two-previous bills LOE and LOGSE. The law restores religion as a mandatory class and imposes qualifying examinations, while also reducing the number of college scholarships, and reducing funding for schools segregated by gender. All political parties, as well as university faculty and students, expressed their opposition to this law.

ORGANIC LAW OF EDUCATION, 2006

Preamble

Contemporary societies regard the education of their youth as most important, with the conviction that their individual and collective wellbeing depends upon it. Education is the best means to build their character, develop their capabilities to the fullest, and configure their own personal identity and comprehension of reality, integrating cognitive, affective, and axiological dimensions. Education is the means to transmit and, at the same time, renew the culture and the values that are part of society, of extracting the maximum possibilities from its fountains of riches; of encouraging a democratic coexistence and respect for individual differences; of promoting solidarity and avoiding discrimination, with the main objective of achieving social cohesion. In addition, education is the best means to achieve and guarantee democratic citizenship, responsible, free and critical, which is indispensable to the evolution of advanced, dynamic, and just societies Therefore, a good education is the best wealth and the principal resource of a country and its citizens.

(...)

The establishment of public educational systems embody a nationalist interest in education. The structures to educate citizens were conceived as essential instruments for the construction of national States. Since then, every country increasingly has paid attention to its educational system, with the objective to adapt them to changing circumstances and corresponding expectations at each historical juncture. (...) In each moment, educational systems had to respond to different priorities. In the second half of the twentieth century, they had to make possible the access of all citizens to education. Universal primary education, achieved in a few countries during the nineteenth century, would be achieved in the following century, incorporating general access to secondary education, which came to be considered an integral part of a basic education. The main objective was to implement a longer period of schooling and with more ambitious goals for both sexes.

At the end of the twentieth century, the goal was to make the instruction top quality and universal. In November of 1990, the ministers of education of the OCDE met in Paris to address the matter of top quality education for all. The more advanced countries devoted themselves to this priority.

Fourteen years later, in September of 2004, the more than sixty ministers that met in Geneva for the 47th International Conference in Education convened by UNESCO expressed the same concerns, reaffirming the challenges from the previous decade. If in 1990 it was the most advanced countries that took the lead on demanding quality and equal access to education, in 2004 it was a greater number of states, of diverse characteristics and levels of development, the ones that posed the same question.

To provide educational opportunities of high quality to all citizens without excluding anyone regardless of their social origins is urgent at this moment. Very different countries with diverse political orientations are seeking this goal, and Spain cannot afford to be the exception.

The extension of basic education occurred late in our country. Although obligatory schooling was promulgated in 1857, and in 1964 it was extended from six to fourteen years of age, it wasn't until the mid 1980s that these goals became a reality. The Law of General Education of 1970 represented the beginning of the end of the historical delay that afflicted the Spanish educational system. (...)

The Law 14/1970, of General Education and the Financing of the Educational Reform and the Organic Law 8/1985, regulating the right to education, declared education as a public service. The Organic Law of Education follows this tradition. The public service of education is an essential service to the community that must make education accessible to everyone without any exceptions, with equal opportunities and regularity and continuity guaranteed, with regular adjustments to social changes. The public service of education may be provided by the public powers and by social forces, as a guarantee of the fundamental rights of the citizens and freedom of instruction. (...)

Three principles guide this law: The first consists of the demand that a quality education must be provided to all citizens of both sexes, in all levels of the educational system. The challenge that this demand represents for today's educational systems and more specifically for the Spanish one, has already been discussed. After having achieved mandatory schooling up until sixteen years of age, the objective is now to improve the general outcomes, and to reduce the still high dropout rates and premature abandonment of education. It is about ensuring that all citizens reach the maximum development possible of all their capabilities, individual, social, intellectual, cultural, and emotional, in order for them to receive a quality education that is adapted to their needs. At the same time, equal opportunity must be guaranteed to them, providing the necessary support to the students who need it and to the centers where they attend school. In sum, it is important to improve the educational level of the student body, reconciling the quality of the education with equal access to it.

The second principle consists in the need of collaboration between all the stakeholders of the educational community to accomplish this ambitious goal. The combination of equality and quality proposed above unavoidably demands the attainment of a shared effort. Very often there is an emphasis on the student effort. This is a fundamental principle that must not be ignored, because without a personal investment, a result of a responsible and committed attitude to self-improvement, it will be very difficult to attain the complete development of individual capacities. However, responsibility for the success of the student body does not rest solely on the individual student, but also on their families, their teachers, the teaching establishments, the educational administration, and ultimately on society in general, which holds the final responsibility for the quality of the educational system.

The principle of effort, essential for obtaining a good quality education, must be applied to all the members of the educational community. Each of them must make a specific contribution. Families should collaborate closely and make the commitment to work every day with their children and with the schools. The schools and teachers must develop a rich, motivational, and challenging educational environment. The educational administrations will facilitate so that all the different components of the educational apparatus have the resources necessary to achieve their goals, demanding at the same time their commitment and applied effort. Society, in sum, should support the educational system and create an environment favorable to personal self-improvement throughout life. Only through commitment and a shared effort will these challenging objectives be accomplished.

One of the most important consequences of this shared effort consists in the need to achieve equal education for all. The Spanish Constitution recognized the existence of a double network of public and private schools, and the Organic Law for the Right to Education mandated a system of agreements to achieve an effective and free implementation of public service and social education, under conditions of equality and within the framework of the general educational program. This model, which respects the right to an education and the freedom of instruction, has been in general functioning satisfactorily, although with the passage of time new needs have become apparent. One of the principal ones has been the equitable distribution of students among the different schools.

With the extension of the mandatory school age and the access to education for new segments of the population, the conditions under which schools must operate have become more complicated. Therefore, it is necessary to attend to the student body's diversity and contribute equally to meet the new challenges and difficulties that this diversity poses. In the end, it is important that all schools, public and private, accept their social commitment to education and accept schooling without limitations, accentuating thus the complementary nature of both educational networks while respecting their uniqueness. In exchange, all the schools sustained with public funds must receive the human and material resources necessary to meet their obligations.

The third principle that inspires this law consists of the serious commitment to the educational objectives proposed by the European Union for the next few years. The process of European integration is leading to a certain convergence of the different educational systems, which in turn has led to the establishment of a series of common educational goals for the twenty-first century.

(...)

It is because of this that, first and foremost, the European Union and UNESCO have proposed to improve the quality and efficacy of the educational systems, which means the improvement of the teaching body's skills, the development of the necessary abilities for the new society knowledge and skills, guarantee access to new information and communication technologies, increased enrollment in science, technical, and artistic subjects, and to take maximum advantage of the resources available, thus increasing the investment in human resources. Second, it has been proposed that it is necessary to facilitate ample access to educational systems, which implies the construction of an environment open to learning, making learning more attractive and conducive to active citizenship, equal opportunities, and social cohesion. Third, the goal is to open these systems to the outside world, which requires strengthening the links with the labor force, with research, and with society in general, so as to develop an entrepreneurial spirit, improve the learning of foreign languages, increase mobility and exchanges, and strengthen European cooperation.

Over the next few years, the Spanish educational system must adjust its policies to achieve these shared objectives with its partners in the European Union. In some cases, the educational system in Spain is close to achieving the objective established for the end of this decade. However, in other cases, the distance is notable. The active participation of Spain in the European Union demands the improvement of the educational levels until they achieve a rank in accordance with its standing in Europe, something which requires a serious compromise and effort, to which this Law also is committed.

(...)

This text has avoided the temptation to completely change our educational system, as if we were starting from zero. It has opted, instead, to take into consideration the experience and the success achieved in the past. In the end, this law is rooted in the conviction that any educational reform must be a continuous process and the role of the legislator and the educational stakeholders is no other than the progressive and permanent improvement of the education citizens receive.

Questions for Discussion:

1. How does the law define education for a democratic society?
2. Who are the different educational stakeholders the law identifies?
3. How does the law intend to subsidise the public and private educational systems? Explain the concepts of equality and equity.
4. Explain the significance of reconciling the Spanish and the European educational systems.

MODULE 6
POLITICAL POWER AND THE LAW

ABSTRACT

During the nineteenth and twentieth centuries, Spain confronted modernization and political democratization through the enactment of laws and constitutions. The nineteenth century opened the modern era of nationalism with the Peninsular War, known in Spanish historiography as the War for Independence (1808–14). The values of the Enlightenment and the French Revolution informed the political conflict among the intellectuals and political elite. Those in favor of change were called "afrancesados" (Francophiles) and characterized as anti-Spanish by those who fought, with the support of the Catholic Church, for the eternal traditions of religion and monarchy. The return of Ferdinand VII in 1814 meant the restoration of the latter, and the rejection of the former as enshrined in the Constitution of 1812.

What followed was a long nineteenth century of constant civil wars centered on claims to the throne by the *Carlistas*—supporters of Don Carlos, brother of Ferdinand VII—against the *Isabelinos*, those supporting Isabel, his daughter, who was able to reign only because the Pragmatic Sanction enacted in 1830 by her father (having no sons), abolished the Salic law that prevented women from becoming heirs to the throne over a male. The wars became the background that informed the political role of the army in the constant *pronunciamientos*, or coups d'état, supporting a series of constitutions throughout the nineteenth century (1820, 1837, 1845, 1856, 1869, and 1876), which led to a tumultuous end of the century; the Glorious Revolution of 1868 against Isabel II was followed by the short Reign of the Italian Amadeo I (1870–3), and the proclamation of the brief First Republic (1873–4), culminating in the Restoration of the Bourbon Dynasty with Alfonso XII after the 1875 coup.

The tensions between the two Spains that Goya allegorically portrayed in his painting "Duel with Cudgels" (1823) would finally explode in the twentieth century. Alfonzo XIII reached the throne in 1902 after the profound crisis of 1898 and the loss of Cuba, Puerto Rico, and the Philippines, the remaining overseas colonies. His reign had to deal with the rise of the labor movement and terrorism, as well as the colonial wars in Morocco. His answer was to appoint a dictator "a la Italiana," General Miguel Primo de Rivera (1923–30). By 1931, the Monarchy was so discredited that the municipal elections of April 14, 1931 gave unquestionable victory to the Republican candidates. Alfonso XIII abdicated and went into exile. The Second Republic was proclaimed in Spain, and a radical constitution that included the anti-Catholic statement and the women's right to vote was approved in Congress.

The centuries-old problems that the country faced included an almost 70 percent illiteracy rate, an impoverish mass of peasants in the south, and industrial workers in Catalonia.

The Spanish Second Republic was an anachronistic democracy in the European context of totalitarianism. On July 18, 1936, a conglomerate of right-wing forces, including the Army, the Catholic Church, and the financial establishment, supported an uprising that turned into a violent three-year-long Civil War, followed by a ruthless dictatorship under General Francisco Franco (1939–75).

Spain was able to establish a democracy after the death of the dictator, and to this day continues to struggle to achieve a better union, respecting the sum of the parts that makes us who we are. The documents included below are but several fragments that illustrate this journey.

DOCUMENT 1
SPANISH CONSTITUTIONS OF 1812 AND 1978

The Constitutions of 1812 and 1978 represent the will of the Spanish people to move from a tyrannical form of government to a more democratic one. In 1812, Europe was fighting against the Napoleonic domination, and the 303 delegates to the Cadiz assembly represented a diverse Spanish population, as it comprised both the Peninsula and its colonies in Africa, America, and the Caribbean. The Cadiz Constitution of 1812 became a model for other countries in Europe, as an expression of anti-French control during the Napoleonic era. However, this document may not be considered a model of radical liberalism as it kept monarchy as the central tenet in the political structure and Catholicism as the religion of the land. The life of this constitution was short, as two years later Ferdinand VII abolished it and restored absolutism. There would be a succession of constitutions enacted throughout the nineteenth century dominated by the military *pronunciamientos* (coups d'état) and the alternation of liberal and conservative forces in power.

Approved on December 6, 1978, the Spanish Constitution has been the longest lasting in the recent democratic history of Spain. It was negotiated between the different political parties, from the most conservatives to the liberals, from the nationalists to the socialists. The text legalized a new administrative organization of the country, conferring regions their autonomous parliament and government. At the same time, the Constitution of 1978 is especially strong in the inclusion of civil and social rights; it guarantees no discrimination on the base of race, sex, religion, creed, or sexual orientation, as well as free public education and equal access to the public health system. Although Catholicism is considered the majority religion, Spain proclaimed itself to be a secular country.

SPANISH CONSTITUTION OF 1812[1]

Chapter 1. Spanish Territories

Article 1
The Spanish territory includes the following lands in the peninsula and adjacent islands: Aragon, Asturias, Old Castile, New Castile, Catalonia, Cordoba, Extremadura, Galicia, Granada, Jaen, León, Molina, Murcia, Navarra, the Basque provinces, Seville, Valencia, the Balearic and Canary Islands, and the rest of the possessions in Africa. In North America, it includes New Spain with New Galicia, the Yucatan Peninsula, Guatemala, the interior provinces of the East and the West, the island of Cuba with the two Floridas, the Spanish part of the Santo Domingo island, and the island of Puerto Rico, with the other islands adjacent thereto and to the continent in both seas. In South America, New

Granada, Venezuela, Peru, Chile, the provinces of the Río de la Plata, and all the islands adjacent in the Pacific and in the Atlantic. In Asia, the Philippine Islands and those that depend on its government. (...)

Article 5

Spaniards are:

1. all free men and their children, who are born and reside in the Spanish domain;
2. foreigners who have obtained naturalization status from the Cortes;
3. foreigners without naturalization status who have been legal residents for ten years in any town belonging to the monarchy;
4. the freedmen from the moment they acquire their freedom in the Spains. (...)

Article 12

The religion of the Spanish nation is and shall always be the Catholic, Apostolic, Roman religion, the only and true one. The nation protects it by wise and just laws and prohibits the exercise of any other religion. (...)

Article 14

The government of the Spanish nation is a moderate hereditary monarchy.

Article 15

The power of making laws resides in the Cortes with the King.

Article 16

The power of executing laws resides in the King. (...)

Article 173

Upon his accession to the throne, and if he is a minor when becoming ruler of the kingdom, the king will take the following oath before the courts: "I, (Name), King of the Spains, by the grace of God and the constitution of the Spanish monarchy, swear by God and the holy Gospels that I will defend and preserve the Catholic, Apostolic, Roman religion, not allowing any other in the kingdom: that I shall keep and defend the constitution and laws of the Spanish monarchy, not doing anything that is not good and advantageous to it: that I shall not alienate, give in, or dismember any part of the kingdom: that I shall never demand any fruits money, or anything but those decreed by the courts: that I shall not take anybody's property; and that I will respect above all the political freedom of the nation, and the personal freedom of each individual. And if I were to do anything contrary to what I have sworn, I should not be obeyed; moreover, whatever I contravened will be void and of no value. (...)"

Article 175

Only legitimate children of one constant and legitimate marriage can be kings of the Spains.

Article 176

In the same degree and line, males are preferred over females, and always from the oldest to the youngest, but females belonging to a better line or degree are preferred over the males of a lower line or degree.

SPANISH CONSTITUTION (1978)[2]

Preliminary Part

Article 1
1. Spain is hereby established as a social and democratic State, subject to the rule of law, which advocates as the highest values its legal order, liberty, justice, equality, and political pluralism.
2. National sovereignty is vested in the Spanish people, from whom the powers of the State emanate.
3. The political form of the Spanish State is that of a parliamentary monarchy.

Article 2
The Constitution is based on the indissoluble unity of the Spanish nation, the common and indivisible country of all Spaniards; it recognizes and guarantees the right to autonomy of the nationalities and regions of which it is composed, and the solidarity amongst them all.

Article 3
1. Castilian is the official Spanish language of the State. All Spaniards have the duty to know it and the right to use it.
2. The other Spanish languages shall also be official in the respective Autonomous Communities in accordance with their Statutes.
3. The wealth of the different language modalities of Spain is a cultural heritage, which shall be the object of special respect and protection.

Article 4
1. The flag of Spain consists of three horizontal stripes: red, yellow and red, the yellow stripe being double the width of each red stripe.
2. The Statutes may recognize flags and ensigns of the Autonomous Communities. These shall be used together with the flag of Spain on their public buildings and in their official ceremonies.
(...)

Chapter 2. Rights and Liberties

Article 14

Spaniards are equal before the law and may not in any way be discriminated against on account of birth, race, sex, religion, opinion or any other personal, social condition or circumstance.

Section 1: Fundamental Rights and Public Liberties

Article 15

Everyone has the right to life and to physical and moral integrity, and may under no circumstances be subjected to torture or to inhuman or degrading punishment or treatment. The death penalty is hereby abolished, except as provided by military criminal law in times of war.

Article 16

1. Freedom of ideology, religion and worship of individuals and communities is guaranteed, with no other restriction on their expression than may be necessary to maintain public order as protected by law.
2. No one may be compelled to make statements regarding his religion, beliefs or ideologies.
3. There shall be no State religion. The public authorities shall take the religious beliefs of Spanish society into account and shall consequently maintain appropriate cooperation with the Catholic Church and the other confessions.

Article 21

1. The right to peaceful, unarmed assembly is recognized. The exercise of this right shall not require prior authorization.
2. In the event of meetings in public places and of demonstrations, prior notification shall be given to the authorities, who may ban them only when there are well-founded grounds to expect a breach of public order, involving danger to persons or property.

Article 22

1. The right of association is recognized.
2. Associations that pursue ends or use means classified as criminal offenses are illegal.
3. Associations set up on the basis of this article must be recorded in a register for the sole purpose of public knowledge.
4. Associations may only be dissolved or have their activities suspended by virtue of a justified court order.
5. Secret and paramilitary associations are prohibited. (. . .)

Article 27

1. Everyone has the right to education. Freedom of teaching is recognized.
2. Education shall aim at the full development of the human character with due respect for the democratic principles of coexistence and for the basic rights and freedoms.
3. The public authorities guarantee the right of parents to ensure that their children receive religious and moral instruction that is in accordance with their own convictions.
4. Elementary education is mandatory and free.
5. The public authorities guarantee the right of everyone to education, through general education programming, with the effective participation of all parties concerned and the setting up of educational centers.
6. The right of individuals and legal entities to set up educational centers is recognized, provided they respect Constitutional principles.
7. Teachers, parents and, when appropriate, pupils, shall share in the control and management of all the centers maintained by the Administration out of public funds, under the terms established by the law.
8. The public authorities shall inspect and standardize the educational system in order to guarantee compliance with the law.
9. The public authorities shall give aid to teaching establishments, which meet the requirements to be laid down by the law.
10. The autonomy of Universities is recognized, under the terms established by the law. (...)

Article 32

1. Men and women have the right to marry with full legal equality.
2. The law shall regulate the forms of marriage, the age at which it may be entered into and the required capacity therefore, the rights and duties of the spouses, the grounds for separation and dissolution, and the consequences thereof.

Article 33

1. The right to private property and inheritance is recognized.
2. The content of these rights shall be determined by the social function that they fulfill, in accordance with the law.
3. No one may be deprived of his or her property and rights, except on justified grounds of public utility or social interest and with a proper compensation in accordance with the provisions of the law.

Article 34

1. The right to set up foundations for purposes of general interest is recognized, in accordance with the law.
2. The provisions of clauses 2 and 4 of Article 22 shall also be applicable to foundations.

Article 35

1. All Spaniards have the duty to work and the right to employment, to free choice of profession or trade, to advancement through their work, and to sufficient remuneration for the satisfaction of their needs and those of their families; moreover, under no circumstances may they be discriminated against on account of their gender.
2. The law shall establish a Workers' Statutes. (...)

Article 45

1. Everyone has the right to enjoy an environment suitable for personal development, as well as the duty to preserve it.
2. The public authorities shall safeguard rational use of all natural resources with a view to protecting and improving the quality of life and preserving and restoring the environment, by relying on essential collective solidarity.
3. Criminal or, where applicable, administrative sanctions, as well as the obligation to make good the damage, shall be imposed, under the terms established by the law, against those who violate the provisions contained in the previous clause.

Article 46

The public authorities shall guarantee the preservation and promote the enrichment of the historic, cultural and artistic heritage of the peoples of Spain and of the property of which it consists, regardless of its legal status and its ownership. Offences committed against this heritage shall be punished under criminal law.

Article 47

All Spaniards are entitled to enjoy decent and adequate housing. The public authorities shall promote the necessary conditions and shall establish appropriate standards in order to make this right effective, regulating land use in accordance with the general interest in order to prevent speculation.

The community shall participate in the benefits accruing from the urban policies of the public bodies. (...)

Article 50

The public authorities shall guarantee, through adequate and periodically updated pensions, sufficient financial means for senior citizens.

Likewise, and independently of the obligations of their families towards them, they shall promote their welfare through a system of social services, which shall provide for their specific problems of health, housing, culture and leisure. (...)

Article 57

1. The Crown of Spain shall be inherited by the successors of H.M. Juan Carlos I de Bourbon, the legitimate heir of the historic dynasty.
   Succession to the throne shall follow the regular order of primogeniture and representation, in the following order of precedence: the earlier shall precede the later

lines; within the same line, the closer degree shall precede the more distant; within the same degree, the male shall precede the female; and for the same sex, the older shall precede the younger.

2. The Crown Prince, from the time of his birth or the event conferring this position upon him, shall hold the title of Prince of Asturias and the other titles traditionally held by the heir to the Crown of Spain.

3. Should all the lines designated by law become extinct, the General Cortes shall provide for the succession to the Crown in the manner most suited to the interests of Spain.

4. Those persons with a right to succession to the Throne who marry against the express prohibition of the King and the General Cortes shall be excluded from succession to the Crown, as shall their descendants.

5. Abdications and renunciations, and any doubt concerning a fact or the law that may arise in connection with the succession to the Crown, shall be resolved by an organic law. (...)

Article 146

The draft Statute shall be drawn up by an assembly consisting of the members of the Provincial Council or inter-island body of the provinces concerned and by the Deputies and Senators elected in them, and shall be sent to the General Cortes for its enactment into law.

Article 147

1. Within the terms of the Constitution, the Statutes shall constitute the basic institutional rules of each Autonomous Community and the State shall recognize and protect them as an integral part of its legal order.

2. The Statutes of Autonomy must contain:
   a) the name of the Community that corresponds most closely to its historic identity;
   b) its territorial boundaries;
   c) the name, organization and seat of its own autonomous institutions;
   d) the powers assumed within the framework established by the Constitution and the basic conditions for the transfer of the services corresponding to them.

3. Amendment of the Statutes shall conform to the procedure established therein and shall in any case require the approval of the Cortes through an organic law.

Article 148

1. The Autonomous Communities may assume competences over the following matters:
   a) organization of their institutions of self-government;
   b) changes in the municipal boundaries within their territory and, in general, the functions appertaining to the State Administration regarding local Corporations, whose transfer may be authorized by legislation on local government;
   c) town and country planning and housing;
   d) public works of benefit to the Autonomous Community, within its own territory;

e) railways and roads whose routes lie exclusively within the territory of the Autonomous Community and transport by the above means or by cable which also fulfills the same conditions;

f) ports of haven, recreational ports and airports and, in general, those, which are not engaged in commercial activities;

g) agriculture and livestock raising, in accordance with general economic planning;

h) woodlands and forestry;

i) environmental protection management;

j) planning, construction and operation of hydraulic projects, canals and irrigation of benefit to the Autonomous Community; mineral and thermal waters;

k) inland water fishing, the shellfish industry and aquaculture, shooting and river fishing;

l) local fairs;

m) promotion of the economic development of the Autonomous Community within the objectives set by national economic policy;

n) handicrafts;

o) museums, libraries and music conservatories of interest to the Autonomous Community;

p) the Autonomous Communities monuments of interest;

q) the promotion of culture, of research and, when applicable, the teaching of the language of the Autonomous Community;

r) the promotion and planning of tourism within its territorial area;

s) the promotion of sports and the proper use of leisure;

t) social assistance;

u) health and hygiene;

v) the supervision and protection of its buildings and facilities; coordination and other powers relating to local police forces under the terms to be laid down by an organic law.

2. After five years have elapsed, the Autonomous Communities may, by amendment of their Statutes, successively expand their powers within the framework established in Article 149.

Questions for discussion

1. Does the Constitution of 1812 truly provide a separation of the legislative, judicial, and executive powers?

2. Is there a position of privilege for the peninsular citizens in the 1812 Constitution? Do you think everybody is considered a full citizen? If not, which groups of people were excluded?

3. Considering the legacy of the Second Republic and the Francoist dictatorship, why is it so important to recognize the autonomy of the regions in the Spanish Constitution of 1978?

4. What makes the Constitution of 1978 last longer than the previous constitutions?

DOCUMENT 2
SPANISH CIVIL CODE 1889 VERSUS SPANISH CIVIL CODE 1958[3]

The Spanish Civil Code of 1889 followed in the tradition of the Napoleonic Code of 1804. It regulated civil society relations not only during the period of the Restoration (1876–1931) of the Bourbon Dynasty, but also after the code of 1889 was restored in 1938 by the Francoist state. It was the civil code in place that would be reformed in 1958. Therefore, these two documents offer us some insight into gender and family relations as well as private property under Spanish law.

Some of the focus we include here is on the regulation of the civil versus Catholic marriage. Likewise, the code regulated gender relations, making women legally minors and therefore always under the guardianship of a male figure (father, husband, brother, or uncle). The social role of women was configured within private family life; they were responsible for taking care of the children and their education to become good citizens. One of the novelties in this code was the regulation of divorce. The United States ordered a translation of this civil code in order to understand the Spanish better when they became owners of Cuba, Puerto Rico, and the Philippines in the late nineteenth century.

In a series of articles, lawyer Mercedes Formica denounced the death of a woman who had been stabbed by her husband. Published in the Madrid daily *ABC* in 1952, this account of domestic violence opened the door to the discussion of the need to reform the Civil Code. Wives could not open a bank account, sell or buy property, testify, or even have custody of their children without the consent of their husbands. The Spanish code of 1958 was approved under the Francoist regime. The Spanish government entered into an agreement with the Vatican to preserve the canonical law and the principles of the Catholic religion. In the spirit of the National Catholic ideology informing the dictatorship during the Cold War, the Civil Code of 1958, in its preface, points out clearly that the main goal was to guarantee the inclusion of this agreement within the Catholic Church in terms of its civil regulation. In the articles included below, we highlight this religious influence in the civil code, which applied to all the citizens, including non-practicing Catholics. The right to get a divorce had been banned by law since 1939. Within marriage the penalty of adultery was more severe in the case of the wife, who could demand separation only if the husband brought the mistress to live in the conjugal home.

CIVIL CODE (1889)

Marriage

Chapter I

General Provisions

First Section

Types of Marriage

Article 42. The law recognizes two forms of marriage: the canonical marriage for all those who profess the Catholic religion, and the civil marriage, to be held as established by this law.

Fourth Section

Rights and Obligations between Husband and Wife

Article 56. Spouses are required to live together, be faithful, and help each other.

Article 57. The husband must protect his wife and she must obey him.

Article 58. The woman is obligated to follow her husband wherever he establishes his residence. The Courts, however, can exempt the woman from this obligation with due fair cause if the husband transfers his residence overseas or abroad.

Article 59. The husband is the administrator of the assets of the spouse, unless otherwise determined by Article 1.384. If under eighteen years of age, the husband may not manage them without the consent of his father in the absence of his father, he needs his mother's consent and in the absence of both, his guardian's. Neither can he appear in Court without the assistance of the above-mentioned persons. Under no circumstances can the husband borrow money, alienate, or encumber real estate without the consent of the above-mentioned persons while he is underage.

Article 60. The husband is the representative of his wife, who cannot appear in a trial, in person or represented by an attorney, unless she has the husband's consent. She does not need, however, his permission to defend herself in a criminal case or to sue or defend herself in any lawsuit she has with her husband, or when she has obtained habilitation according to whatever civil prosecution law establishes.

Article 61. Nor can the woman, without license or permission from her husband, purchase, profit, or dispose of assets, nor be bound in any other way unless in cases and with the limitations established by the law.

Article 62. Acts performed by the woman against the provisions presented in the previous articles are null, unless in the case of things that, by their nature, are intended for the ordinary consumption of the family, in which case purchases made by women will be valid. Purchases of jewelry, furniture, and precious objects, can only be validated when the husband has given his wife consent for the purchase, use, and enjoyment of those objects.

Article 63. The wife will be able to do the following without her husband's consent:

1. Execute her will.
2. Exercise the rights and fulfill the duties that apply to her in regards to the legitimate or natural children born to a different father, and to their possessions.

Article 64. Women will enjoy the honors given to their husbands, except those who are strictly and exclusively personal, and she will retain them unless she remarries. (...)

Chapter II

Canonical marriage

Article 75. The requirements, form, and solemnities for the celebration of the canonical marriage are governed by the provisions of the Catholic Church and the Sacrosanct Council of Trent, which are considered laws in the Kingdom. (...)

Fourth Section

Divorce

Article 101. The common life of two married persons can only be suspended by divorce.

Article 105. Legitimate causes of divorce are:

1. All cases of adulterous wives and, in the case of husbands, when adultery results in public scandal or the denigration of wives.
2. Serious insults or physical abuse.
3. Violence exercised by the husband over his wife in order to force her to change her religion.
4. The husband's proposal to prostitute his wife.
5. The husband or wife's attempt to corrupt their sons or prostitute their daughters, and the collusion in their corruption or prostitution.
6. The condemnation of the spouse to life imprisonment.

Article 106. Divorce can only be requested by the innocent spouse. (...)

Article 320. The age of majority is twenty-three. (...)

Article 321. Notwithstanding the preceding article, the daughters who have come of age, but are less than twenty-five years old, are not allowed to leave their paternal house without permission from the father or the mother they live with, unless it is to marry or when the father or mother have remarried.

CIVIL CODE AMENDMENT (1958)

The present amendment of the Civil Code, the most extensive one introduced so far, mainly affects the marriage regime, to adjust our legal system to the Concordat signed on August 27, 1953, between the Holy See and the Spanish State; it introduces some novelties in matters related to adoption that, although they had fallen into disuse when the code was written, have acquired now a thriving vitality; it addresses the problem of women's legal capacity which long ago was raised, and it modifies the regulation of inheritance rights of the surviving spouse, establishing a simpler regime and at the same time increasing the participation of the widow.

(...)

In articles 42 and 86, which are now reformed, the nature of civil marriage is clearly established. Therefore, as long as one of the intending spouses professes this religion, the canonical marriage is the only option. That is, civil marriage is only possible when both intending spouses are not Catholic and this condition has to be proved.

(...)

Thus, it has been estimated that the civil law should not dictate any sanctioning rule if the union has been contracted with full legitimacy in the eyes of the Church. The union would be illegal only in the case of minor children who do not ask for their parents' consent or if parents are justly opposed to the future marriage.

(...)

The term divorce and its derivatives have been banned from the code, which has resulted in the simple editing of some articles and headings of sections and a general provision in which the term "divorce" is replaced with the expression "personal separation."

After explicitly recognizing the competence of the Church regarding the canonical marriage, the State is limited to regulate the civil effects, which are produced from the celebration of the canonical marriage, but the inscription in the Civil Registry in the terms expressed in the final Protocol of the Concordat are required.

(...)

While it is true that gender itself should not lead to differences or unequal legal treatment, it seems equally clear—to the point of considering it a fundamental principle—that the family, as the most intimate and essential of all communities, cannot cause inequalities, but it allows for certain organic differences derived from the responsibilities that pertain to all its members, with the aim of achieving the best moral and social purposes that, in accordance with natural law, the family is called to attain. Therefore, the peculiar position the married woman has in the conjugal society is contemplated. Due to the demands of the unity of marriage, there is a power of command that is given to husbands by nature, religion, and History, within a regime, which follows faithfully the Catholic tradition that has always inspired and should inspire in the future the relationship between the spouses.

(...)

Serious efforts have been made to ensure the rights and legitimate interests of spouses, particularly those of women, which are ordinarily more apt to succumb. And always guided by the wellbeing of children, who embody the most important asset that must be saved when the marriage is in crisis.

Law of May 17, 1958

The Spanish nation considers it a true honor to comply with the law of God, per the doctrine of the Holy Roman Catholic and Apostolic Church, the only and true faith, inseparable from the national consciousness, which will inspire its legislation.

V

The national community is founded on the man, as the bearer of eternal values, and in the family, as the basis of social life; but the individual and collective interests must be subordinated to the common good of the nation, made up of past, present, and future generations. The law will protect the right of all Spaniards alike.

(...)

VII

The Spanish people, united in an order of law, informed by the postulates of authority, freedom, and service, constitute the national State. Its political form is—within the immutable principles of the National Movement and as determined by the Law of Succession and other fundamental laws—the traditional, Catholic, social, and representative Monarchy.

VIII

The representative character of the political order is the basic principle of our public institutions. The participation of the people in the legislative tasks and other functions of general interest will take place through the family, the municipality, the Union, and other bodies with organic representation accorded by the laws for this purpose. All political organizations of any kind outside of this representative system will be considered illegal.

(...)

IX

All Spaniards have the right to an independent justice, which will be free for those who lack financial means; a general and professional education that will never fail to be received due to lack of material means; the benefits of social assistance and security; and to an equitable distribution of national income and tax burdens. The Christian ideal of social justice, reflected in the labor jurisdiction, will inspire the policy and laws.

Questions for discussion

1. Do you think that the principles of the French Revolution (Enlightenment) are reflected in these civil codes? Why do you think they are or why not?

2. How are gender roles regulated in both Civil Codes? Focus on the issue of marriage and divorce.

3. "The Spanish nation considers it a true honor to comply with the law of God, according to the doctrine of the Holy Roman Catholic and Apostolic Church, the only and true faith, inseparable from the national consciousness, which will inspire its legislation." How does the religious spirit of the law inform gender relations?

4. Explain this statement: "[T]he peculiar position the married woman has in the conjugal society is contemplated. Due to the demands of the unity of marriage, there is a power of command that is given to husbands by nature, religion, and History, within a regime which follows faithfully the Catholic tradition that has always inspired and should inspire in the future the relationship between the spouses."

DOCUMENT 3
CONSTITUTION OF THE SPANISH REPUBLIC (1931)

The short-lived First Republic (February 11, 1873–December 29, 1874) was abruptly terminated by General Martínez Campos' coup d'état on December 29, 1874. The restoration of the Bourbon Dynasty would last until 1931 with the proclamation of the Second Republic. King Alfonso XIII had been unable to solve centuries of structural problems, even after imposing the dictatorship of General Miguel Primo de Rivera (1923–30).

The Spanish Second Republic (1931–9) was proclaimed on April 14, 1931, after municipal elections gave the majority to republican candidates and forced King Alfonso XIII (1902–31) to abdicate and go into exile.

The Constitution of 1931 represents an example of more progressive politics as it proclaimed the freedom of religion, thus alienating millions of Spaniards that felt the Catholic Church represented the essence of Spanishness. It was also a constitution that responded to the commitment to the betterment of the poor through education and economic improvement, as well as equality between the sexes, with the ratification of female suffrage.

However, only five years into existence, the Second Republic, commonly known as "La niña bonita" ("the beautiful girl"), would face a military uprising that led to a three-year civil war. The western democracies declared a policy of non-intervention in the hopes of appeasement against Nazi Germany and the prevention of a second world war. The Second Republic was left to the mercy of the Soviet Union military support against Nazi and Fascist forces, and military equipment supported the Francoist side.

The promise of a progressive Spanish democracy was violently eradicated and put on hold for thirty-six years with the victory of the dictatorship of Francisco Franco.

PRELIMINARY TITLE

General Disposition

Article 1. Spain is a democratic republic of workers of all kinds, organized under a regime of Freedom and Justice.

The powers of all its bodies emanate from the people.

The Republic is an integral state, compatible with the autonomy of municipalities and regions.

The flag of the Spanish Republic is red, yellow and purple.

Article 2. All Spaniards are equal before the law.

Article 3. The Spanish State has no official religion.

Article 4. Castilian is the official language of the Republic. All Spaniards have the obligation to know this language and the right to use it, regardless of the rights that state laws give to the languages of the provinces or regions.

Except as provided by special laws, the knowledge or use of any regional language is not mandatory.

Article 5. The capital of the Republic is Madrid.

Article 6. Spain renounces war as an instrument of national policy.

Article 7. The Spanish State complies with the universal norms of international law incorporating them into its positive law. (...)

Title III

Rights and Duties of the Spaniards

Chapter I

Individual and political guarantees

Article 25. No legal privilege will be acquired on the grounds of nature, descent, gender, social class, wealth, political ideas, or religious beliefs.

The State does not recognize distinctions and titles.

Article 26. All religious denominations will be considered Associations ruled under a special law.

The State, regions, provinces, and municipalities will not support, favor, or give economic help to churches, or religious associations and institutions.

A special law shall regulate the total elimination of the Clergy budget within a maximum period of two years.

Religious orders that include within their statutes special obedience to an authority other than the legitimate state will be dissolved. Their assets will be nationalized and dedicated to charity and education. (...)

Article 27. Freedom of conscience and the right to profess and practice any religion freely are guaranteed in the Spanish territory, provided that public morality is respected.

Cemeteries shall be subject exclusively to the civil jurisdiction. Separate sections within cemeteries cannot be created for religious reasons.

All religions may exercise their worship privately. Public manifestations of worship must be authorized by the Government on a case-by-case basis.

No one may be compelled to officially declare his or her religious beliefs.

Religious condition shall not constitute modifying circumstance of a civil or political person, except as provided in this Constitution for the appointment of President of the Republic and President of the Council of Ministers.

Article 36. Citizens of both genders, aged at least twenty-three, have equal voting rights, as determined by law. (...)

Article 38. The right to assemble peacefully and without weapons is recognized. A special law shall regulate the right of outdoor meetings and demonstrations.

Article 39. Spaniards may join or organize unions freely for different purposes of human life, under the laws of the State.

Unions and Associations are required to register with the relevant public Register, in accordance with the law. (...)

Chapter II

Family, economy and culture

Article 43. The family is under the special protection of the State. Marriage is based on equal rights for both sexes, and may be dissolved by mutual consent or at the request of either spouse who pleads a just cause.

Parents are obliged to feed, assist, educate, and instruct their children. The State shall ensure the fulfillment of these duties and obligates itself to its subsidiary execution.

Parents have the same duties with respect to children born in or out of wedlock.

Civil laws will regulate the investigation of paternity.

Any statement about the legitimacy or illegitimacy of birth or the civil status of the parents may not be entered in the registers or in any other document related to parentage.

The State will assist the sick and elderly, and will provide protection to mothers and children, endorsing the "Geneva Declaration," on children's rights.

Article 44. All the country's wealth, whoever may be its owner, is subordinated to the interests of the national economy and affects the sustainability of public burdens in accordance with the Constitution and the laws.

The ownership of all kinds of goods may be subject to expropriation, with adequate compensation, if they are considered of social utility, unless otherwise directed by a law passed with the votes of the absolute majority of the Parliament.

Utilities and farms affecting the common interest may be nationalized in cases where the social necessity so requires. (...)

Article 46. Work, in its various forms, is a social obligation and shall enjoy the protection of the laws. The Republic will ensure every worker the conditions necessary for a dignified existence. Its social legislation will regulate the following: medical insurance, accidents, unemployment, old age, disability, and death; the work of women and young people, and especially maternity protection; working hours and minimum and family wages; paid vacation; the conditions of Spanish workers abroad; the institutions of cooperation, the economic and legal relationship of all the factors that make up the production; the participation of workers in management, administration, and corporate profits, and everything regarding the defense of workers.

Article 47. The Republic will protect peasants and it will legislate to this purpose, among other things, on the indefeasible family property which will be exempt from all taxation, on agricultural credits, compensation for loss of crops, production and consumer cooperatives, savings banks, agricultural schools and experimental farms, irrigation works, and rural roads. The Republic will safeguard the fisherman on equivalent terms.

Questions for Discussion:

1. "Article 1. Spain is a democratic republic of workers of all kinds, organized under a regime of Freedom and Justice./The powers of all its bodies emanate from the people." This article rejects the monarchy as the form of government of Spain. Compare this with the Constitutions of 1812 and 1978.

2. Women's right to vote was recognized in Article 36 of the Constitution of 1931 in Spain. How does it compare with other countries in Europe and the rest of the world?

3. Should religion be a main point to include in the Constitution? How is religious freedom better protected while at the same time guarantying separation of Church and State?

4. Do you think the Constitution of 1931 was conciliatory? In what ways do you see the Constitution of 1978 being more conciliatory?

DOCUMENT 4
LAW OF POLITICAL RESPONSIBILITIES (1939)[4]

On April 1, 1939, Franco delivered his last war address. The war had ended but the suffering of the vanquished had not. While Europe was entering the Second World War in September, Franco decreed a law of political responsibilities to articulate the repression of dissidents. With this law, the fascist regime established who were politically responsible for the Civil War. The dictator and his supporters considered their uprising a crusade against those on the side of the Republic, and who therefore represented an attack against the eternal idea of Catholic Spain.

Condemned by the law were all the members of the *Frente Popular* (Popular Front, a left-wing coalition that won the elections in February of 1936) and the nationalist parties from the historical regions of Catalonia, the Basque country, and Galicia. This law remained in place for thirty years and prohibited all exiles from returning to the country until Franco's death in 1975.

Based on the principles of the Movimiento (the Fascist party—Falange Española Tradicionalista, that informed the regime's policies) and also on conservative Catholic beliefs, the law prohibited political dissent and assembly and made political participation possible only through the political and social structure controlled by the dictatorship: family, syndicate, and municipality.

The law was the instrument to implement the regime's repression of political opposition during the long period of the regime. Everyone who had participated actively in politics during the Republic was declared an enemy of Spain, and when some of these dissidents could not be located, their families were made the target as a social example.

LAW OF POLITICAL RESPONSIBILITIES (1939)

Now that the total liberation of Spain is about to become a reality, the Government is aware of its duties in the spiritual and material reconstruction of our country, and therefore considers that it is the appropriate time to enact a law of political responsibilities that serves to address the political faults incurred by those who contributed—by acts or serious omissions—to forge the Red subversion, to keep it alive for more than two years, and to hinder the providential and historically inevitable triumph of the National Movement. This law will deal with the civil responsibilities of convicted persons and will finally allow those Spaniards who, by tightly joining together, saved our country and our civilization, and will also allow others that have paid for their misdeeds through just sanctions and the commitment to never go astray, to coexist, so that they can dedicate all their efforts and sacrifices to the service of a great Spain.

The aim of this Law and its development go beyond the harsh concepts of a criminal provision that would be embedded into molds that have become outdated. The magnitude, intention, and material consequences of the injuries inflicted upon Spain are such, that it is impossible to have a proportional punishment and reparation for them. These would go against the deep meaning of our National Revolution, which does not want to punish cruelly, nor bring misery to households.

Therefore, this Law, which is not vindicatory but constructive in nature, mitigates, on the one hand, the disciplinary rigor, and on the other, it seeks to fairly harmonize the sacred interests of the Homeland with the will not to bankrupt the economic life of individuals.

Economic sanctions are regulated with humane moderation, and are exemplified by the precepts designed not to restrict the activities of those who base their livelihood on modest business. And these sanctions—in those cases where the danger of possible future actions of those indicted should be prevented—may be accompanied by others, which, strictly speaking, are security measures that will include the ineligibility for holding certain offices, and the displacement from their previous residences; in cases of extreme gravity, individuals that do not deserve the honor of being Spaniards will lose their Spanish citizenship. (...)

The Courts in charge of imposing sanctions shall be composed of representatives of the Military, the Judiciary, the *Falange Española Tradicionalista*, and JONS (Traditionalist Spanish Phalanx of the Juntas of the National Syndicalist Offensive), which will provide their joint action with the tone that inspired the National Movement. And so that all courts and agencies entrusted to implement the law work in perfect harmony, a high court and an adjacent administrative body will be created, so that under one direction, and in accord with the Government, the necessary unity is created, in order to achieve the desired results in both the legal and the economic orders. (...)

Title I. Substantive Part

Chapter I. General Statements

Article 1. We hereby declare the political responsibility of persons—both physically and legally—that since the first of October of nineteen thirty-four and before July 18th of the year one thousand nine hundred and thirty-six, helped to create or aggravate the subversion of which Spain was a victim, and those others that, from the latter date have, opposed or will oppose the National Movement with specific acts or serious passivity.

Article 2. As a consequence of the previous statement and ratifying what has been mandated in Article 1 of Decree one hundred and eight, dated the thirteenth of September of one thousand and thirty-six, we hereby outlaw all political parties and associations that have integrated the so-called Popular Front since the elections held on February sixteenth of one thousand and thirty-six, as well as parties and groups attached to it by the mere fact of being so, separatist organizations and all those who have opposed the triumph of the National Movement. (...)

Article 3. Parties, groups, and organizations that are declared outside the law will suffer the absolute loss of all kinds of rights and the total loss of their property. The above will become entirely State-owned. (. . .)

Chapter II. Causes of Responsibility and Circumstances Affecting It

Article 4. Pursuant to Article 1, all individuals who are included in any of the following categories are considered to be politically responsible and will be subject to the sanctions imposed upon them during the proceedings against them:

a) those convicted by the military jurisdiction for any offense related to rebellion—including joining, helping, aggravating, or encouraging others to such a rebellion—or for any acts of treason that are considered to be criminal under the Glorious National Movement.

b) those who have held leadership positions in the parties, groups, and associations as established in Article 2, and those who have been the representatives of such parties in any type of corporation and organization, both public and private. (. . .)

g) the members of Parliament of one thousand nine hundred thirty six who, betraying their constituents, have contributed, by action or abstention, to the implementation of the ideals of the Popular Front and its programs.

h) those who belong or have belonged to the Freemasonry, with the only exception being those who voluntarily left the sect before the eighteenth day of July of the year one thousand nine hundred and thirty-six, thus explicitly breaking with it, or those expelled from such sect for having acted against the principles that inspire it or the purposes pursued by it. (. . .)

l) those who have actively opposed the National Movement. (. . .)

m) those who have remained abroad since the eighteenth day of July of the year one thousand nine hundred and thirty-six without returning to the national territory within a maximum period of two months, unless they have established their usual and permanent residence abroad or have been entrusted with a mission by the authorities of the liberated Spain, or those who were physically unable to return to the national territory, or who can prove that there is an extraordinary and substantial cause that can sufficiently justify his stay abroad. (. . .)

o) those who have accepted any of the red authorities, foreign missions, except in the case that, once involved, they did not carry them out and only accepted the missions as a way to escape enemy territory, and who presented themselves in the country as soon as they were able to leave.

Questions for discussion

1. Nazi Germany enacted the Nuremberg laws against the German-Jewish population in 1935. How do these laws compare with the Spanish law of political

responsibilities? What is it that makes the vanquished Spanish population non-Spanish just like the Jews who were declared non-German?

2. What was the idea of nation that Franco tried to preserve with this type of law?

3. Explain this article: "Parties, groups and organizations that are declared outside the law, will suffer the absolute loss of all kinds of rights and the total loss of their property. The above will become entirely State-owned." Is this exclusive of fascist dictatorships?

DOCUMENT 5
FUNDAMENTAL PRINCIPLES OF THE STATE (1958)

Franco's dictatorship received international recognition with the signing of two major diplomatic agreements in the summer of 1953: the Pact of Madrid with the United States and the Concordat with the Vatican. Franco was welcomed into the United Nations in 1955. In the eyes of the Western world, the Cold War facilitated his transition from fascist dictator to anti-communist "Sentinel of the West" in the words of the official propaganda. No doubt the Falangists had to be pushed into the background of the political stage, and the regime rapidly adopted the National Catholic technocratic identity that the Opus Dei provided, to better administer the American dollars. To show this change to the world sitting in the audience of the political theater, the regime published in 1958 the Fundamental Principle of the State as one of the eight main laws, which at that time, lent it some sort of constitutional nature. Scholars would start referring to the regime as authoritarian rather than totalitarian, because they regarded it as an example of "limited pluralism" rather than as ruled by a crude single dictator. Everybody with a public responsibility had to swear to accept the contents of this bill. Franco recognized the law as the principles of the Movimiento, the political framework of his regime. It renewed Spain's identity as Roman Catholic; family was recognized as the main social institution, and the syndicate as the only venue for labor bargaining. These were Falangist so-called "sindicatos verticales"; every professional group and trade had to obtain a membership card to get a job. Centralized Nationalism—rather than respect for the historical regions' identities—National Catholicism, and devotion to the Caudillo were some of the main principles of this law. Even though Article IX declared the right to free justice for everybody, free social security, and education, citizens had to pledge allegiance to the National Catholic principles delineated in the law.

The Regime of Franco developed a strong legislative apparatus to control and legitimize its principles based on the "law of God." In the future, the only form of government that would be tolerated would be that of the traditional Monarchy. No other religious freedom, no democratic participation, no dissent was accepted.

FUNDAMENTAL ACT OF MAY 17, 1958

By which the Principles of the National Movement Are Enacted[5]

I, Francisco Franco Bahamonde, Caudillo of Spain, aware of my responsibility before God and History, in the presence of the Council of the Reign, enact the following principles of the National Movement, which should be understood as the union of all Spaniards in the support of the ideals that gave life to the Crusade:

I. Spain is one in its universal destiny. Service to the country's unity, greatness, and freedom is a sacred duty and a collective undertaking for all Spaniards.

II. The Spanish nation considers it an honor to obey the law of God, according to the Holy Catholic Apostolic and Roman Church, the one and only true Church, whose faith is inseparable from the national consciousness and will inspire its legislation.

III. Spain, as the foundation of a great family of peoples, to whom it feels bound in indissoluble brotherhood, aspires to the establishment of justice and peace among the nations.

IV. The unity between the land and the men of Spain is inviolable. The integrity of the homeland and its independence are both supreme demands on the national community. The Armed Forces of Spain must possess the strength required for the best service of the homeland since they are the guarantee of national security and are the expression of our people's heroic virtues.

V. The national community is founded on men as bearers of eternal values, and on the family as the basis of social life; but individual and collective interests will always be subordinate to the common welfare of the nation, formed of past, present, and future generations. The Law safeguards the rights of all Spaniards alike.

VI. The natural entities of social life—family, municipalities, and the workers' union—are the basic structures of the national community. Institutions and corporations of other character that meet general social needs shall be supported, so that they may participate effectively in the improvement of the aims of the national community.

VII. The Spanish people, united in an order of Law informed by the postulates of authority, freedom, and service, form the National State. Its political form is—within the immutable principles of the National Movement and the provisions of the Succession Act and the other fundamental laws—that of the traditional, Catholic, social, and representative Monarchy.

VIII. The representative character of the political order is the basic principle of our public institutions. The participation of the people in legislative tasks and the other fundamental functions of general interest shall be provided through the family, the municipality, the labor union, and other bodies that the laws may recognize as having organic representation for such purpose. All other political organizations of any kind that fall outside of this representative system shall be deemed illegal. All Spaniards will have access to public office and functions, according to their merit and ability.

IX. All Spaniards are entitled to the following: independent justice, which will be free for those who lack financial means; a general and professional education, which nobody will fail to obtain due to lack of material means; the benefits of social assistance and social security; and an equitable distribution of the national income and tax burdens. The Christian ideal of social justice, reflected in the Labor Charter, will inspire State policy and laws.

X. Work is recognized as the origin of the hierarchy, duty, and honor of Spaniards, and private property in all its forms is recognized as a right conditioned by its social function. Private enterprise, the basis of economic activity, shall be encouraged, channeled, and if necessary, supplemented by State action.

XI. The Corporation, an association of men and means of production, forms a community of interests and a unity of aims. The relationships between its components must be based on justice, on mutual loyalty, and economic values shall be subordinate to the human and social order.

XII. The State shall endeavor, by all means in its power, the following: to improve the physical and moral health of Spaniards and to ensure them the most decent working conditions; to promote the economic progress of the nation by improving agriculture, improving irrigation, and promoting a rural social reform; to seek the fairest use and distribution of the public credit; to safeguard and promote the prospecting for and exploitation of the mines; to intensify the process of industrialization; to sponsor scientific research, and to promote maritime activities, as it is suitable for the large sea-faring population of Spain and our naval record.

Questions for discussion

1. How was religion utilized by totalitarian regimes before World War II? Take into consideration Italy, Germany, and Spain.
2. How did Franco utilize religion as a principle of governance in the country during the Cold War?
3. What was the difference between the communist regimes and the fascist regimes at that time in Europe? Consider Spain versus Poland.
4. Why do you think Franco became a benign dictator in the eyes of the United Nations when he had been allied with Hitler and Mussolini during the Spanish Civil War?

DOCUMENT 6

LEY DE RECUPERACIÓN DE LA MEMORIA HISTÓRICA (LAW OF HISTORICAL MEMORY, DECEMBER 26, 2007)⁶

There is no doubt the Spanish Civil War represents to this day the most dramatic conflict between Spaniards. The ensuing dictatorship of Francisco Franco perpetuated, through the law of political responsibilities, the repression against those who lost the war. Many today regard the Transition to democracy framed under the Constitution of 1978 as another victory on the side of the right, and consequently, an imperfect outcome based on what has been called "the pact of silence." In 2007, with the PSOE (*Partido Socialista Obrero Español*) in power, then Prime Minister José Luis Rodríguez Zapatero passed a law of Historical Memory to address the issue of reconciliation. This law became a source of multiple juridical disputes after its implementation, opening a heated debate around the Transition and the baggage of the civil war and the dictatorship.

LAW OF HISTORICAL MEMORY

Juan Carlos I

King of Spain

To all who might see and understand.

Let it be known: That the General Cortes have approved, and I sanction, the following law.

Explanatory Preamble

The spirit of reconciliation and peace, respect for pluralism, and the peaceful defense of all ideas that guided the Transition, allowed us to bestow upon ourselves a Constitution in 1978, which legally transformed the will of reunification of Spaniards, articulating a democratic social State under the law, with an inclusive vocation.
(. . .)
This law honors the proposal of the Congress Constitutional Commission, which on November 20, 2002, passed unanimously a Proposition, not a law, in which the body of citizenship representation reiterated: "no one can feel that he has the right, as it happened in the past, to utilize violence to impose his political convictions and establish totalitarian regimes contrary to the dignity and liberty of all citizens. That deserves condemnation and rejection by our democratic society." The present Law assumes this Declaration and

the condemnation of Francoism contained in the Report from the Parliamentary Assembly of the Council of Europe, signed in Paris on March 17, 2006, in which the grave violations of Human Rights committed in Spain in the years 1939 to 1975 were denounced.

It is time, therefore, that Spanish democracy, and the living generations who enjoy it today, may honor and recover forever all of those who directly suffered the injustices and aggressions produced by various political or ideological reasons, or due to religious beliefs during those painful periods in our history. Unquestionably, [especially] those who lost their lives and their families. Also those who lost their freedom, suffering imprisonment, deportation, confiscation of property, forced labor or internment in concentration camps inside or outside our borders. Also, those who lost their fatherland, when they were pushed into a long, heartbreaking, and in some cases irreversible, exile. And finally, those who at different times fought in defense of democratic values, like the members of the Corps of Riflemen, the International Brigade, the guerrilla fighters, whose restoration was unanimously requested by Congress on May 16, 2001, or the members of the Democratic Military Union that became dissolved with the first democratic elections.

Therefore, this Law establishes the basis for the public powers to implement public policies that spread the knowledge of our history and the encouragement of a democratic memory.

The present Law bases itself on the consideration that the different aspects concerned with personal and family memory, particularly when they have been affected by conflicts of a public nature, are also part of a democratic citizenry's legal rights, and as such these concerns are addressed in the law. Therefore, we recognize the right to personal and family memory of each citizen (. . .) in article 2.

In effect, there is a general proclamation of the unjust character of all the sentences, sanctions, and the personal violence against individuals for ideological and political reasons during the Civil War, as well as those inflicted, for the same reasons, during the dictatorship that followed.

This general declaration contained in article 2 is supplemented with the provision of due process to obtain a personal Declaration whose substance is both rehabilitative and restorative. This is offered as a right to all who are wronged and are entitled to it individually or as a family.

Article 3 of the Law declares as illegitimate all courts, juries, or bodies of any administrative nature created without the most basic guaranties of the law for due process. Likewise, it declares null and void the sentences and penalizations of a personal nature imposed for political, ideological, or religious reasons. We emphasize, in an unequivocal manner, the present lack of legal validity of those dispositions and resolutions that are contrary to human rights, and we thus contribute to the moral rehabilitation of those who suffered unjust punishments and convictions.

(. . .)

In articles 5 to 9 the recognition of the improvements of a variety of economic rights already planned in our Ordinances is established. In the same way, it provides the right to compensation in favor of those people who lost their lives defending the democracy we all enjoy today, and who had not received the appropriate compensation until now (art. 10).

Various mandates are adopted (articles 11 to 14), that address the fact that in this environment there is a legitimate demand from, not just a few citizens who do not know the location of the remains of their loved ones, some still in common graves; measures and instrumentations are provided for the public administrations to facilitate the location and, for some, identification of the missing for those interested, and who apply for it, being this proof of respect for them.

There are a series of provisions established (arts. 15 and 16) with regard to commemorative symbols and monuments of the Civil War and the Dictatorship, based on the principle that we must avoid all exaltation of the military uprising, the Civil War, and the repression by the Dictatorship, and on the conviction that the citizenry has the right to public symbols that are an occasion for unification rather than confrontation, offense, or injury.

Legislators consider it just to express two recognitions in one. First, to the volunteers of the International Brigades, who will be allowed to receive Spanish citizenship without having to renounce their own (art.18); and also, to the citizen associations who have distinguished themselves in defense of the victims of political violence to which this law refers.

With the objective to facilitate the compilation and the right to access historical information about the Civil War, this Law reinforces the role of the current General Archive of the Spanish Civil War located in Salamanca, which will be integrated with the Documentary Center of Historical Memory, also located in Salamanca, establishing that all documentation be transferred there from all other state institution (arts. 20 to 22).

The present law expands the possibility of bestowing Spanish citizenship to the descendants, up to the first degree, of those who were originally Spanish citizens. With this it satisfies one of the legitimate expectations of Spanish emigration, and specifically includes the descendants of those who lost Spanish citizenship as a result of the exile forced upon them during the Civil War and the Dictatorship.

Finally, the present Law wants to contribute to the healing of the still open wounds among Spaniards, and give satisfaction to those citizens who suffered directly—or to members of their family—the consequences of the Civil War tragedy and the repression of the Dictatorship. It wants to contribute to this sentiment, based on the conviction that by deepening the Transition's spirit of reunification and harmony, not only are those citizens recognized and honored, but also the Spanish democracy as a whole. It is not the legislator's task to impose a prefixed collective memory. But it is the legislator's duty, and the purpose of the law, to provide reparations to the victims, consecrate and protect, with the utmost normative vigor, the right to personal and family memory as an expression of full democratic citizenship, to foment constitutional values, and promote the knowledge and reflection about our past, so that we may prevent the repetition of situations of intolerance and violation of human rights like those experienced before.

This is the commitment to which this legal text and its judicial consequences respond. (...)

Therefore,

I order all Spaniards, individuals and authorities, to enforce and ensure that this law is enforced.

Madrid, December 26, 2007

Juan Carlos R.

Prime Minister
Jose Luis Rodriguez Zapatero

Questions for discussion

1. Explain the following statement: "no one can feel that he has the right, as it happened in the past, to utilize violence to impose his political convictions and establish totalitarian regimes contrary to the dignity and liberty of all citizens. That deserves condemnation and rejection by our democratic society." What are the limits on freedom of expression that guarantee peace and inclusion of all citizens?

2. Why do you think individual and family memories are characterized in this law as democratic rights? Is it possible to build a national unified narrative with only one set of values?

3. Why is the law considering access to historical documents as part of the historical reconciliation? Do you think the implementation of this provision might be problematic when the rights of the perpetrators and the victims collide at the local level?

4. Look for information about Judge Baltasar Garzón, who was removed from office due to his involvement in investigating the crimes of the dictatorship, and explain how this statement has played out:

"Consequently, the present law wants to contribute to heal the still open wounds among Spaniards and satisfy those citizens who suffered directly—or to members of their family—the consequences of the Civil War tragedy and the repression of the Dictatorship."

MODULE 7
RELIGION

ABSTRACT

The Iberian Peninsula may be considered the medieval final frontier in Western Europe. For almost eight hundred years (711–1492), the forces of Christianity and Islam fought to regain control over the land. After 1492, Catholicism became synonymous with Spanish identity. The Catholic monarchs launched their matrimonial policy with their daughter, Catherine of Aragon, but she would not be able to keep her husband, Henry VIII, after he became smitten with Anne Boleyn. Catherine's support from her uncle, Charles V, and the Pope did not prevent the schism between the Anglican and the Catholic Church.

The Reformation and the Counter-Reformation defined the confrontation across the European continent for most of the early modern period and became the Spanish Empire's *raison d'etre*. Therefore, religion represents a most important aspect of study to understand the history and culture of the Hispanic worlds. During the Enlightenment in the eighteenth century, and exacerbated by the Napoleonic War of Independence (1808–14), the tension between the enlightened thinkers and those who held essential absolute divine monarchy started to delineate what in traditional historiography has been called the two Spains. The confrontation between the forces of tradition and liberalism continued into the nineteenth century. Anticlericalism became increasingly more violent in the first third of the twentieth century. The lower classes, whether factory workers in Catalonia or the Basque country or the landless peasantry in southern Andalucía, regarded the Catholic Church as a powerful and privileged institution allied with the landowners and big business.

The Spanish Civil War (1936–9) and the ensuing long right-wing dictatorship of General Francisco Franco reinforced the polarization between the two Spains, giving the victory to the conservative Catholicism until the 1970s when the Second Vatican Council principles reached Spain and split Catholics across generational lines.

DOCUMENT 1
CONCORDAT CONCLUDED BETWEEN HIS HOLINESS AND HER CATHOLIC MAJESTY, SIGNED IN MADRID ON 16 MARCH, 1851[1]

A concordat is an agreement between the Catholic Vatican State and another country. This agreement is also a legal document, which delineates the terms of Catholic Church and Civil State relations. The nineteenth century in Spanish history saw a series of civil wars between the Carlists[2] supporting the right to the throne of Don Carlos, brother of Ferdinand VII, and the liberals supporting the reign of Ferdinand's daughter, Isabel II (1834–68), appointed by the Pragmatic Sanction of 1830, which, following king Ferdinand's wishes (as he had no sons), repealed the Salic Law that prevented women from being heirs to the throne even when there was a male direct heir, which was the position of the Carlists.

The Carlists were ultra-Catholics but so was the Isabeline monarchy. In March 1851, the Concordat signed with Pope Pius IX guaranteed that Catholicism would be the only religion of the land in Spain. The Church oversaw the educational system, and the agreement converted the Church into a special interest group along with others such as the military and the financial elites. This agreement reflects the relationship that the Church and the moderate liberals had up to the early twentieth century and it regulated the relations between Spain and the Vatican until it was terminated by the Second Republic (1931–6). The dictatorship of Franco reactivated the Concordat in 1941 and eventually entered a new agreement in the summer of 1953.

CONCORDAT OF 1851

[Came into force on May 11, 1851 upon the exchange of the instruments of ratification, which took place in Madrid, in accordance with Article 46.]

His Holiness the Supreme Pontiff Pius IX, strongly desiring to provide for the good of the religion and the utility of the Church of Spain with the pastoral solicitude with which he tends to all faithful Catholics and with especial benevolence toward the illustrious and devout Spanish Nation, and Her Majesty the Catholic Queen Isabel II, being possessed of the same desire owing to the piety and sincere adherence to the Apostolic See inherited from her ancestors, have decided to conclude a solemn concordat to govern all ecclesiastical affairs in a stable, canonical manner.

To this end, His Holiness the Supreme Pontiff has appointed as his Plenipotentiary His Excellency Mr. Juan Brunelli, Archbishop of Salonika, Domestic Prelate of His Holiness, Assistant to the Pontifical Throne and Papal Nuncio to the Kingdom of Spain with the powers of legate *a latere*, and Her Majesty the Catholic Queen has appointed Mr. Manuel Bertran de Lis, Knight Grand Cross of the royal and distinguished Spanish order of Charles III, of the order of Saint Maurice and Saint Lazarus of Cerdena and of the order of Francis I of Naples, member of Parliament and her Minister of State, who, having exchanged their full powers, found in good and due form, have agreed as follows:

Article 1. The apostolic Roman Catholic religion, which, to the exclusion of any other cult, continues to be the sole religion of the Spanish Nation, shall be preserved always in the dominions of Her Catholic Majesty, with all the rights and prerogatives which it should enjoy per the law of God and the provisions of the sacred canons.

Article 2. Consequently, instruction in universities, colleges, seminaries, and public or private schools of any nature shall be in all respects in keeping with the doctrine of the said Catholic religion; to that end, bishops and other diocesan prelates charged by virtue of their ministry with watching over the purity of the doctrine, the faith and mores and over the religious education of the youth shall in no way be hindered in the exercise of that charge, even in public schools.

Article 3. Nor shall the said prelates or other sacred ministers be hindered in any way in the exercise of their functions, nor shall anyone disturb them under any pretext about the performance of the duties of their office; rather, all the authorities of the Kingdom shall take care to give them and see to it that they are given due respect and consideration in accordance with the divine precepts and that nothing is done which might cause them to suffer any blemish or scorn. Her Majesty and her Royal Government shall, moreover, grant their mighty patronage and support to the bishops where they so request, principally where they need to oppose the malignancy of men who try to pervert the minds of the faithful and corrupt their mores, or where the publication, introduction or circulation of wicked and noxious books must be prevented.
(...)

Article 31. The stipend of the Most Reverend Archbishop of Toledo shall be 160,000 reals yearly.

That of the archbishops of Seville and Valencia shall be 150,000.

That of the archbishops of Granada and Santiago shall be 140,000.

And that of the archbishops of Burgos, Tarragona, Valladolid, and Saragossa shall be 130,000.

The stipend of the Right Reverend Bishops of Barcelona and Madrid shall be 110,000.

That of the bishops of Cadiz, Cartagena, Cordova and Malaga shall be 100,000.

That of the bishops of Almeria, Avila, Badajoz, the Canaries, Cuenca, Gerona, Huesca, Jaén, León, Lérida, Lugo, Majorca, Orense, Oviedo, Palencia, Pamplona, Salamanca, Santander, Segovia, Teruel, and Zamora shall be 90,000 reals.

That of the bishops of Astorga, Calahorra, Ciudad Real, Coria, Guadix, Jaca, Minorca, Mondonedo, Orihuela, Osma, Plasencia, Segorbe, Sigüenza, Tarazona, Tortosa, Tuy, Urgel, Vich, and Vitoria shall be 80,000 reals.

That of the Patriarch of the Indies, being neither archbishop nor bishop proper, shall be 150,000, there being deducted from that amount any other which he may collect, by way of ecclesiastical pension or otherwise, from the State.

Prelates who are cardinals shall have the benefit of 20,000 reals in addition to their stipend.

The auxiliary bishops of Ceuta and Tenerife and the priors of orders shall have 40,000 reals yearly.

These stipends shall not be subject to any discount either because of the cost of papal bulls, which shall be defrayed by the Government, or owing to any other costs to which such bulls may give rise in Spain.

In addition, archbishops and bishops shall keep their palaces and the gardens, orchards, or houses that have been destined for their use and recreation in any part of the diocese and have not been alienated.

Archbishops and bishops may, in derogation of the present legislation relative to their *spoila* freely dispose, in accordance with the dictates of their conscience, of whatever they may leave at the time of their decease, and their legitimate heirs shall succeed to them *ab intestato* with the same obligation of conscience, with the exception, in both cases, of sacred vestments and pontifical, which shall be deemed as belonging to the mitre and shall be transferred to their successors therein.

Article 32. The first chair of the cathedral church of Toledo shall have a stipend of 24,000 reals; those of the other metropolitan churches, 20,000; those of suffragan churches, 18,000; and those of collegiate churches, 15,000.

The dignitaries and major canons of metropolitan churches shall have 16,000 reals; those of suffragan churches, 14,000; and the major canons of collegiate churches, 8,000.

The remaining canons shall have 14,000 reals in metropolitan churches, 12,000 in suffragan churches, and 6,600 in collegiate churches.

Assistant chaplains or beneficiaries of metropolitan churches shall have 8,000 reals; those of suffragan churches, 6,000; and those of collegiate churches, 3,000.

Article 33. The stipend of parish priests in urban parishes shall be from 3,000 to 10,000 reals; in rural parishes, the minimum stipend shall be 2,200.

Coadjutors and administrators (*ecónomos*) shall have from 2,000 to 4,000 reals.

In addition, rectors and coadjutors, if any, shall have the benefit of the houses intended for their abode and such gardens, orchards or estates as have not been alienated and are known by such names as *iglesarios, mansos* or others.

Rectors and their coadjutors shall also have the benefit of their rightful share in surplice-fees and alterage.

Article 34. To defray the costs of worship, metropolitan churches shall have from 90 to 140,000 reals annually; suffragan churches, from 70 to 90,000; and collegiate churches, from 20 to 30,000.

For administrative expenses and extraordinary visitation expenses metropolitans shall have from 20 to 30,000 reals and suffragans, from 16 to 20,000.

For the costs of parochial worship the respective churches shall be allotted a yearly amount of no less than 1,000 reals in addition to any emoluments and the fees fixed or to be fixed for certain functions in the tariffs of the respective dioceses.

Article 35. The conciliar seminaries shall have from 90 to 120,000 reals yearly, according to their circumstances and needs.

Her Majesty's Government shall provide, by the most conducive means, for the subsistence of the religious houses and congregations discussed in article 29.

As for the maintenance of religious communities, the provisions of article 30 shall be observed.

The property belonging to those communities which is in the hands of the Government and has not been alienated shall be returned to them immediately and without delay, and on their behalf to the diocesan prelates in whose territory the convents are situated or were situated before the most recent changes. His Holiness, however, bearing in mind the present state of that property and other particular circumstances, orders the prelates, on behalf of the owner religious communities, to proceed immediately and without delay to sell the said property at public auctions conducted in accordance with canonical precepts and with the participation of a person designated by Her Majesty's Government, in order that with the proceeds thereof the expenses of worship and other general expenses may be met with greater uniformity. The proceeds of such sales shall be converted into non-transferable 3% Government bonds, the principal and interest of which shall be distributed among all the above-mentioned convents in proportion to their needs and circumstances with a view to meeting the said expenses and paying the pensions of nuns entitled to receive them, provided, however, that the Government shall supply, as hitherto, whatever is necessary for the complete payment of such pensions until the decease of the pensioners.

Article 36. It is to be understood that the amounts allocated in the preceding articles for expenses of cult and clergy do not preclude increases in those amounts where circumstances so permit. Nevertheless, where for special reasons any of the allocations specified in article 34 does not suffice in a particular case, Her Majesty's Government shall provide accordingly; similarly, it shall provide for the costs of repairs to temples and other edifices consecrated to worship.

(...)

Article 45. The laws, orders, and decrees published hitherto in any manner or form in the dominions of Spain shall, in pursuance of this Concordat, be deemed repealed in so far as they are opposed thereto, and this Concordat shall hereafter govern forever as law of the State in those dominions. Both Contracting Parties therefore promise, on their own behalf and on behalf of their successors, the faithful observance of each and every one of the articles of which it consists. Should any difficulty occur in the future, the Holy Father and Her Catholic Majesty shall come to an understanding to resolve it amicably.

Article 46 and last. The exchange of ratifications of this Concordat shall take place within a period of two months or, if possible, earlier.

IN WITNESS WHEREOF, we the undersigned plenipotentiaries have signed this Concordat and sealed it with our own seals in Madrid on 16 March 1851.
Juan Brunelli
Archbishop of Salonika
Manuel Bertran de Lis
[Spanish Minister of State]

Questions for discussion

1. In 1848 the Communist Manifesto is published, and there is an expansion of the labor movement across Europe, including Spain. Explain the following statement from the document: "Her Majesty and her royal Government shall, moreover, grant their mighty patronage and support to the bishops where they so request, principally where they need to oppose the malignancy of men who try to pervert the minds of the faithful and corrupt their mores, or where the publication, introduction or circulation of wicked and noxious books must be prevented."

2. How does the state guarantee the economic wellbeing of the Catholic Church as an institution? Explain articles 31 to 36.

3. What is the length of time the agreement is signed for?

4. How does the State guarantee the freedom of expression and creed under the legal limitations of the Concordat of 1851?

DOCUMENT 2
CARTA COLECTIVA DEL CLERO (BISHOPS' COLLECTIVE LETTER), 1937[3]

The Spanish Catholic Church hierarchy expressed publically their support to the generals who rose up on July18, 1936, against the democratically elected government of the Second Republic (1931–9). The country plunged into a violent three-year civil war characterized by the nationalists as a crusade against the reforms of the Second Republic. Particularly contentious was Prime Minister Manuel Azaña's proclamation that Spain no longer was a Catholic country but rather there was to be freedom of religion. The conflict unleashed a vicious anticlericalism with the profanation of sacred sites and the assassination of priest and nuns by uncontrolled masses. The collective pastoral letter of the bishops, published in 1937, represents a public declaration from the Spanish Catholic Church supporting the so-called crusade. We reproduce here an excerpt of the letter.

COLLECTIVE LETTER FROM THE SPANISH BISHOPS TO THE BISHOPS OF THE WORLD REGARDING THE CIVIL WAR IN SPAIN

Pamplona—Gráficas Descansa

July 1, 1937

Venerable Brotherhood

1°. The Rationale of this Document

It is customary that Catholic peoples help each other in turbulent moments, in the name of the law of mercy and fraternity, which unites us all in one mystic body and the love for Jesus Christ. The bishops are the natural authority of this spiritual exchange, to which the Holy Spirit entrusted Our Lord's Church. Spain, undergoing one of the most severe tribulations in its history, has received multiple gestures of affection and condolences from the foreign Catholic Episcopate, either in collective messages, or by individual Bishops. The Spanish Episcopate, so tragically tested in its members, its priests, and its churches, wants to reciprocate the great mercy received from all parts of the world with this collective document.

Our country is suffering a profound upheaval: it is not only this cruelest civil war that fills us with tribulation; it is also a tremendous commotion shaking the foundations of social life and endangering the existence of our nation. You have understood, Venerable Brethren, and "your words and hearts have opened [our eyes]" we will say with the

Apostle, allowing us to see your charity towards our dear fatherland. May the lord reward you.

But along with our gratitude, Venerable Brethren, we must also proclaim our pain for the lack of knowledge about the truth of what is happening in Spain. This is a fact that we know based on abundant documentation, that the majority of foreign opinion does not know the reality of the events taking place in our country. As a result of this misinformation it is possible that an anti-Christian spirit has advanced in the conflict with opposite political doctrines in favor and against the religion of Jesus Christ and Christian civilization. The opposite political doctrines aspire to dominate the world with the tendentious aid of hidden foreign forces. The anti-patriotism that preys on gullible Spaniards has caused harm to the true Spain hiding behind the shield of their ill-understood Catholicism. Even more painful for us, is how the foreign Catholic Press has contributed to this mental deviation, something that could prove to be fatal to the most sacred interests being made public across our fatherland.

(...)

Therefore, the Spanish Episcopate is obliged to address collectively our Brethren in the world, with the sole purpose of clarifying the truth, obscured, due to indolence or malice, and to ask for help in spreading the truth. This is a most important matter in which several political and national interests intersect along with the providential foundations of social life: religion, justice, authority, and citizens' liberties.

With this we intend to fulfil our pastoral mission—whose main goal is the administration of the truth—with a triple duty: religious, patriotic, and humanitarian.

(...)

2°. Nature of this Letter

(...) [T]he war is the result of the battle of two irreconcilable ideologies. In its origins are the gravest of questions regarding moral, judicial, religious, and historical orders. (...)

Therefore this document has an assertive and categorical character of empirical nature. This is so in two ways: the judgement of the legitimate evaluation of the situation, and *per oppositum* the way in which, with mercy, we will undo the false affirmations and twisted interpretations of this year in the history of Spain.

3°. Our Position about the War

It must be asserted that the war could have been avoided in 1931 when the national spirit suffered a rude attack, which the Spanish Episcopate addressed then with the highest examples of apostolic and civic prudence. Following the Church tradition and the Holy See rulings, we sided with the establishment in power, and worked to cooperate for the common good. Despite the repeated assaults on the people, property, and rights of the Church, we maintained the goal of harmony. To the humiliations we responded with the example of loyal submission within boundaries, through serious, reasonable protests or apostolic measures whenever possible. Exhorting repeatedly our Catholic faithful to be submissive, to pray, to be patient, and peaceful. And the Catholic faithful acquiesced, making our intervention a contribution to national harmony at a time of profound social and political crisis.

With our commitment to peace we offer our pardon to those who hunted us and our sentiments of mercy for all. And we say over the battlefields to our progenies on both sides the word of the Apostle: "The Lord knows how much we love you all in the heart of Jesus Christ."

But peace is the harmony of "Divine, national, social, and individual order, which guarantees for each one their place and provides what each deserves making God's glory the top of all priorities and from His love derives all fraternal service." (...) War being one of the cruellest blows to humanity, it becomes sometimes the only historical remedy, to restore everything to its just place and return to the kingdom of peace. This is the reason why the Church, while being the daughter of the Prince of Peace, has blessed the emblems of the war, founding Military Orders and organizing Crusades against the enemies of faith.

This is not the case here. The Church did not want this war and did not seek it, and we are not vindicating it as has been asserted in some foreign newspapers that condemn the Spanish Catholic Church. It is true that thousands of our faithful, obeying their conscience and their patriotism and only under their personal responsibility, rose in arms to save their religious principles of Christian justice, which had informed our national life for centuries. However, all those who accuse the Church of provoking this war, or to have partaken in a conspiracy to seek it, and even of not having done anything to prevent it, those not only do not know the reality but also are falsifying it.

This is the position of the Spanish Church Hierarchy on the current war. It has been humiliated and persecuted before the conflict broke out. It has been the prime victim of the fury between the contenders. And it has not stopped in pursuing, with its prayers, pleas, and influences to ameliorate its damages and abbreviate the days of trial. (...)

No; this is the freedom we demand for the exercise of our ministry. In this freedom reside all the liberties of the Church. By its virtue, we have not endorsed anybody—people, powers or institutions—even when we are grateful for the protection of those who have liberated us from the enemy and, as Spanish Bishops, we are willing to collaborate with those ready to restore in Spain a regime of justice and peace. No political power will be able to say that we departed at any moment from this goal.

4°. The Quinquenium Preceding the War

(...)Our political regime of democratic liberties splintered due to the arbitrary administration of the state and the governmental coercion that dislodged the popular sovereignty, turning it into a political machinery against the national political majority. Therefore, in the latest general elections, February 1936, with more than half a million votes over the to left, the right obtained 118 deputies less than the Popular Front because capriciously the results of entire provinces were annulled, and resulted in the de-legitimization of the Parliament.

(...)

The legal means exhausted, there was no other option but to resort to force to sustain order and peace which powers unfamiliar with the legitimate authority decided to subvert the established order and violently impose communism. Logically, Spain had no other choice: either succumb to the planned and orchestrated destructive blow of communism, or try through the titanic effort of resistance to free ourselves from the terrible enemy and to save the fundamental principles of its social life and its national character.

5°. The Military Uprising and the Communist Revolution

On July18 last year the military uprising took place and the current war broke out. But note first, that the military insurrection, from the very beginning, did not happen without the collaboration of the good people who joined the movement in mass. Therefore, this uprising must be considered civil and military. Second, this movement and the communist revolution are two facts impossible to separate if we want to understand judiciously the nature of the war—coinciding in the very first clash, they mark from the beginning the profound division of the two Spain(s) that will fight each other in the battlefields.

(...)

And because God is the most profound foundation of an orderly society—it was so in the Spanish nation—the communist revolution allied with the government's army was, above, all anti-God. Thus ended the cycle of the lay Constitution of 1931 with the destruction of everything God-fearing.

(...)

That is why there was a religious reaction in our soul, against the nihilist destruction of those without God. And Spain was divided into two large militant sides, each becoming the agglutinant of deep-seated popular tendencies; and around it and collaborating with them, they polarized, in the form of voluntary militia and rear-guard services, the opposite forces that had the nation divided.

The war is, therefore, an armed plebiscite. The struggle of the 1936 elections, in which the lack of political integrity of the national government arbitrarily gave the victory to the revolutionary forces when they did not earn it in the ballots, was transformed, by way of the civic-military conflict, in the cruel clash of a people divided into two tendencies: the spiritual one was on the side of the rebels who rose in defense of order, social peace, traditional civilization, and fatherland, and was mainly and very visibly in favor of the defense of religion. On the other side, there were the materialist, which may be called Marxist, communist or anarchist, that wanted to substitute the old Spanish civilization and all its factors, with the novice "civilization" of the Russian Soviets.

(...)

7°. The National Movement: Its Character

Let's explain now the character of the so-called "national" movement. We believe this denomination is just. First, due to its spirit; because the Spanish nation was fractured in its majority as a result of a government that could not realize its most profound needs and aspirations; and the nation accepted the movement as a hope. In those regions not liberated it only hopes to break the shield of the communist forces that oppress them. It is also national because of its objectives, because it aspires to save and sustain for the future the essence of a people, articulating it under a State able to continue its history with dignity. We manifest a reality and a general hope for all Spaniards without proposing the means to achieve it.

The movement has strengthened the sense of patriotism against the exoticism of the forces that oppose it. The Fatherland implies a fatherhood [sic]; it is a moral environment as if it were an extended family in which citizens achieve their complete potential. The national movement has encouraged a flow of love that has materialized around this name and was based on Spain's historical substance rejecting foreign elements that brought us ruin. And when the patriotic love is sanctified by the love of Jesus Christ, our God and Lord, it reaches the pinnacle of Christian compassion. We have witnessed an explosion of true mercy through the ultimate expression in the blood of thousands of Spaniards who cry, "Long Live Spain! Long Live King Jesus Christ!"

Within the national movement we have experienced the marvelous phenomenon of martyrdom—true martyrdom as the Pope has asserted—thousands of Spaniards and priests, religious and secular. This bloody testimony must determine the future, under the weight of immense political responsibility, of those who will take up arms to build a new state in peace and harmony.

(...)

This situation promises a regime of justice and peace for the future (...) We have the hope that with the forceful imposition of the enormous sacrifice we will find anew our true national essence.

(...)

We address you from Spain, in the memory of the Fatherland's dead and missing brethren, on the festivity of the Most Precious Blood of Our Lord Jesus Christ, July 1, 1937

ISIDRO, Cardinal GOMÁ Y TOMÁS, Archbishop of Toledo, et al.

Questions for discussion

1. Who is the audience the bishops are addressing in this letter?

2. What is the international political context in Europe and in the United States during this time?

3. The Bishops utilize the religious narrative of Cain and Abel to describe the conflict between the two Spains. How is this effective in terms of propaganda for the Francoist side after the war is finished?

4. Explain the term "martyrdom" in the context of the Spanish Civil War and in the context of the non-intervention policy by Western democracies.

DOCUMENT 3
ENRIQUE TARANCÓN, *EL PAN NUESTRO DE CADA DÍA* CARTA PASTORAL (*OUR DAILY BREAD*, 1951)[4]

In March 1950, Monsignor Enrique Tarancón, Bishop of Solsona (1907–94), published a critical pastoral letter in condemnation of Franco's regime's abuses in rationing. The black market had led to the enrichment of a few at the expense of the misery and hunger of most of the population. The 1940s were known as the Hunger Years and the ration books would remain in circulation until 1952. In September 1953, a Concordat with the Vatican followed the Pact of Madrid, an agreement signed with the United States in August of the same year, which ended a period of almost total isolation for Spain. The Vatican continued to support the regime and National Catholicism opened the door of the United Nations. The bold criticism of Monsignor Tarancón would result in being disciplined by the authorities, who for years would not confer upon him any episcopal appointments. However, Tarancón became cardinal in 1969 and would play a key role in the transition to democracy as Archbishop of Madrid (1971–83). Cardinal Tarancón officiated at the funeral of Dictator Francisco Franco at the Mausoleum of the Valley of the Fallen under the watchful eyes of the "Franquistas," who witnessed how King Juan Carlos I and Queen Sofia would lead Spain into a delicate democratic transition.

OUR DAILY BREAD

Introduction

We cannot be silent. We must not be silent any longer. We hear the supplication of the masses. The anguish and miseries our children suffer break our Fatherly heart and an unavoidable duty places the pen in our hands.

We might not accomplish anything with these words. Perhaps men's selfishness and malice drown our voice. But we want, in fulfilment of our responsibility which we deem most sacred, to reinforce with our voice and our authority the imploration of our children.

We want to say publicly that it is a matter of conscience to attend their pleas and petitions. We want to say that it is not only Christian justice and mercy, but also humanity itself that demands that their pleas for a piece of bread be heard.

Because we do not step outside of our area when we confront the problem and write a Pastoral Letter to defend the rights of the poor and the workers to eat bread in abundance and whatever they need to carry on a dignified and humane life. We do not go beyond our episcopal mission when we ask for plenty of bread and sufficient food and decent shelter for all our children. We do not depart from our proper conduct as Minister when we proclaim anathema against those who are responsible for workers and the poor not having what they need to live.

(...)

And we do not want to carry in our conscience the weight of their destruction, and much less their apostasy and, who knows, even their own despair. And, not being able to do anything else, we want to put at their service all we are and all we are worth. We want them to see that the heart of a Bishop feels pain for their anguish and the voice of their Bishop rises, brave and defiant, to defend their cause.

(...)

We write a Pastoral Letter knowing well the character, orientation, and even the tone that these religious documents must demonstrate. And we realize this is a delicate and difficult matter that must be treated with the highest vision and mercy with which a Bishop must address all problems, looking only for the Glory of God and the wellbeing of the souls because many susceptibilities may be hurt, even when proceeding with the utmost tact and the purest intention.

It is not our purpose to study the problem from a technical or economic perspective, since this aspect does not pertain to our ministry and, additionally, we do not have sufficient preparation for it. Nor do we want to make easy and demagogic literature, which indeed would lead to ignite passions; this would be improper for a Church Bishop and for any honest person.

We only intend to highlight a wrong, present the problem in its desperate reality and to point out the great responsibility of those guilty of it before God and the Fatherland, and in this way contribute as much as possible to a solution.

(...)

Outwardly we appear to live in abundance, with happiness and peace. Our stores appear to be fully stocked and the people enjoy themselves, perhaps to an extreme. We cannot deny, or have any interest in doing so, that we cannot complain about our situation and that other nations would like to have the peace and abundance we enjoy, even when the circumstances have been particularly adverse. But maybe that is why the contrast is harder and more anti-Christian.

For those with much money, and unfortunately there are many who have become tremendously rich in the past few years, there is no deprivation. Currently, with money you can buy everything necessary to live and even many frivolous things. There are many who live a euphoric life, without having to renounce any desire or caprice. But the laughter of some cannot drown out the implorations of the many who suffer hunger and live in misery. There are also among us many children who beg for bread and nobody gives it to them. There are many families without the most essential food. There are many parents who cannot give bread to their children every time they are being asked for it. Most workers are hungry for bread and lack many necessities.

And we do not mean only those unemployed or those who for whatever reason cannot earn a wage to purchase the bare necessities. It is also the situation of those workers who are employed and supposedly earn a living wage but cannot have the bread they need or buy the necessary food. Today the problem of the working class is not usually a problem of wages, but rather that those salaries should be fair and adequate. The problem is deeper and very serious.

Essential food staples are not rationed in a sufficient amount at all to sustain families. And although it is possible to find bread and other food in abundance at high prices, workers and anybody who receives a minimum wage cannot buy those products at those extremely high prices set by the selfish majority. And the problem is tragic, not only for working class families, but also and perhaps even more so for the middle class who want to keep up appearances and cannot pay for the bare necessities of life.

This is the hard and painful reality, and it is silly and ridiculous to close our eyes and pretend that an idyllic happiness reigns over our people.

As a result of this reality, which has become more and more difficult as times goes on, even if only for its persistence, a seed of discontent that might have devastating consequences has been planted in many places. Because this discontent engenders suspicion, mistrust, and resentment. Today, let's not deceive ourselves; there are many who mistrust the State and its social and political organizations. And there is also a mistrust of the Church and its true desire to look after the well being of all. (...) Today, a large number of workers and even the middle class does not believe either in the Government's good intentions nor in the Bishops' sincerity, because all judge us with the same criteria, and we all feel their suspicion, precaution, and perhaps their scorn. (...)

Causes of this Problem

After the war our nation was impoverished. The calamities that every civil war brings with it were aggravated by the conduct of those who, after destroying many sources of wealth and infrastructure, also stole Spain's treasures and reserves. It was necessary to think of reconstructing our agriculture, our industry, our entire economy, and this could not be accomplished without titanic efforts and great sacrifice on the part of everyone.

Nobody was surprised that after the war we suffered many deprivations (...) But it has been more than ten years since [the end of the war] and the sacrifice we all accepted at first with resignation and even with joy, grows heavier every day. (...) During these ten years there are many who have taken advantage of the scarcity to make big business. Some have not been able to solve the problems with the authority bestowed on them, and instead have aggravated them with their conduct.

We Lack Christian Conscientious Individuals

The main cause of this reality (...) resides in the lack of true Christian consciences. (...)

And this is what has happened among us. Selfishness has become worse in the hearts of men after the war. We are surrounded and imprisoned by an immoral environment in business and customs, result of such egotism, which has such an overwhelming strength and whose current takes with it even good and honest people (...) That environment destroys and brings failure to even the best-intentioned society.

(…)

The Remedy

(…)

The remedy resides in the reign of sincerity, of honesty, of justice, of charity. And therefore, authorities and all who hold a position of responsibility in society have a most important and urgent task. Those above are the ones who may be able to counteract and even destroy this prevailing egotistic and immoral environment. Those above, are the ones that need to impose honesty, sincerity, justice and charity for all people.

(…)

Everyone in office or in a position of responsibility or of some social status should serve as an example of austerity, honesty, spirit of justice, and charity. Because, how are they to impose and demand austerity and honesty in others if they themselves do not practice it?

(…)

There is no other way to achieve it but by their own example and extreme good conduct. Those in office, right now, must not only be honest and worthy but must also demonstrate it, avoiding all behavior that may lead to distrust of them. (…) The abandonment of principles has very serious consequences because it awakens suspicion in simple people about the moral authority of their government. This obviously leads to the loss of credibility of those in power.

(…)

Mission of the Civil Authority

(…)

The direct mission of civil authorities, their main purpose for which they have been appointed and been granted power, is to achieve the natural and human destiny of Man: his material welfare and moral and spiritual betterment within the human order. Therefore, an authority will not fulfil his mission if they neglect this as their primary and specific objective, even if they have another spiritual and moral objective.

(…)

While the State has a human and natural mission, the Church's purpose is divine.

(…)

Conclusion

We have written this Pastoral Letter guided exclusively by our divine interests.

God's glory and the good of the souls have been the two powerful reasons that put the pen in our hands.

Likewise, we believe this is a social and patriotic service.

As a citizen and as Bishop we also have the obligation to seek society's common good. This is the society we are a part of, and we must take an interest in the welfare of our brethren as well as the prosperity and peace of the Fatherland.

Questions for discussion

1. How does Monsignor Tarancón justify this pastoral letter?

2. Tarancón asserts: "Selfishness has become worse in the hearts of men after the war. We are surrounded and imprisoned by an immoral environment in business and customs, result of such egotism, which has such an overwhelming strength and whose current takes with it even good and honest people." What other causes of such selfishness does he mention?

3. In his opinion, what is the role of the civil authority in alleviating the misery of the many?

4. What does he consider to be his duty as a citizen and as a bishop? How does this document anticipate the ideological openness of the Second Vatican Council (1962–5) convoked by Pope John XXIII (1958–63)?

DOCUMENT 4
FRANCO AS MEDIEVAL KNIGHT

The Francoist propaganda presented the figure of Francisco Franco as the savior of the motherland from the Second Republic, presented as the anti-Spain incarnated in the official propaganda. In 1939, Franco became the Caudillo or the Generalissimo for the next thirty-six years. In the image of the Apostle Santiago, Spain's patron saint, known as the Moor-slayer who, according to legend, appeared in the mythical Battle of Clavijo on the side of the Christians fighting the Muslims in the ninth century. The Republicans were regarded as the new infidels of the twentieth century and Franco as the savior of the authentic Spain.

Figure 9. Franco as Medieval Knight. Detail of painting from the Archivo Histórico Militar, Madrid.

It is not the first time that a dictator is represented in medieval armor. Adolph Hitler was also painted in this guise as a propaganda tool for the masses to contemplate the idealized image of their leader.

Questions for discussion

1. Describe the composition of the painting. How does the artist represent the present and the past as well as the earthly and the heavenly realms?

2. How is Franco represented in terms of size and posture with respect to the other men in the image?

3. As an allegorical representation of a savior, what are the religious overtones that you find here and that point to the concept of Crusade expressed in the previous document, the Bishop's Pastoral Letter of 1937?

4. From a gender perspective, what are the elements that define the strength of the nation: masculinity or femininity?

DOCUMENT 5
"THE SOCIO-RELIGIOUS CHANGE IN SPAIN: THE MOST SIGNIFICANT FACTS," AND "THE CHRISTIAN LIFE COMMITMENT IN SPAIN"[5]

One of the most important tenets of a modern democratic Western nation since the Enlightenment was the separation of Church and State. The process of secularization that Spain experienced in the 1960s after the accords with the United States had a very important impact on the religious beliefs and practices of Spaniards. The FOESSA Foundation published an in-depth study of this phenomenon in 1975, extracts of which are reproduced here.

"THE SOCIO-RELIGIOUS CHANGE IN SPAIN: THE MOST SIGNIFICANT FACTS"

It is evident that the most predominant characteristics in Spain in 1974 are the changing conditions in a more "accelerated" and "irregular" fashion than other countries have experienced under similar circumstances.

In Spain the change is more notorious with regard to religious aspects, what today is called the "secularization process."

In general, all of those who have analyzed dynamically and meticulously the topic of religion among the Spaniards, recognize there has been at the beginning a slow and difficult evolution from the bottom up, due to the vital strength of the grassroots community, accepted reluctantly a posteriori by the institutional religious hierarchy. Likewise, the studies recognize that in the last few years, and now with the support of the hierarchy, the transformation has accelerated and given way to a new situation that is characterized by a profound revision of Spanish traditional Catholicism, a mix of some fears and success, tensions, hindrances, and liberations.

This era, particularly characterized by the "socio-religious crisis" that we are referring to, corresponds to a period that we may call "Post-Conciliar," which covers the years after 1966 and especially since 1971.

Certainly, Pope John XXIII and the Second Vatican Council, along with economic development and the resulting cultural changes that have taken place, mark a new stage in Spanish religious history. The documents about the "religious freedom of the Church and the world" pose severe problems to the Spanish religious consciousness.

Since then, there has been a series of developments in Spain, which by simple enumeration manifest the accelerated and irregular change. Regarding the institutional

Church, represented by its hierarchy (bishops and the most significant part of the clergy) these developments indicate three phenomena that begin to have relevance and will create tensions and conflicts: a) a change in mentalities more in the post-conciliar line and spirit; b) an increasing distance from power, and c) a real connection with the people. Regarding the faithful, it is important to point out the existence of two opposing mentalities: the post-conciliar, represented by very small groups, and the traditional where most Spaniards find themselves. Both positions are a constant source of tension within the Church and in the labor, political, and social realms, which have important impacts on the country.

From this new situation of "socio-religious change" in Spain during the period called "post-conciliar" arose some developments of special significance, enumerated below:

- In May1966 a silent march of 130 priests and clergy took place in Barcelona to protest against the Police Superintendent for presumed mistreatment of a student. Two months earlier, the same policeman had raided the Capuchins in Sarriá.

- On June 19 of the same year, the Permanent Spanish Episcopal Commission expressed its opposition to the protest in Barcelona.

- There is an important development of the so-called "preterjerarquismo." Some Christian groups—clergy and secular people—start to think, live, and act in the margins of the official Church. Many of the "grassroots communities" emerging during this time followed this option.

- Since 1968, the hierarchy begins to express itself in the post-conciliar spirit. This year an episcopal document about trade unionism is published.

- In 1969, a pastoral letter by Monsignor Cirarda, by then Bishop of Bilbao, is made public, expressing the rejection of violence coming from "whomever or wherever."

- The following year, several highly significant events take place. Particularly important are: The episcopal document concerning the right to association and assembly; the declaration of the auxiliary Bishop of Pamplona against the mistreatment of political prisoners which led to the retaliation of the minister of justice; the declaration of the Bishop of Oviedo that "the Church does not create problems when it denounces problems"; the declarations of Cardinal Tarancón analyzing Spanish Catholicism; the document by the Commission "Justitia et Pax" and the pastoral letter of the Tarragona Episcopal Conference about pluralism.

In 1971, it is important to especially highlight the Joint Assembly of Bishops and Priests celebrated in Madrid after two years of county, dioceses, and national planning.

Since the 16th Plenary Episcopal Conference celebrated in March 1972, a new phase of the Spanish episcopate begins. The line called *aperturista* [meaning "in favor to open up"] achieved a majority.

The Concordat and its implications are of special significance. Very important changes take place in relation with this agreement.

(…)

THE CHRISTIAN LIFE COMMITMENT IN SPAIN

Conclusions: Political Significance of the Change in Spanish Catholicism

Even when some still pretend that the situation remains the same (and affirm the war has not finished yet) it is evident that:

1. There has been a structural, economic, and social change in the country (although the change has not yet impacted the superstructures) situated within the decisive European and world historical transformation. We are now, simply, "in another epoch" regarding 1936–9, and those who are nostalgic forget this and remain fixed in that remote past.
2. The overcoming of extreme positions accentuated in 1934–36 that led to the Civil War and today are minority behaviors, marginal, residual (unless they may be opening the door to those types of extremisms again, of course, due to new economic crisis and violent pseudo-populist demagogies—either fascists or from extreme left groups—have an impact on a population with no real grassroots anchor).
3. Fundamental structural change of Spanish Catholicism, which undergoes a profound transformation in the current political behavior.

Questions for discussion

1. What are the most significant transformations pointed out by these documents that led to a change in religious behavior in Spain?
2. How did the economic crisis of the 1970s facilitate the secularization of Spaniards? What similar circumstances can we find in countries struggling economically today?
3. Is there a latent generational gap in the developments described in the documents? How is the Church hierarchy responding to the socio-economic changes?
4. Explain the difference between post-conciliar and traditional outlooks. How did the Second Vatican Council transform the global church?

DOCUMENT 6
GAY PRIEST ON THE COVER OF *ZERO* MAGAZINE (2002)[6]

Homosexuality had been illegal and was persecuted and punished with prison under the Franco's regime. National Catholicism considered it a moral disorder and a political offense. Catholic priesthood is still today exclusively male and celibacy the main vow to uphold. In the early transition to democracy, sexual behavior experienced a profound transformation and liberalization. In 1979, homosexuality was no longer illegal in Spain and in 2005 the socialist government of José Luis Rodríguez Zapatero approved the first gay marriage law in Europe. However, the Catholic Church continues to reject homosexuality as a moral offense.

Zero, a gay monthly magazine, published its first issue in 1998. We reproduce here the 2002 cover and part of the interview with a priest who declared: "I give thanks to God for making me gay."

"SPAIN'S GAY PARISH PRIEST",[7] JUAN PÉREZ CABRAL

February 2, 2002. José Mantero, the parish priest of the Andalusian town of Valverde del Camino, has outed himself in style. "I thank God for being gay," the intrepid priest told the Spanish gay magazine, *Zero*, which features him on its cover this month. He was "fed up," he said, with the silence and the guilt that surrounds gayness in the Catholic Church. "God may be asking me to take this step," he said yesterday after his decision to make history as the first Spanish priest ever to publicly declare that he is gay. In a nationally broadcasted interview on the Cadena SER radio network, quickly picked up by the rest of the Spanish media, thirty-nine-year-old Mantero, said that he had not outed himself "for psychological relief; I did it because I had to do it, because something like this could also answer a call from God saying: you have to face this."

"This kind of issue has to be defended from the inside. From the outside, it's impossible. And this struggle from the inside implies an essential factor: love for the institution," explains Mantero. "I'm neither rancorous nor some kind of pervert. To the contrary, I'm a regular guy. I adore the Church. And love must be belligerent."

Mantero also said that, "I wouldn't have done this at a time when my faith was weak. It's precisely because my faith is very strong, fresh, and warm that I'm doing this. It's motivated by my faith: it's not just purely a matter of social conscience."

The parish priest, who admitted that he had not always remained celibate, added, "I'm fairly realistic, but I'd like this to be like a tiny germ, a tiny seed, so that one day we'd see homophobic statements disappear from the Church, we'd see this accepted as something absolutely natural; more than tolerable—natural."

Mantero realized he was gay when he was twelve, but it was not until he was thirty or thirty-one, and already a parish priest, that he did something about it. "That was when I met someone who, well, I kind of fell in love with, and from that point on, a new, different, at times strange, and, of course, very fulfilling process began in my life," he told Cadena SER.

To add piquancy to the tale, *Zero* editor-in-chief, Carlos Alberto Biendicho, warned in the same radio program that if there were any church reprisals against the Andalusian parish priest, he'd reveal the names of three Spanish bishops with whom he, Biendicho, has had sex. In an added, ironical twist, Biendicho chairs the gay caucus of the conservative Popular Party of Prime Minister José María Aznar, whose relations with the Spanish gay community are tepid at best.

Questions for discussion

1. If the main vow of a priest is celibacy, how does Mantero justify his coming out of the closet?

2. How might the discussion on homosexuality gain social acceptance through the public declarations of priests like Mantero?

3. Is homosexuality a right or a left wing political issue?

4. Is homosexuality a religious or a medical issue? What does Mantero mean when he says it is a "natural" thing?

MODULE 8
PUBLIC HEALTH

ABSTRACT

The Catholic Monarchs, via a Royal Decree on March 30, 1477, established the office of the *Tribunal de Protomedicato* (Health Practitioners' Tribunal), a body to grant accreditation to those providing medical assistance throughout the realms of Castile and Aragon. In addition to accreditation, the *Tribunal* guaranteed the subjects' health by prosecuting cases of malpractice and/or practicing without a license. *Protomedicatos* were established throughout the Spanish Empire and in 1588 underwent reforms under Phillip II. During the eighteenth and nineteenth centuries, there were several reforms. These *Protomedicatos* are the precedent to the Ministries of Public Health.

In this module, we compiled six different legal and educational texts that illustrate the significant interest in the public health and welfare of the Spanish citizens since the Enlightenment constitutional debates during the War for Independence (1808–14) against the Napoleonic invasion, and up until the legalization of abortion in 1985.

DOCUMENT 1
ON THE OBSTACLES THAT NATURE, OPINION, AND LAWS POSE TO THE PUBLIC HAPPINESS, WRITTEN BY COUNT OF COBARRÚS TO SR. DON GASPAR DE JOVELLANOS (1808)

Francisco Cobarrús Lalanne (1752–1810) was an important industrialist and financier during the reign of Charles III. He was part of the Enlightenment circles and forged friendships with other illustrious reformers and free thinkers like Gaspar Melchor de Jovellanos, the Count of Campomanes, and the Count of Floridablanca. His financial talent led him to found the first Spanish central bank, Banco de San Carlos, which later became the Banco de España. He was also interested in the development of hydraulic infrastructure in the country. The so-called Cobarrús Chanel was finished and enhanced under the reign of Isabel II and bore the name of the queen. In 1789, Charles IV conferred upon him the title of count for his services. Accused of embezzlement, he was imprisoned in 1790 for two years. The document below contains Cobarrús' thoughts on public health and social happiness. It contains letters written in 1792 to his friend Gaspar Melchor de Jovellanos. They were published in 1808, the year that marked the six-year Napoleonic invasion, which became known in Spanish historiography as the Spanish War for Independence (1808–14). Cobarrús supported the new king of Spain, Joseph I, Napoleon's brother, and was viewed as an "*afrancesado.*" He died in 1810, before the end of the war, and was buried in the Chapel of the Concepción in Seville's Cathedral.

The document below is a letter written in 1792 to Jovellanos, on the obstacle that nature poses to progress and some proposals to solve those problems. The segment below focuses on the best way to help the poor, from the Enlightenment perspective.

FIRST LETTER[1]

I am now going to deal with (public relief services) distribution, because this explanation will undoubtedly be necessary regarding its ability to meet all needs, and not least regarding the ease of its administration.

The Distribution of Relief

The protection of society begins at the moment of birth; (…) for nature (…) entrusted to maternal love the care, nurture, of the sweet and restless needs that we all require during those (first moments).

The Foundlings

This truth does not allow more exceptions than for those sad victims of a terrible calamity, who, having found an empty and unprotected crib, (...) call upon society for a more efficient care, and beg not only for (their) protection, but also for charity, (and) gentleness. (...)

I see it as a great benefit that the priest serves as one of the members of the charity: his ministry obligates him to secrecy, gives him influence over the unhappy mother, over the family members, and over (their) opinion: he can without (causing) scandal, and in agreement with the family, take away and hide the mother, provide her with all the aids that her state requires: protect the birth and the nutrition of the infant, either provided by the mother herself, or by a stranger; he can reconcile decorum with charity, and the strictness of morality with the interests of the State. All women should be aware that their spiritual councilor will comfort them and will be the keeper of their fragility, and that they will not live as disgraced (women) if they religiously observe a mother's obligations (...).

This is the structure that we must follow: if the mother cannot be surrounded by her own (family), the ingenious charity will substitute another type of family during those critical moments; yet not a family of mercenary employees, in whom the continuation of the same spectacle has destroyed the sensitivity that inspires, but rather a selected family; and of course, it will not be one of the poorest families where less humanity and virtue is found.

If the mother cannot bring up the baby, the adoptive family will oversee making the wet-nurses meet their obligations, her salary, (will be higher and not inferior to what one would expect for (raising) any other child (...) (and whose) soul will be rewarded upon presenting a healthy and strong child at twenty-four months (...).

Nature already made wet-nurses prone to love their offspring; what would happen when interest, far from changing this tendency, actually confirms it; when after (p. 46) a long cohabitation and custom is added; when reciprocal love between parents and children is ingrained; (...).

All these consequences are undeniable (... but) most our legislators seem to have forgotten, when it comes to applying it to government, what they have observed, and what they feel inside.

Questions for discussion

1. When does Count Cobarrús consider the obligation to the social wellbeing of citizens start? Frame your answer within the historical context of 1792.
2. Explain why the Enlightenment thinkers placed great importance on the reforms of public necessities such as health and assistance to the poor.
3. Is Cobarrús singling out poor single mothers for their misfortunes? How does he propose they are guided and assisted out of their misery?
4. Why do you think Cobarrús considers the priest as the most useful aid in change?

DOCUMENT 2
JUAN GINÉ PARTAGÁS, *CURSO ELEMENTAL DE HIGIENE PRIVADA Y PÚBLICA* (BASIC COURSE IN PRIVATE AND PUBLIC HYGIENE, 1871-2)

Juan Giné Partagás (1836–1903), a Catalan physician during the second half of the nineteenth century, became a renowned professional in the areas of psychiatry and dermatology. He graduated from the University of Madrid in 1862 and was appointed professor at the University of Barcelona a year later, after spending some time as a rural doctor. In 1866, he spent two years at the University of Santiago de Compostela before returning to Barcelona to serve as the Chair of Hygiene and head of the surgical clinic. He founded the medical journal *La Independencia Médica* (The Medical Independence) in 1869 in Catalonia, known for its experimental nature. Giné Partagá's innovative scientific approach led some of his pupils to establish the prestigious Catalan medical association called *El Laboratorio* (The Laboratory) in 1874.

Giné Partagás is one of the Spanish pioneers of organic psychiatry in Spain. In 1864, he directed the Asylum of New Bethlehem in Barcelona, where he established a chair in Psychiatry (*Frenopatía*). It would become the origin of the first Spanish school for the study of mental illnesses.

While occupying his chair of Hygiene at the University of Barcelona (1867–71), Giné Partagás published several works on the subject: *Tratado de higiene rural* (A Treaty on Rural Hygiene,1860), based on his experience after graduation, and the more significant *Curso elemental de higiene privada y pública* (An Elementary Course on Private and Public Hygiene, 1871-2), from which an excerpt is included below. Giné also published three science fiction novels: *Viaje a Cerebrópolis* (A Trip to Brainopolis, 1884); *La familia de los onkos* (The Onko's Family, 1888); and *Misterios de la locura* (The Mysteries of Madness, 1890).

BASIC COURSE IN PRIVATE AND PUBLIC HYGIENE (1871–2)[2]

Lesson I: The History of Public Hygiene

Wherever humans have convened in social relationships, they had to create customs and establish laws and regulations with the goal of protecting themselves from the inherent dangers of overcrowded or too dense grouping of populations, with the final objective of increasing the advantages of these same ties, which, in the human species respond to a group of necessities, more compelling, if possible, than the fundamental ones expressed by the instinct to comfort. Therefore, then, anyone that aims to know the history of public hygiene, will be obligated out of necessity to study it in the codes and customs of different peoples, whose civilizations have remained imprinted on the general history of humanity, never losing sight of the fact that the laws and customs have always emerged from the impulse of its own instinctual conservation, manifested as much in the individual, as in the human collectives that make up the nationalities.

(...)

In Western civilizations, there are no remains of public baths, which were so popular among the Romans; only the Russians and the Turks have public establishments for bathing or perhaps for saunas, dry or wet, followed by a shower, and a massage or flagellation, practices reminiscent of Spartan habits and the Romans' *laconicum*.

It can be noted, then, that the insatiable aspiration for material accumulation and corporal vigor that was so prominent in Antiquity has disappeared from the hygienic customs of modern peoples. Our institutions are taking a higher road; the hygiene (movement) has been spiritualized; inspired by Gospel maxims; it values its efforts in the protection of the underprivileged; takes charity as its ensign, and merges in a single epithet Charity and Health. Modern peoples' public hygiene is the official practice of Christian morality. The hospital, the charitable shelter for the poor, the leper hospital, the dungeon turned into a healthy prison, the asylum, vaccinations, international health conferences, and the study of the causes of insalubrity of the different industries, in order to lessen or correct them completely, are the main objectives of the health administration these days.

Spain can be proud of having been the origin of many of these institutions. Alfonso VI ordered the destruction of public baths, that the Romans and the Arabs had caused to become so widespread, whereas in the eleventh century, Cid Campeador erected in Palencia the first hospital for lepers under the name of St Lazarus; and later Alfonso the Wise[3] erected another one in Seville. The first hospital order, called *the Antoninos*, was Spanish; it was founded by knights of the order of Delfinado Gaston y Girondo, who attributed to the intercession of St Anthony their salvation from an epidemic known as *sideración* or *fuego sagrado* (sacred fire) that had spread in the eleventh century. Thus, they dedicated a temple and a hospital in the city of La Mothe to this saint, and dedicated themselves to serve the sick and to establishing a great number of hospitals throughout Europe, which were in operation up until 1767, when, at the request of Charles III, Pope VI decreed its extinction.[4]

Neither can the glory of the Spaniards be denied for having been the first to build comfortable shelters for the moral treatment of mental illnesses. The first house for the insane was the so-called Hospital of the Innocents, in Valencia, erected in 1409; the second, with the same name, was founded in Seville, in 1436 by Marcos Sanchez; the third one was built in Zaragoza in 1829. (...)

Regarding hospitals, a big change in thinking is taking place: extraordinary dimensions and magnificence are no longer reasons for which to admire a hospital; hygiene requires more establishments that are proportionally reduced, salubrious, ventilated, strategically spread throughout the population and ready to host less sick people in each of them, so that mephitis and infection due to overcrowding are avoided. A result of these will be specialty hospitals, maternity houses, nurseries, or foster homes, and shelters for the old and handicap. But this is not enough (. . .).

(. . .) [T]he literature on modern public hygiene is very significant. (. . .) [T]he magnificent *Diccionario de higiene pública y de salubridad* (Dictionary of Public Hygiene and Healthy Conditions), by M. Ambrosio Tardieu, (. . .) the incomparable treatise of *Higiene pública y privada* (Public and Private Hygiene), by Miguel Levy, (. . .) the *Tratado de higiene industrial*, by Max. Vernois.

But special mention must be made of Dr D. Pedro Felipe Monlau. A first class talent, of whom is proud, not only the city of Barcelona, his place of origin, but the whole nation, and a life of incessant labor, principally dedicated to fostering health sciences and its diffusion across all levels of society.

Questions for discussion

1. What does the author mean by the following statement: "the hygiene movement has been spiritualized; inspired by Gospel maxims; it values its efforts in the protection of the underprivileged; takes charity as its ensign, and merges in a single epithet Charity and Health. Modern peoples' Public Hygiene is the official practice of Christian morality"?

2. How has Giné Partagás' argument about public hygiene at the end of the nineteenth century evolved from Count of Cobarrús' reasoning in 1792?

3. What are the different public institutions, mentioned by him in this excerpt, that will benefit from a rationalization of hygienic measures?

4. Why do you think Giné Partagás includes mental hygiene and mental institutions in his analysis to improve the national health? What historical references does he mention to enhance his praise of the Spanish nation?

DOCUMENT 3
GYMNASTIC PHOTOGRAPHS. WOMEN'S SECTION OF THE FALANGE (1960S)

The Women's Section of the Falange was established in 1934 by a small group of university women led by Pilar Primo de Rivera (1907–91), José Antonio Primo de Rivera's (1903–36) sister, who had founded the Falange party only a year earlier. By a decree on December 28, 1939, the Francoist dictatorship made the Women's Section the only official organization for women. In this way, the regime rewarded their services in the front and the rearguard during the Spanish Civil War. They would manage the national duties of Spanish women until 1977 through the Social Service, a six-month service to the state, and through the instruction of National Catholic Principles of Domesticity, as well as physical education, two mandatory subjects in the educational system, from elementary school to the university levels. Gymnastics and folkloric dances through the Choirs and Dances Secretariat were outlets for some middle-class women who were able to travel within the country and abroad as ambassadors of traditional values that epitomized what it meant to be Spanish. The photographs included here show a gymnast with castanets and a group of the Choirs and Dances Secretariat, created to recover the traditional folklore (song and dances) of the different regions of Spain. These young women became the embodiments of the fatherland with their international tours through Europe and the Americas. The Law of 1961 regulated physical education. Chapter I of the law defines physical education as "a school of virtues, an indispensable part of man's complete instruction" and to promote public health. Women's physical education was designed to make them healthy mothers for the fatherland.

Figures 10.1 and 10.2. Gymnastic Photograph. Women's Section of the Falange (1960s).

Questions for discussion

1. Why was it important for the Francoist dictatorship to make physical education and National Catholic principles part of the mandatory school curriculum?

2. How does physical prowess and political strength become synonymous in totalitarian and nationalist propaganda? How do the dancers represent the traditional Spanish national values?

3. Describe the photograph of the gymnast with the castanets. Is this a masculine or a feminine gymnastic pose? How would you describe this pose in the photograph?

4. How have female athletes' bodies changed over time? Compare the image of the gymnast with female Olympic athletes of today.

DOCUMENT 4

TOMÁS CARO PATÓN, *LA MUJER CAÍDA. MEMORIAS Y REFLEXIONES DE UN MÉDICO EN LA LUCHA ANTIVENÉREA* (THE FALLEN WOMAN. MEMOIRS AND REFLECTIONS OF A PHYSICIAN INVOLVED IN THE FIGHT AGAINST ANTI-VENEREAL DISEASE, 1959)

Until 1956, the policy of the Francoist dictatorship (1939–75), towards prostitution was that of tolerance. The Catholic values of the regime represented prostitution as a necessary evil—to sustain the double morality that expected men's sexual prolificacy. State-run clinics sought to prevent the expansion of venereal diseases. Every two weeks a state certified physician examined the women who worked in authorized brothels. If "clean," the doctor would stamp their state-issued health cards so they could continue working. Otherwise, they were required to stay in the hospital for treatment. A decree on March 3, 1956, made prostitution illegal. Article 1 stated that the goal was to "ensure women's dignity and the interest of social morality." The prostitution abolitionist movement prevailed after Spain was welcomed into the international arena, after signing the Pact of Madrid with the United States in 1953. Within two years, the regime was rehabilitated and welcomed into the United Nations.

Tomás Caro Patón was a doctor in the state clinics for thirty-seven years and a committed abolitionist. Here we include an excerpt from his memoirs, *The Fallen Woman. Memoirs and Reflections of a Physician Involved in the Fight against Anti-Venereal Disease*, published in 1959.

THE FALLEN WOMAN[5]

Shortly after I entered the anti-venereal campaign as head of a rural clinic, they brought me a wounded prostitute. Some youngsters had followed and thrown stones at her, causing an injury to her forehead. The wound was bleeding profusely; an artery had been broken, and intermittent jets of blood pumped to the rhythmic impulses of her heart beat. I had to perform a ligature and suture, and then proceeded to put a circular dressing resembling a crown. Under the bandage, her straight, bobbed bloody hair fell. The poor woman, blood-spattered, pale, her eyes wide open, showing some tears, she did not groan, did not say anything; she was motionless like a statue. It was hot;

the window was open and the blinds down, and outside the youngsters still shouting angrily: "Die you bitch!" (. . .) And I looked at her sad figure; she seemed to be the picture of martyrdom.

1. Look at women in general, and at those you work with in particular, with the eyes of your soul and with your reason, not with your senses.

2 Despise women's "Muñequismo" (excess of makeup and artifice, doll-like).

3. Be Catholic feminists; recognize women as capable human beings, able to perform activities beyond those domestic ones historically assigned to their sex.

4. Combine this feminist concept with the love of virtue, with motherhood, with the rearing of children and the domestic administration of the home, because they are functions specific to women.

5. Respect women's virtue, not just as a matter of courtesy and good manners, but rather because you seek your own virtue, your own chastity, and repress your passions.

6. Avoid with contempt those frivolous male friends who love women as sexual objects, and try to attract them to your way of thinking.

7. Deeply feeling and practicing these pieces of advice, you will not have any problem in socializing with girls who practice them as well. Socialize with them not only at work, but also during leisure time, in walks, parties, during sports, avoiding the sad misogyny. With your full of grace interactions, the healthy happiness of youth will flourish, and love will be real, not as a vice, but as God's blessing.

8. Look at women in general, and to those you work with in particular, with the eyes of your soul, and with your reason, not with your senses.

Questions for discussion

1. In the first paragraph of the excerpt, Dr Caro Patón describes the injured woman he is treating. Is he sympathetic? How does he represent her?

2. Explore the distinction between regulation and abolishment of prostitution. What are the moral arguments? What are the public health concerns?

3. Dr Caro Patón offers some recommendations to improve relationships between the sexes. Choose two that you consider feminist and two you consider obsolete.

4. What do you think he means by "sad misogyny"? How are the prostitute and the pure woman bound to each other?

DOCUMENT 5

SOCIOLOGY OF HEALTH CARE. 1. DOCTRINAL PRINCIPLES. INFORMES FOESSA, MADRID 1975[6] AND CAUSES OF DEATH 1968–70. SOURCE: INSTITUTO NACIONAL DE ESTADÍSTICA (INE, NATIONAL INSTITUTE OF STATISTICS, MADRID, 1973)[7]

After the implementation of the Stabilization Plan in 1959, the Spanish economy took off and the country entered a process of urbanization and social transformation, stimulated by American loans in the wake of the Pact of Madrid (1953). Improvements in the quality of life due to the transition from autarky to consumerism had a significant impact on the health of Spaniards. While the 1940s were branded as the "Hunger Years," the 1960s turned out to be the "Development Years" or the "Miracle Years."

To better maximize the investment of dollars and rationalize the modernization of the country, several five-year development plans were initiated in the 1960s. We include here an excerpt from FOESSA, a foundation established in 1965 as a charity-teaching institution by Catholic Charities Caritas. Following the United States' philanthropic foundation model, the purpose of FOESSA was to advise the Francoist state in their social duties. From its very beginning, the goal of FOESSA was "to align itself with modernity and efficacy."[8] The members of the FOESSA foundation were: economists, researchers, and sociologists who collaborated to build a more just society. Here we include an excerpt from FOESSA's 1975 sociological studies on health care, and also a 1970s table from the National Statistics Agency.

SOCIOLOGY OF HEALTH CARE

I. Doctrinal Principles
    1.1   Health issues as part of the social context
    1.2   The model and ways in which a country's population gets sick as a result of a series of interconnected variables:
        1.2.1 Geographical and environmental
        1.2.2 Population distribution and age. Relation between rural and urban population
        1.2.3 Cultural level and health education

1.2.4 Health care infrastructure and the capability of the state to compensate for individual or regional income inequalities

In general, we can say that as a country develops economically, socially, and culturally, exogenous diseases, such as infections, decrease, while exogenous (degenerative, neoplastic) disorders, such as accidents, increase, along with social rehabilitation and integration of the invalid and the infirmed. On the other hand, economic development with more industrialization and an increase of the urban population manifest health problems not evident before: sub-normality of physical disabilities and mental illness, which make it difficult for individuals to adapt, and lead to neurotic disorders, including alcoholism and drug addictions.

(...)

II. Mortality in Spain

2.1 Evolution of mortality in Spain

In Table no. 1, we can see the considerable decrease of mortality in Spain in less than a century, moving from a rate of 30 per 1,000 inhabitants to less than 9 per 1,000. However, if we were to add the number of children's deaths before they reach twenty-four hours of life, these figures are higher, and thus lower the life span projections. (...)

Nonetheless, the net mortality figures tell us very little about the state of the population's health care, except in very underdeveloped countries, because those figures are determined by the aging of the population, in other words by pyramid's structure.

In Spain, as in other countries, the decline in mortality is due, above all, to the fight against infant mortality, as we can see in Table no. 2. Children dying under one year of age decreased from 6.48 per 1,000 inhabitants and 185.9 per 1,000 born alive in 1901, to 0.44 per 1,000 inhabitants and 22.1 per 1,000 born alive in 1969. If we consider the age group 0 to 5 years old, the decrease has been 12.0 per 1,000 inhabitants or 346.8 per 1,000 born alive in 1901, to 0.52 per 1,000 inhabitants or 28.8 per 1,000 born alive in 1969. In other words, almost a fifteen times decline, considering the rates of 1,000 inhabitants, or more than nine if we refer to infants born alive, in the age group 0-1.

If we focus on the age group 0–5 years old, the rates show a twenty-two times decline (per 1000 inhabitants) or almost fifteen times (per 1000 born alive).

(...)

2.3 Causes of mortality in Spain

The model of mortality in a country is fluid due to multiple factors, but it varies per its socio-economic evolution.

(...) In developed countries the predominant causes of mortality include degenerative diseases of the heart and blood vessels, malignant tumors, and accidents. In some of them, like Denmark and France, we can highlight hepatic cirrhosis, which in France in 1959 caused no less than 2.4 per 100 of the deaths.

Table no. 1: General figures on birth and mortality rates in Spain

Year	Birth Rate	Mortality Rate
1880	35.4	30.0
1890	34.3	32.0
1900	33.8	28.8
1910	32.6	22.9
1920	29.3	23.2
1930	28.2	16.8
1940	24.8	16.5
1950	20.0	10.8
1955	20.8	9.2
1960	21.6	8.6
1965	21.1	8.4
1968	20.2	8.5
1970	19.5	8.4

M. Mezquinta López, "Demographic World's Profiles," *Tribuna Médica*, March 17, 1972[9]

In Colombia, the predominant cause is contagious diseases, in comparison with other countries, including illness due to infections and eating ailments in newborns and lactating infants.

In Spain, the situation is intermediate. (...) Tuberculosis, lactating infant gastritis, duodenitis, and enteritis are among the ten most significant causes of death.

(...)

Malignant tumors and heart and blood vessels diseases are, along with senility (a diagnosis that has decreased), the four most significant causes of death.

The percentage of flu and pneumonia has decreased from 7.0 per 100 in 1959 to 4.6 in 1967. Bronchitis has remained the same, but we know that exogenous factors, such as (asthmatic reactions), cardiac, and environmental (pollution), are the cause, persistence, and fatal evolution of this disease.

There is an eradication of tuberculosis and lactating infant's gastritis, enteritis, and duodenitis. But, in turn, the mortality due to accidents has increased from 3.1 per 100 to 4.1 per 100 and hepatic cirrhosis emerges as one of the ten causes, influenced, as is known, by the consumption of alcohol.

The model of, and the structure of mortality are more and more similar to that of Western European industrialized countries or North America.

(...)

At age fifty-four there is a significant increase in cancer and heart diseases. The latter is increasingly more prevalent in the later years of life.

Chapter X
Causes of Death

5.1.2 Eight Revision 1965

	1968		1969		1970	
	Total number	Increase percentage	Total number	Increase percentage	Total number	Increase percentage
Total	277 357	100.00	297 169	100.00	280 170	100.00
B 1 Cholera	—	—	—	0.01	—	—
B 2 Typhoid fever	43	0.02	37	—	33	0.01
B 3 Bacillary dysentery and amebiasis	2	—	11	—	5	—
B 4 Enteritis and other diarrheal diseases	1363	0.49	1234	0.45	1147	0.41
B 5 Tuberculosis of the respiratory system	3990	1.44	3809	1.28	3202	1.14
B 6 Other tuberculosis including late affects	527	0.19	456	0.15	394	0.14
B 7 Plague	—	—	—	—	—	—
B 8 Diphtheria	14	—	7	—	5	—
B 9 Pertussis	14	—	21	0.01	9	—
B 10 Streptococcal angina and scarlet fever	2	—	3	—	4	—
B 11 Meningococcal infections	181	0.07	168	0.06	259	0.09
B 12 Acute poliomyelitis	33	0.01	43	0.01	21	0.01
B 13 Smallpox	—	—	—	—	—	—
B 14 Measles	113	0.04	134	0.05	95	0.03
B 15 Typhus and other rickettsiosis	—	—	—	—	—	—
B 16 Malaria (1)	—	—	4	—	—	—

			Count	%	Count	%	Count	%
B	17	Syphilis and its sequelae	314	0.11	311	0.10	258	0.09
B	18	All other infectious and parasitic diseases	1719	0.62	1751	0.59	1834	0.65
B	19	Cancer tumors including neoplasm of the lymphatic tissue and hematopoietic organs	43512	15.69	43653	14.69	45631	16.29
B	20	Benign tumors and unspecified tumors	390	0.14	390	0.13	324	0.12
B	21	Diabetes mellitus	4130	1.49	4930	1.66	4543	1.62
B	22	Avitaminosis and other nutritional deficiencies	87	0.03	77	0.03	82	0.03
B	23	Anemia	669	0.24	723	0.24	724	0.26
B	24	Meningitis	466	0.17	446	0.15	475	0.17
B	25	Active rheumatic fever	769	0.28	582	0.26	479	0.17
B	26	Chronic mitral valve prolapse	10021	3.61	10329	3.48	7480	2.67
B	27	Hypertension diseases	5137	1.85	5170	1.74	4664	1.67
B	28	Ischemic heart diseases	14403	5.19	16985	5.45	15692	5.60
B	29	Other heart diseases	31482	11.35	30570	10.29	33834	12.08
B	30	Cerebrovascular diseases	36052	13.00	39474	13.28	38417	13.71
B	31	Influenza	3219	1.16	5167	1.74	1949	0.70
B	32	Pneumonia	10615	3.83	9734	3.28	9981	3.56
B	33	Bronchitis, emphysema and asthma	10446	3.77	13021	4.38	11448	4.09
B	34	Peptic ulcer	1854	0.67	1995	0.67	1916	0.68
B	35	Appendicitis	209	0.08	201	0.07	184	0.06
B	36	Intestinal obstruction and hernia	1875	0.68	1931	0.65	1901	0.68
B	37	Cirrhosis of the liver	7045	2.54	7644	2.57	7219	2.58

(continued)

Chapter X
Causes of Death (*continued*)

5.1.2 **Eight Revision 1965**

		1968		1969		1970	
		Total number	Increase percentage	Total number	Increase percentage	Total number	Increase percentage
B	38	Nephritis and nephrosis	4501	1.62	4537	1.53	4077	1.45
B	39	Prostatic hyperplasia	611	0.22	576	0.19	576	0.20
B	40	Abortion	14	–	17	0.01	15	0.01
B	41	Pregnancy, childbirth and postpartum complications	238	0.09	204	0.07	202	0.07
B	42	Congenital abnormalities/birth defects	1709	0.62	1733	0.58	1643	0.59
B	43	Birth injuries, complicated births, anoxic and hypoxic perinatal conditions	706	0.25	685	0.23	666	0.24
B	44	Other causes of perinatal mortality	3005	1.08	2890	0.97	2711	0.97
B	45	Other unhealthy states and ill-defined diseases	22808	8.22	23988	8.07	22634	8.08
B	46	All other diseases	40370	14.56	48562	16.34	39920	14.25
ACCIDENTS, POISONING AND VIOLENCE (EXTERNAL CAUSES)								
BE47		Motor vehicle accidents	3405	1.23	4323	1.45	4583	1.64
BE48		All other accidents	7848	2.83	7774	2.62	7296	2.60
BE49		Suicide and self-inflicted injuries	1413	0.51	1476	0.50	1424	0.51
BE50		All other external causes	33	0.01	83	0.03	214	0.08

(1) Cases originated outside the national territory

(...)

As mentioned above, there is a fallacy in the Spanish figures for infant mortality, as the number of deaths within the first twenty-four hours of life is not computed, and if it were factored in, the Spanish infant mortality rate would increase to close to 25 per 100.

Questions for discussion

1. Identify the three major causes of death in Spain in the late 1970s. Compare these figures with the information about previous decades in the first document by FOESSA.
2. What diseases showed an increase and which of them showed a decrease?
3. What are the figures pertaining to women's health in table 2?
4. Explain the figures pertaining to accidental or violent deaths.

DOCUMENT 6
ORGANIC LAW FOR THE LEGALIZATION OF ABORTION 9/1985

During the Spanish Civil war (1936–9), and under the first female Minister of Health, anarchist Federica Montseny, abortion was legalized in 1937 in the Republican side. Under the Francoist dictatorship (1939–75), contraception and abortion were illegal, in accordance with the National Catholic precepts regulating family and gender relations.

However, illegal abortions continued to happen, and were difficult to quantify. According to the FOESSA health study in 1975, abortion was "extraordinarily frequent,"[10] responding to multiple factors. Abortions were only identified when complications took place. Per the study, in 1941 the number of "legal" "abortions were 16,605, 3.27 per 100 born alive, while in 1970 the number was 16,810, 2.56 per 100 born alive. The medical journal *Tribuna Médica* reported an approximate figure of 70,000 to 100,000 per year in Spain.

The feminist movement emerging in the early 1970s fought actively for the legalization of abortion and denounced the class bias and injustice behind the issue. Many middle-class women were able to have a safe procedure by traveling to England or The Netherlands, where they paid expensive hospital fees. Most lower income women were risking their lives by trying to get abortions illegally. The struggle for reproductive rights culminated in a very difficult and controversial law that de-penalized abortion under certain conditions in 1985.

I. GENERAL PROVISIONS[11]

HEAD OF STATE

14138   STATUTE 09/1985 of July 5 amending
                   the text of Article 417 bis of the Criminal Code

Juan Carlos I
King of Spain
   Know All Men by Those Present.
   Be it known that the Parliament has approved and I hereby enact the following Statute Law:

Sole Article:

Article 417 bis of the Criminal Code shall be worded as follows:

1. An abortion performed by a physician or under the direction of a physician, in an accredited private or public health center or treatment facility and, with the voluntary and informed consent of the pregnant woman, shall not be punishable if any of the following conditions are fulfilled:

1st. The abortion is necessary to avert a risk to the life or a risk of serious damage to the physical or mental health of the pregnant woman, provided that this circumstance has been previously determined and supported by the expert medical opinion of the relevant specialty, other than the physician performing the abortion, or under whose direction the abortion procedure is done.

The voluntary and informed consent, as well as the expert medical opinion, may be omitted in the event of an emergency that constitutes a life-threatening condition to the pregnant woman.

2nd. The woman's pregnancy is a result of the crime of rape on the grounds of Article 429, provided that the abortion is performed within the first twelve (12) weeks of gestation and that the sexual assault had been reported to law enforcement authorities.

3rd. There exists the presumption that the fetus has an irreversible medical condition or abnormality, provided that the abortion is performed within the first twenty-two weeks of gestation, and that the expert medical opinion has been issued by two specialist physicians from a private or public health center or facility authorized for this purpose, other than the physician who is to perform the abortion, or under whose direction the abortion procedure will be performed.

2. In the cases referred to in the preceding sub-sections, no penalty shall be imposed on the pregnant woman, even if the abortion procedure is performed in a private or public health center or treatment facility not accredited for such purpose and, if the required medical opinion has not been issued.

Wherefore,

I hereby command all Spanish citizens and public authorities, to comply with this law and ensure its compliance.

Palacio de la Zarzuela, Madrid, July 5 of 1985.

JUAN CARLOS R.

Felipe González Márquez
Prime Minister

Questions for discussion

1. Explain the conditions imposed by the law to be able to abort legally.

2. Look for the legalization or de-penalization of abortion in the United States' case Roe v. Wade (1973) and the Act of 1967 in the United Kingdom. Compare them with the Spanish law.

3. How do you explain the evolution in Spanish mentality regarding this law, in view of the stronghold of Catholicism in cultural and moral values?

4. How does the issue of separation of Church and State influence citizens' rights versus their private religious beliefs?

MODULE 9
GENDERED SEXUALITIES

ABSTRACT

This module examines the importance of sexuality in articulating social relations. The title "gendered sexualities" intends to address the problematic binary sex/gender that feminist scholars have studied for the last four decades. Central to the breaking down of this binary is the understanding of how our bodies represent a crucial site of political power. Our biology became our destiny with the shift to a scientific rather than a religious centered worldview during the Enlightenment. Physicians determined who was normal and fit for political participation and what represented standard, productive sexuality and not an aberration. Biological determinism—that is, the idea that biological features such as male or female chromosomes and sex organs control our destiny—was widespread up to the twentieth century. Heterosexuality was equated with normalcy and respectability. Likewise, citizens were assigned gender specific roles in society. Our gender (and race, of course, as well as class) determined our socio-economic and political opportunities and expectations. The different documents compiled in this module address the different debates around sexuality in Spain in the last century. The intention is to reflect on our embodied historical experiences.

DOCUMENT 1
GREGORIO MARAÑÓN, *LA EVOLUCIÓN DE LA SEXUALIDAD Y LOS ESTADOS INTERSEXUALES* (THE EVOLUTION OF SEX AND INTERSEXUAL CONDITIONS, 1930)[1]

Gregorio Marañón (1887–1960) was an internationally renowned physician and scientist whose present relevance is due to the numerous historical, philosophical, and literary essays that he published throughout his career. Ideologically, he can be considered a liberal humanist, who fought against Primo de Rivera's dictatorship and was also critical of both the Republicans and the Nationalists during the Spanish Civil War.

Marañón was a prominent figure in the sexual reform movement that took place in early twentieth-century Spain. He is considered the founder of endocrinology and one of the most renowned theoreticians about endocrinology of sex and sexual differentiation. Throughout his writings we can appreciate Marañón's mixed attitudes towards gender roles. On the one hand, he was part of national eugenicist projects; he supported women's rights to birth control and childcare, was an advocate of divorce, and criticized double moral standards. On the other hand, he defended traditional family values and insisted that women's biological fate was motherhood. One of his best-known books is *Los estados intersexuales en la especie humana* (Intersexual Conditions in Humans, 1929). The first edition included controversial pictures of clinical cases of intersexuality and hermaphroditism, and a year later he published a second edition entitled *La evolución de la sexualidad y los estados intersexuales* (The Evolution of Sex and Intersexual Conditions) from which all pictures were removed.

In this book, Marañón describes his famous theory of sexual hybridity by blending biological and psychological explanations. Marañón affirms that to understand the complexity of many physiological and pathological sexual issues, we should understand sex not as an immutable value, but as an evolutionary one, and therefore "feminine" and "masculine" should not be understood in terms of opposition, but gradation. In the preface to the English edition of the book, Marañón writes: "It is essential to recognize that differentiation between the man and the woman does not imply different sexual value. It results simply from the fact that in each of the two sexes the succession of phases of sex is not accomplished in the same way."[2] While women go through the "viriloid" phase during climacterium, men have a "feminoid" phase during adolescence. In Marañón's view, there is a constant predisposition to intersexuality and cases of sexual purity are exceptional in humans. On the one side of the spectrum of intersexual states we find hermaphroditism, and on the other, virilization in women and feminization in men. Marañón's theories on homosexuality are derived from this view of evolutionary sexuality; homosexuality is a state of immaturity or emotional stagnation; that is, a phase that has to be overcome, but never a permanent state.

THE EVOLUTION OF SEX AND INTERSEXUAL CONDITIONS

Chapter XIV

Secondary Functional Intersexualities (Psychical, Affective Intersexuality, etc.)

Concept

In our classification of sexual characters, we have defined *functional secondary characters* as a certain number of human activities whose sexual significance we consider undeniable. Of course, in these characters sexual indifferentiation (intersexuality) can also be seen. However, they mainly involve modalities of psychology, character, and social conduct, which are beyond the direct influence of primary sexuality. This is the reason why their interpretation as sexual phenomena is at times difficult and problematic, especially the interpretation of its abnormal forms as intersexual conditions.

We must admit, however, with all the caveats, that there is a *psychology, affectivity, and an intersexual conduct*; as there is *an intersexual form of the instinct* (homosexuality) as well as a variety of forms of anatomical intersexuality.

Often, they are all related. It is common knowledge that a morphologically effeminate man may be homosexual and conduct himself psychologically and socially like a woman. The same can happen to the woman invert, who might be morphologically, erotically, psychologically, and socially invert. But in other cases, we can observe the same dissociation that we already mentioned about homosexuality. Just as higher degrees of homosexuality do not coincide with the maximum degrees of morphological intersexuality (hermaphroditism, pseudo hermaphroditism, extreme virilization, and feminizations) but with the discreet forms, so it is also very common to find these stigmata of psychological inversion not in men and women of striking intersexuality, but in those cases of attenuated intersexuality.

One can even dissociate—as actually occurs in countless cases—the psychical forms of intersexuality, as far as erotic intersexuality is concerned, from homosexuality. In sum, we find men or women with sexually perfect morphology and with correct sexual instinct, yet who are endowed with emotional and psychological traits, as well as traits of social behavior which are distinctly invert. That is, psychological inversions can be strictly partial.[3] (...)

Psychical inversion in men

The most typical sexual characteristic of the men's psychology is, as I said, their tendency and aptitude for social activities, which involves the defense and material prosperity of the household; and in the case of the most capable men—in a sense the most virile—the acquisition of wealth and glory that widen their own circle of material and spiritual welfare as well as that of their families. However, this kind of aptitude is not present in many healthy men, who are unfit for social success from its minimum degree—the acquisition of life's bare necessities—to the maximum degrees of affluence and celebrity. In my judgment, the hypovirile signification of this deficiency is conclusive, not only in those cases in which it is accompanied by doubtful particulars of the libido or the morphology, but also in those cases where there is not the least physical or erotic deviation from the normal type.[4]

It is common for men subject to this incomplete form of virile differentiation to seek—as is the case with those with equivocal libido—other types of activities that substitute the genuinely masculine ones. The most frequent one is *sport*, which is, as I suggested elsewhere, a substitute for real work.[5] These men frequently dedicate themselves to dilettante activities, especially artistic ones. These are amateur writers, poets, painters, and sculptors, who do not create truly original works, since they are not able to do so; at the same time they do not need the remuneration that ennobles all human activities, even the artistic ones, no matter how mediocre they might be. (. . .)

It is also typical of this modality of masculine psychology the presence of traits corresponding to the secondary sexual activity of the woman: especially the inclination and the aptitude for the meticulous arrangement and decoration of the house, which are so characteristic of eunuchs.[6] The frequency of intersexual psychology—even true homosexuality—among men employed in domestic service may be associated with this type of masculine psychology. We are not including the direct care of children among these excessive tendencies to domesticity since both the maternal instinct and the paternal tenderness are separate from intersexuality.

Since in these cases the erotic tendency may be normal, men who have a feminoid psychology cohabit easily with women. However, a great number of these men do not get married. These men have a difficult time genuinely falling in love since they do not need or find a highly differentiated type of woman. In addition, their libido needs are not urgent and often they are sexually timid.[7] The social and economical problem of marriage overwhelms them. Finally, they are often infertile or lack a deep desire to become parents.

In all these cases, it is well known that men concentrate their affection on their mothers. Filial love becomes for them an idolatry that excludes any other affection. Therefore, a large proportion of *unrepentant bachelors* belong to the group under study. We will see now that in many cases their celibacy is encouraged by their inclination towards a polygamous and Donjuanesque type of love.

But many others do marry or have long-term monogamous relationships. *In such individuals this almost always occurs through a process of domination by women.* Indeed, one of the psychosexual characteristics of these men is the transfer of the management of conjugal matters to the women, whose instincts, always alert to the discovery of stable partners, usually detect the existence of the weak males with wonderful intuition. That is the reason why, very often, male psychosexual laxity is matched by compensating viriloid energy in women. Coexistence favors this displacement of the controlling energy towards the female. In these circumstances, weak males tend to compensate their specific energy deficiencies—even in the indirect form of lack of social success—with all kinds of concessions to their spouses. These concessions can become weaknesses that at times lead them to ridicule, and other times to breaking the law. Cases of men who steal, swindle, or kill, pressed by a woman, always belong to this category of dominated hypoviriles. We must add that this phenomenon can also occur in men of normal constitution, whose virility has been weakened as a result of pathological causes. This is the case with old men or those in decline, who are so prone to violent and submissive love, usually with young girls.[8]

Another type of hypovirile conduct is, in my opinion, Donjuanesque love, a topic I dealt with repeatedly elsewhere. In chapter XIII, I explained the mechanism by virtue of which the instinct of a man, in cases of maximum differentiation—maximum virility— changes gradually until the object of his instinct is an absolutely individualized type of woman. Monogamous love would therefore be the prototype of normal love for men; and it surely will become more frequent every day, as humanity, still in its adolescence, evolves towards perfection, towards maturity. On the contrary, the epidermic and superficial love that does not originate in a profound libido, but on a wise technique in the art of seduction and the mechanics of the amorous relationship, is typical of men of hypo virile psychosexual conduct; and often even undifferentiated, cynical libido, if not of equivocal morphology.[9]

Questions for discussion

1. Gregorio Marañón has been considered a reactionary by some and a liberal reformist by others. Explain your position based on the above selection.

2. Based on this selection, would you say that Marañón's views on sex roles are biologically determined?

3. In an essay published in 1924, Marañón writes: "each man—or at least an immense majority of men—carries within him the ghost of a woman; not in the imagination, from where it would be easy to expel it, but running in the blood." Five years later, he urges both men and women to kill the ghost of the other sex that each of them carries within. Comment on this statement in view of the text that you have read.

DOCUMENT 2
HILDEGART RODRÍGUEZ, *EL PROBLEMA SEXUAL TRATADO POR UNA MUJER ESPAÑOLA* (THE SEXUAL PROBLEM EXAMINED BY A SPANISH WOMAN, 1931)[10]

Hildegart Rodríguez (1914–33) was a herald for the sexual revolution, an activist for sexual reform, and probably the only Spanish young girl at the time writing extensively and doing research on human sexuality. Hildegart was conceived by her mother, Aurora Rodríguez Carballeira, after carefully selecting, and soon discarding, a biological father in what would become a tragic eugenic experiment. More than a daughter, Hildegart became her mother's project—a real-life doll. She became someone that, in the mind of this delirious and staunch believer of eugenics, had only one mission in this world: to become the model of the New Woman and savior of women in their struggle to free themselves from men's control.

During Hildegart's infancy, she seemed to be the perfect puppet for her mother's plan. She was a truly gifted child, who could read when she was twenty-two months old, and already writing when she was three. At the age of ten, she was translating books from Latin, and could speak German, English, and French fluently. By the time she was fifteen, she was lecturing on feminist issues and had achieved international recognition. She corresponded with H.G. Wells and Margaret Sanger, as well as with English physician and social reformer, Havelock Ellis, becoming a translator of his essays on human sexuality. In Spain, she soon found a place in the academic world—graduating at age seventeen from the Complutense University of Madrid with a Law degree—and in the political arena too, becoming affiliated with the Socialist Party, PSOE, the *Federación Nacional de Juventudes Socialistas* (National Federation of Socialist Youth), and the UGT (Socialist Workers Union). She was also chosen as Secretary of the *Liga Española por la Reforma Sexual* (Spanish League for Sexual Reform), an association presided over by well-known Spanish physician, Gregorio Marañón. This astonishing political and intellectual career was cut short, when, at the tender age of nineteen, Hildegart's mother, not being able to control her daughter's personal and public life any longer, decided to shoot her while she was sleeping.

Hildegart was a prolific writer, who managed to publish fourteen books in a very short period, including: *La rebeldía sexual en la juventud* (The Sexual Rebellion of Youth, 1931), *Profilaxis anticoncepcional* (The Prophylaxis of Contraception, 1931), and *Malthusismo y neomalthusismo* (Malthusianism and Neo-Malthusianism, 1931). In these books, she presents compelling arguments in defense of abortion, eugenic methods, the death penalty, free love, and independent education. The excerpt below is part of her chapter on freedom in love, included in one of her most reprinted books: *El problema sexual tratado por una mujer española* (The Sexual Problem Examined by a Spanish Woman, 1931).

THE SEXUAL PROBLEM EXAMINED BY A SPANISH WOMAN

Prostitution

When dealing with prostitution, we are facing an institution that is as old as civilization itself; we do not say older because we have proof that among savages, due to freedom in romantic relationships, prostitution was completely unknown. When we discover in a primitive village the presence of prostitution, we realize immediately that these people have had some contact with civilization. Thus, up until 1879 (the time in which the Omaha Indians became Christians and sent their children to Sunday school), there was not among them, as Reverend Owen Dorsay attests, the institution called Minckoda. Even then, it was formed only by two or three women who could be called "prostitutes."

Its origin in religion

Prostitution has its unquestionable origin in religious customs. The sacred prostitute was part of religious practices in ancient civilizations, and Herodotus tells us that "almost all peoples, except for Egyptians and Greeks, had relationships with women in sacred places." In the fourteenth and fifteenth centuries, prostitution enjoyed special tolerance by the religious authorities. In a very curious case mentioned in *Sex and the Law*, Huntington Cairns relates that in the city of Avignon, there was a brothel (sponsored by Queen Juana of Naples) that followed the same rules as those of monasteries. Briffault[11] adds more details about this very curious fact, saying: "Only good Christians were admitted there, rejecting Jews and infidels, and it closed its doors on Holy Friday and during Easter." Lay prostitution was simply a consequence of the religious one. In the coastal cities frequented by foreigners, the priestess, who sold herself in the past to convey the favors of the goddess, surrendered herself in exchange of money. Ulpian[12] defines the prostitute as a woman who "openly surrenders her body to a great number of men, without choosing them, in exchange of money." And the problem that Ulpian faced then continues today with the same unquestionable gravity.

Teachings

We see how, even within the critical and objective impartiality of history a lack of moral founding in analyzing prostitution is born to the beat of religion. The concepts of a false morality, of an absurd honesty, that constrain women fearing scandal—the only teaching that the Church has made sure to provide—would later force the males (whose liberties the Church tolerated and even glorified), to search for satisfaction of their sexual drive before forming a family. The Church itself, always alert to the smallest necessities of its worshippers, satisfied also their legitimate aspirations, and created prostitution indirectly, and with it, one of the most terrible afflictions of present society. (. . .)

The abolitionist campaign

Many years have passed since Josephine Butler started abolitionism in England, and tried to redeem a few women from this terrible life that affected their physical body, conscience, and dignity. The abolitionist struggle against the lack of legislation about prostitution is spreading. Will it succeed? The day in which women will be free to love wherever they want, in whatever way they want, and whoever they want, will see the end of that secret desire to find in the prostitute, a satisfaction that men's economic or moral incapacity cannot find at home. It is not by chance that Nietzsche said, "the age to marry comes much earlier than the age to love."

Its realization

For men who have not acquired the commendable role of achieving a manual or intellectual work that occupies their whole existence; those whose physical or economic situation does not allow them to have and support a child, the freedom to love, the free sexual experience in their youth (without consequences and compromises), will be an undeniable solution.

It will be an experience in which everybody will have the security of not coming across women who sell their love like mercenaries, or are infected and wounded by terrible sexual diseases. On the contrary, the experience will be with young women belonging to the same economical and moral situation, who will satisfy, in the same way men do, a logical aspiration in those who have not had the sufficient capacity to direct their education and activities to benefit humanity, not worrying about the sexual practice that so often delays this performance and sometimes invalidates it completely. (. . .)

Sex and science

The topic of sex is always relevant, from kindergarten to university. Biology includes the study of the reproduction processes and growth; genetics is dedicated exclusively to the mechanisms of the cell reproduction process.

Hygiene, as an academic subject, aims to give students a general, and in most cases routine, notion of the structural base of sexual functions. Psychology has to study the problems of sexual emotion, psychosexual development, sexual love, repressions, and frustrations. Social psychology deals with the effect of all these sexual activities on the collective existence.

Mental hygiene and abnormal psychology revolve around sexual life, particularly its aberrations and inadequate expressions. Social sciences must constantly deal with sexual topics. History remembers the great legends and sexual feats of the past, indicating the influence they had in the development and circumstances of events. Thus, as with the case of Henry VII, his religious politics, or Charles II's diplomacy, an explanation would be lacking, without the sexual motif behind them. Anthropology dedicates a large part of its studies to the rites related to sexuality that are preserved among primitive people, since they explain their religions, along with their mysteries and political situations. Sociology, when dealing with sex, family, reproduction, and education, should study sexual issues more in-depth than any other science. Criminology, a special branch of sociology, includes a detailed study of the sexual crimes or offenses due to sexual impulse, even in cases where such an urge appears to be instrumentally hidden. Political economy, that science which deals with speculation and bank entities (consequently, even more distant from sexuality), understands in all its weight the problem of the relationship between life patterns and the population. This relationship poses the necessity of limiting population growth if prosperity and the effects of the feminist advances are to be perpetuated; an especially prime example is women's accessibility to male professions. Political sciences and jurisprudence study the legislation and government apparatus, that is, the legalization of sexual problems in the fields of Law and the State.

Ethics seemed to be limited until recently, almost exclusively, to sexual issues such as marriage and divorce.

In literature and the arts, sex and love motives have been pervasive in such a way that, even in the Anglo-Saxon and Scandinavian countries (colder by nature), the discussion and interpretation of sexual topics have been given a space and freedom that is occasionally remarkable.

The transcendence of the problem of love

All this only proves the transcendence of the problem of love, which is studied by the sciences from all points of view. Precisely because of this transcendental importance, religion has done everything within its power to try to dominate it, subjugate it, and make sure that individuals only have their spiritual directors as personal guides. However, love issues/dilemmas are so personal that, no matter how much they are socialized, the individuals, when facing love conflicts, resolve them by themselves and under their own responsibility; this is how the Church has gradually lost power over love and sex, with the release of humans from their slavery, and with newfound freedom. However, this is a freedom in which a harmonious disposition exists between the two individuals to coordinate their mutual interests and aspirations. It is a freedom that does not become debauchery, as it does for many young people who are too affected by those anarchist-like readings that support a free love that is false and complicated; on the contrary, that brings a better sense of responsibility. A freedom that will always be on alert, because it will be the source of all human complications, a source of conscious paternity, if it is desired and can be physically tolerated; a freedom that can overcome social class impediments—only good to hamper the true mission of human beings—so that people can pay homage to an existence whose only limitation is that dictated by *individual* consciousness.

Tolerance and freedom

Ethereal and impalpable love cannot be owned because its nature makes it elusive and free. Tolerance for all the attitudes should be adopted when facing this *complicated* and personal problem. Tolerance while understanding the social problem does not deteriorate by bringing more babies to the world than the State's capacity can endure, or when individuals with a physical condition force the State to spend more in healing the handicapped and sick, who are not going to bring any future benefits. Freedom is conditioned by consciousness and an innate sense of justice for those very few people who can understand it. It is not by chance that many think that "free love" is something like turning all homes and traditional families into brothels. Freedom should be regulated by the State, if it is negatively affected by it. While the State, as a collectivity, has the obligation (rightly demanded by the people), of providing schools, and capital to have a greater number of workshops and factories, it will also have the obligation to ask, as a logical and legitimate guarantee, that only a specific number of citizens is entrusted to the State. Those will be the citizens that can be saved with decorum and whose future and prosperity the State will be responsible for.

A hundred strong, healthy, and hard-working citizens are worth more than a thousand individuals, if five hundred out of those are admitted to hospitals, three hundred to mental asylums, and the other two hundred brought up as vagrants and rogues (due to the State's lack of attention), most of whom will ultimately end up in jails and gallows.

Freedom in love without responsibility? As much as the individual wants. All that he personally needs, and that which the chosen partner will allow him.

Freedom with consequences? Only the freedom that "should" be allowed, not the one that "can" be achieved. Nobody is asking to limit pleasure, but rather to regulate responsibility. To this end, although it might sound paradoxical, one must foster a sense of responsibility, so that people become accustomed to being accountable for their acts, conscious about their promises, and in short, humans; that is, creators under the intense bridle of their sovereign will.

Consequences

The goal that the freedom in love pursues is to try to reform and organize the future society under a regime with wider and indisputable scope. By defending this proposal, we have never meant to put forward and recommend to future generations something that we would have considered an immorality. On the contrary, we estimate that if we develop in people the power of choice by any possible means that we may have, we will be offering them one of the best gifts. To achieve it, freedom in love should be accompanied by a previous preparation that is efficient and indispensable. It cannot be preached and brought into practice if one does not have a sufficiently clear and explicit knowledge of the responsibility that comes with it. For many, especially unscrupulous youngsters, the problem of freedom in love would end in a brutal and promiscuous romp lacking all purpose. For those who are aware (since they are given freedom), society also has the right to guarantee its use; freedom in love will not mean more accessibility to sex, but rather a larger responsibility. Before, all commitments were cancelled with marriage; nobody was responsible for what happened after the spouse's illness, squandering, insolvency, domestic abuse, or incompatibility of characters. In free union, when each person can break the merely moral tie that connects them, there is a greater incentive on both sides to maintain/preserve the relationship, while also being held responsible as required by that impartial society. Through freedom in love, individuals will pursue the reproduction goal of the species, or satisfaction of their necessities and desires. What they will not do is commit a series of crimes under the shameful scrutiny of a self-centered law that destroys the rights of the weak to protect the strong. Clearly, the men who have created such law have done so, logically, for their own benefit.

When these sentences reach you in a better period, remember (those who aspire to practice one day), this freedom in love will not be a means to achieve satisfaction, without hindrances. Those who see it already near or try to exercise it now, even with restrictions, must remain mindful of such limitations, when it is in place. On the contrary, freedom in love (since it will be a revolutionary acquisition), should offer the society that promotes it sufficient guarantees that it will result in improvements to the tragic institution of the family, whose influence over the universal social organization has been so bleak.

Questions for discussion

1. According to Hildegart Rodríguez, why is the scientific study of sexuality important in our society?

2. What does she understand by the expression "freedom in love"?

3. Hildegart Rodríguez entwines topics of marriage, love, human sexuality, gender, eugenics, and reproduction in this essay. What are your own views on these issues?

4. In an essay entitled "On Women," Arthur Schopenhauer refers to prostitutes as "bloody sacrifices on the altar of monogamy." A few years later, anarchist writer Emma Goldman writes: "To the moralist, prostitution does not consist so much in the fact that the woman sells her body, but rather that she sells it out of wedlock." How are these two views about marriage and prostitution related to the ideas that Hildegart Rodríguez puts forward in this essay?

5. Hildegart Rodríguez's life has been compared to Mary Shelley's novel, *Frankenstein; or the Modern Prometheus*. In ancient Greek mythology, Prometheus gives mankind knowledge and enlightenment in the form of fire. Explain why Hildegart Rodríguez can be considered a modern incarnation of Prometheus. How do power and knowledge play a role in her assassination?

DOCUMENT 3
DR. RAMÓN SERRANO VICENS, *INFORME SEXUAL DE LA MUJER ESPAÑOLA* (SEXUAL REPORT ON SPANISH WOMEN, 1978)[13]

Dr. Ramón Serrano Vicens was born in Zaragoza in 1908 and died in 1978. He was the author of the most important study about female sexual behavior in Spain. The first study, entitled *La sexualidad femenina: una investigación estadística* (Female Sexuality: A Statistical Research), covered the period between 1940 and 1961. Dr. Serrano sent his study to Alfred Kinsey (1894–1956) in the United States who praised his rigor and interesting results, which were very like the discoveries Kinsey published himself in 1953 on the same subject in Female Sexual Behavior.

Kinsey had promised to help with the English translation of Serrano's study when he visited Spain in 1956; however, Kinsey's death also meant the death of the project. The excerpt presented here is the prologue to the second book entitled *Informe sexual de la mujer española* (Sexual Report on Spanish Women) published shortly before Serrano Vicens' death in 1978. While the first was a statistical study, which suffered under Francoist censorship, this second work collected forty-two clinical histories of Serrano's patients as a gynecologist. He made clear that despite the iron-control of the National Catholic morality, the reality was more liberated, much in the same way that Kinsey's work would show for the United States.

PROLOGUE

We cannot assert any longer that women are an enigma, as it was affirmed emphatically until recently. On the contrary, today women have claimed and conquered their right to express themselves, who they are and what they feel. Above all, in the area that concerns this book, there have been numerous reports about female behavior, as if suddenly there were an increased interest in the topic, "Mysterious female reality" so openly discussed throughout history.

It is evident that things are different now. (. . .) Today there is no hiding the immense capability for pleasure a woman holds. That is not to say that women's liberation has been achieved, even in the sexual realm. However, the data we have today is very illuminating. There are not very many scientific studies, but rather many opportunistic attempts to examine a topic now in demand in the wake of the women's liberation movement.

Dr. Ramón Serrano Vicens is one of the most relevant scholars on the topic, who has contributed to the discussion with his rigorous studies, meticulous and tested. With only one book published on the topic, he has become an authority on female sexuality here and abroad. He is a peer specialist with William Masters and Virginia Johnson, as well as Alfred Kinsey. (...)

Dr. Serrano Vicens has devoted forty years to the study of female sexuality, and he reveals his findings in this book. His first book on the topic, entitled Female Sexuality, has had several editions and received the praise of the critics. (...) Nobody doubts that with the information provided in that first study, Dr. Serrano Vicens shattered and almost destroyed the prevailing naive theories about female sexuality. Due to obvious censorship, it took some time to be printed and even for it to contain the complete information. (...)

Dr. Serrano Vicens' research covers 1,417 women from all socioeconomic backgrounds and different ages, from adolescence to elderly. When he interviewed these women the breakdown of the population studied was: 347 single, 995 married, 71 widows, and four nuns.

(...) All these women felt safe and confident in sharing their information with Dr. Serrano Vicens because they knew he would keep the professional confidentiality and offered them thoughtful solutions since their testimonies revealed very intimate details. (...)

When Professor Alfred Kinsey visited the author in Spain, Dr. Serrano Vicens had already conducted 1,300 interviews, representing the most complete study on the topic in Europe. But even with the support from Prof. Kinsey, these results could not be published until some years later.

As in his first book, the author emphasizes the statistical analysis—with a focus on masturbation, premarital petting, premarital and marital intercourse, as well as extramarital, and finally homosexual relations. His Report on the Sexual Behavior of the Spanish Woman was written with the intention to cover all the areas of female sexuality, as well as to explore the evolution of experience among Spanish women in the last few years. To accomplish these goals, the author offers several clinical histories, which reflect explicitly and thoroughly the secret sexual behaviors of Spanish women.

Therefore, we can say that with the forty-two clinical histories collected in the book, Dr. Serrano Vicens offers an accurate and broad vision of the diverse conduct of Spanish women from a purely sexual perspective, and the results are surprising and therefore revealing.

(...)

The statistical data may be synthesized as:

The main sexual outlet for Spanish women is solitary masturbation. This same form of sexual gratification occupies the second place in the total number of orgasms among married women as well.

A 61.8 percent of Spanish women discovered masturbation spontaneously, the majority between the age of puberty and twenty years old. Another revealing figure is that 9.6 percent discover it through a homosexual encounter.

At the age of 20, 49.8 percent practice masturbation and experience one orgasm per day, and 21.8 percent enjoy between one and three per day. A 2.2 percent of them experience up to ten daily. (...)

Among single women, heterosexual petting is practiced by 90 percent, but only 30 percent experienced orgasm due to male incompetence. (...) Among married women, 38.3 percent practice masturbation, although 81.2 percent report they experience pleasure during intercourse as well. (...) Among women under 45 years of age, 31.2 percent have had sex outside of marriage and 57.7 percent expressed having had extramarital desires, but repressed them due to moral conventions.

Of those married women who had sex outside of marriage, 28 percent did it freely and the rest for different reasons. Of all of them, 50 percent had only one lover and the rest more than one. Also, 30 percent were unfaithful only once, while 70 percent were unfaithful on several occasions.

Sixty-six percent of the single women had had desires to enter into a lesbian relationship. (...)

Obviously, Spanish women are not so different from any others. However, we have been conditioned to regard them as "different." Above all, Spanish women are not frigid, which is made very clear in the work of Dr. Serrano Vicens, particularly in the present book, *Report on the Sexual Behavior of Spanish Women*. Other authors have studied the incompetence of some Spanish men as lovers, due to their long disregard for the true desires of women. But these are conclusions for the readers to reach on their own, based on the information provided by the author. This study will be valuable for further scientifically sound research.

Dr. Serrano Vicens' honesty, tenacity, and research ethic contributed to keeping the information private until all the work was done. However, it will cause surprises. Everything he documents about Spanish women's sexuality represents an endorsement of the importance of this topic, especially today, when there is a wave of eroticism that invades our daily routines.

This is, therefore, the first report on the female sexual behavior in Spain.

The editors

Questions for discussion

1. The new democratic constitution was approved in December of 1978. What is the significance of this book in the context of the post-Franco era?

2. How are the relations between men and women portrayed in this excerpt?

3. The scientific emphasis in the tone of the text tries to put a distance between women's sexual behavior as a conversation between doctor and patient, versus sinful behavior that would inform the conversation between priest and penitent. Identify some of the language and explain how the transformation was possible after the death of Franco.

4. What are the works published by Masters and Johnson and Alfred Kinsey mentioned in the text? What do the editors mean when they state that Spanish women are no different than other women?

DOCUMENT 4
ESPERANZA VAELLO ESQUERDO, *DELITOS DE ADULTERIO Y AMANCEBAMIENTO* (THE CRIME OF ADULTERY AND COHABITATION, 1976)[14]

The Franco regime's legislation considered three fundamental units of social and political interaction: Municipality, Syndicate, and Family. While family may be considered a private realm, it represented the most important unit of indoctrination and control of the dictatorship. Women's sexuality revolved around their biological destiny as mothers within marriage, and Catholic moral values further legitimized the way the relationship between the spouses would be for the sole purpose of procreation. Heterosexual mandate and a dysfunctional double standard for sexual behavior and expectations of husband and wife penalized contraception, adultery, abortion, and divorce.

Franco died on November 20, 1975, the same year the United Nations declared as International Women's Year. Hence, in Spain the period of transition to democracy coincided with the emergence of a vibrant feminist movement. Spanish feminists organized themselves and launched campaigns against the penalization of abortion and adultery and demanded the right to contraception and divorce. While a husband could publicly entertain a mistress and even move his lover into the conjugal home without paying more than a minor fine, wives faced severe punishment for any kind of the extramarital relations with other men. Women had no legal protection against an abusive husband and risked losing custody of their children. These legal constraints made many women stay and endure the infidelities of their husbands, while only a few would risk social ostracism and shame by separating and starting new lives.

The document here is an excerpt from a dissertation presented in 1976 in the School of Law at the University of Granada, which represents the importance of the legal transformations the country was facing during the immediate post-Francoist era in the area of sexual relations and moral values.

ESPERANZA VAELLO ESQUERDO. *DELITOS DE ADULTERIO Y AMANCEBAMIENTO* (THE CRIME OF ADULTERY AND COHABITATION, 1976)

It would not be an exaggeration to state that the crime of adultery is an anachronistic legal concept, a type of offense completely outdated within the current social and cultural context, given the fact that it implies a total lack of awareness with respect to the changes that perceptions regarding sexuality and family have experienced.

Indeed, the importance of its analysis, as well as the difficulty of said legal concept, lies in the fact that it is a type of sexual criminality—a subject area of Criminal Law particularly confusing—which directly targets the family, a social unit that finds expression in a diversity of legal domains.

Another interesting issue in the analysis of the crime of adultery is related to the limited effectiveness that its existence seems to have, as evidenced by the fact that marital infidelity is far from being an infrequent occurrence and yet, crime statistics show a number of legal proceedings for adultery that do not reflect reality in any way whatsoever. There is a peculiar "dark number" in this field that can be partly explained by the fact that the crime of adultery is an offense which may be prosecuted only at the request of a party, and this party on many occasions chooses to ignore the affront in order to avoid intimate marital disputes coming to light, with its consequent feelings of embarrassment and humiliation. In addition, the party initiating the action may conclude that achieving a conviction for the crime of adultery does not provide an adequate solution to the problem itself.

The *historical background* of the crime of adultery is influenced by excessive rigor in its repression, which perhaps may be explained by the fact that ethical and religious values are not missing elements in the sphere of Criminal Law. For a long time, the notions of crime and sin have been confusing, similar as the ascetic mission of Morality and Religion with the political mission of criminal justice. Another feature also to be highlighted within these historical notes is related to the discriminatory treatment that the spouses received, usually detrimental to the wife.

Fortunately, in recent times, not only is discrimination based on gender being banished—by means of the proclamation of Constitutions in all countries, as well as the Declaration of Equality of all individuals under the law, made by international organizations—but also repression itself has been tempered, to the point that there are only a few instances in which adultery is still severely punished; on the contrary, each day the number of laws that have eradicated said offense from their list of crimes is increasing.

The stance adopted is the result of a series of sociological factors reflecting the changes that the concepts of ethics and sexuality have undergone, as well as the new ideas regarding family and sexual morality. Certainly, it is a consequence of the crisis experienced in the methods that traditionally have been implemented to resolve these kinds of issues.

In fact, within the current order of things and, considering that adultery constitutes a crime, the criminalization of the unfaithful behavior of a partner should be made on grounds of absolute equality between the two spouses. However, the most important question to be determined is related to the appropriateness and opportuneness of the accusation.

We have adopted an *abolitionist position* since we believe that there are critical issues with respect to the punishable nature of adultery. In addition to this circumstance, we consider that civil sanctions are adequate to deal with these behaviors. It is worth noting that petitioning for the suppression of a category of offense does not imply accepting the very action regulated as morally good; however, the duplicity of an action is not sufficient for such an action to be considered punishable, nor is the criminal law the right instrument to impose morality.

The number of issues that have been so far mentioned are the following:

1) Sanctions may become unfair because most of the time the legal proceeding for adultery aims only to obtain a conviction for the other spouse—thus preparing the path for divorce or civil separation—or rather, what is even worse, to obtain merely financial advantages. Other times, vengeance is the motive that prompts the legal action and therefore, criminal justice is not achieved; instead, the course of action becomes the instrument of pressure and extortion.

2) Sanctions are ineffective. It seems unlikely that someone will refrain from committing adultery considering a distant possibility of being caught or facing an even more distant eventuality, that of being punished with a sanction, which in most the countries is a short-term penalty or simply a financial compensation.

Moreover, family turns out to be inefficiently protected. Adultery is a type of offense that does not include in its specificity many related infringements to the duty of faithfulness that spouses owe each other, since the legal action is limited to extramarital sexual relations. Likewise, the clandestine nature of such behavior is another reason that it diminishes the efficacy of Criminal Law. At the same time, as attitudes and customs have changed, a general preventive demeanor is not attained, because a large segment of public opinion is not favorable towards the criminalization of some acts that are tolerated or accepted as normal.

3) Another problem worth mentioning—arising from the new ethical and social conceptualizations—is the fact that the criminalization of adultery widens the gap between real and legal life regulations.

4) Lastly, we cannot fail to mention the difficulty in providing evidence to support a legal cause of action for adultery. Also, the humiliating nature of the means of proof makes the chance of reconciliation even more problematic for the spouses.

We can thus conclude that civil sanctions are adequate to regulate adultery, since the severity of criminal law is not in agreement with familial affections. In addition, the active party in legal cases of adultery—the offended party—presents a minimal degree of danger. At the same time, statistics show inconsistencies between actual and ostensible crime rate, leading to criminal law being discredited and consequently the power of authority of the law diminishes.

Ultimately, the crime of adultery should not be set forth under a punitive regime. Criminal law must be limited to ensure and protect the rights of citizens to a peaceful coexistence. The efficacy of criminal law as guardian against moral infringements should be restricted to a lesser sphere of influence only when its applicability is possible and with a certain degree of effectiveness. We must not forget that based on current criminal law, this legal area aims to be respectful regarding the sexual freedom in the relationships between consenting adults; consequently, it must take a cautious stance against interfering with the family or the individual's privacy.

If the above mentioned is not the aim to be pursued but instead, it is considered pertinent that adultery should persist as a category of offense, then rather than desirable, it would be necessary to penalize, under the same conditions and with the same type of sanctions, the infringement to the duty of fidelity by either spouse. A different legal framework would violate the most basic principles of justice that today demand absolute equality between men and women, more than ever before.

Questions for discussion

1. Who is the audience this document addresses? What is the impact on the legal community to accept a topic such as this one as a dissertation for a doctoral degree in the immediate post-dictatorial era?

2. What are the main arguments put forward to justify the de-penalization of adultery?

3. Explain the significance of the Catholic morality in the acceptance of the double standard morality between husband and wife.

4. Is this consideration of adultery more heinous in the case of the wife than the husband only exclusive of the Spanish culture?

DOCUMENT 5
PEDRO ALMODÓVAR, *LA LEY DEL DESEO*
(THE LAW OF DESIRE, 1987)

Internationally acclaimed director Pedro Almodóvar (1949) filmed *La ley del deseo* in 1987 with two of his favorite actors: Carmen Maura (1945) and Antonio Banderas (1960). This is the first movie in which the Spanish filmmaker openly explores homosexuality. The film addresses the different facets of human desire through the triangle relation of three men, and a transgendered person with a history of incest with her father.

Almodóvar is one of the most popular directors of the democratic transition, forming part of Madrid's cultural movement called "la Movida," regarded as a new form of expression in the arts, music, literature, and cinema. In 1982, the Socialist Party in Spain (PSOE) won the elections with overwhelming majority, signaling the first time in contemporary Spanish history that a political organization that had been declared illegal during the Francoist regime won the government. The PSOE ruled the country until 1997, a period regarded as progressive in the enactment of fundamental legal changes, including the controversial divorce and abortion laws. Professor Enrique Tierno Galván (1918–86), as mayor of Madrid, the capital of Spain, became instrumental in the progress of "la Movida" because of his open mind and tolerance of all ideas. Cultural life turned into the means to find new ways of expression and to present a new modern face of post-Franco Spain. Almodóvar, a former employee of Telefónica (a national telephone company), started filming as an amateur. He also tried being a singer in a band that played in different underground venues in Madrid. Now he is an icon of the new Spanish cinema, and owns his own production company called El Deseo (The Desire). Well known and acclaimed in the most important cinema festivals in the world, his filmography examines intimate themes of desire and gender ambiguity. *La ley del deseo* represents a good example of the transition's transformational period in terms of gender and social conventions in Spain. A movie that talks openly about sex, about homosexuality, and transgender(s) matters made the more conservative and Catholic segments of society critical of its contents, but this was part of Almodóvar's plan and film production. He represents a new kind/brand of cinema in Europe, as evidenced in France, where he is always welcomed at the renowned Cannes film festival, probably the most important cinema event in the European Union. Actors casted by him ensure international projection, as demonstrated by the careers of Penélope Cruz (1974), Antonio Banderas, and Javier Bardem (1969).

Figure 11. Pedro Almodóvar. *La ley del deseo* (The Law of Desire, 1987).

Questions for discussion

1. How can plastic arts, cinema, and literature help us learn more about the historical context of a country?

2. Spain is part of the "Third Wave" transition to democracy model presented by political scientist Samuel Huntington, referring to Portugal in 1974, and Spain and Greece in 1975. Are there any similarities between Almodóvar's films and those of other European directors in the 1980s?

3. Why does Almodóvar choose "desire" as one of the main themes for his movies? Is desire related only to homosexuality? How does it complicate the concept of family and Catholicism?

4. What has been the role of cinema in the politics of the twentieth century? Think about how Hitler, for example, utilized the work of filmmaker Leni Riefenstahl or how political campaigns cannot function without a well-orchestrated visual apparatus.

DOCUMENT 6
LEY DE MATRIMONIOS HOMOSEXUALES (GAY MARRIAGE LAW, 2005)[15]

Most members of the Spanish Parliament approved the gay marriage law on June 30, 2005, the day before the annual Gay Pride Parade in Madrid. The only political groups who voted against it were the conservative Catalan party UDC and the conservative Popular Party (PP) who appealed to the *Tribunal Constitucional* (Supreme Court) to declare it unconstitutional. Prime Minister José Luis Rodríguez Zapatero of the Socialist party (PSOE) had won the elections a year earlier and was instrumental in the passing of the law. This was one of his main promises as a candidate during the electoral campaign, and a part of an ambitious package of civil rights including a special law for people with disabilities, the law of equality between women and men, the law against social/gender violence (one of the first in Europe), and the law to guarantee free health assistance and care for the infirm and the disabled (Law of Dependents).

Spain was the third country in the world with a sanctioned gay marriage law. The most important thing in this bill is that the term "union" between same sex couples is recognized as a marriage, unlike other names utilized in countries like Italy or Chile that refer to it as Civil Unions. Another important novelty in this law is the right to adopt children. Every couple has the right to adopt regardless of the gender of the individuals. The Catholic Church and the extreme right represented in some segments of the conservative party (PP), organized large demonstrations all over the country, complaining about the law, the government, and the progressives in Parliament. The PP's opposition at the time proved futile, as five years later the Supreme Court rejected their appeal of unconstitutionality and the law was officially recognized as constitutional.

The day that the law was approved there were many gay people, activists, and LGBT movement representatives as guests at Parliament. In his speech to the Spanish Parliament, Rodríguez Zapatero addressed the law as part of a historical moment during his administration.

LEY DE MATRIMONIOS HOMOSEXUALES (GAY MARRIAGE LAW, 2005)

I. General Provisions
        HEAD OF STATE
11364   STATUTE 13/2005, of July 1st amending the text of the Civil Code in the matter of rights to contract marriage.

Juan Carlos I

King of Spain

Know All Men by These Presents.

Be it known that the Parliament has approved and I hereby enact the following Statute Law:

I

The relationship and coexistence of couples based on affection is a genuine expression of human nature, and it constitutes a significant path towards the development of personality, which our Constitution establishes as one of the fundamental pillars of political order and social harmony. As a result, marriage has been considered a manifest expression of such relationships, recognized by the Constitution in Article 32 and deemed by our constitutional jurisprudence as a legal concept with social relevance, that allows for couples to make a statement of cohabitation.

Whereas matrimony is considered a constitutional right, the legislator shall neither be unaware of the institution of marriage nor fail to regulate it in accordance with the supreme values of our legal system, given the nature of an individual's right granted by the Constitution. Consequently, the law must formulate this fundamental right within the legal options allowed by the Constitution, which will determine the legal capacity to contract marriage, as well as its content and legal framework, taking into consideration the historical moment and prevalent values in society.

The regulation of marriage in contemporary civil law has reflected the dominant models and values of European and western societies. Its origin can be traced back to the French Civil Code of 1804, which unquestionably gave rise to the Spanish Civil Code of 1889. In this regard, marriage has been configured not merely as an institution, but also as a legal relationship allowed to be established only between two people of different sexes. In fact, it is such sexual distinctions that traditionally have been defined as essential for the institution of marriage to be recognized by both the State and the canonic law. For this reason, the legal codes of the last two centuries reflected the dominant culture and thus, they did not have to prohibit or even refer to a marriage between two people of the same sex, since it was not contemplated in any way that such a relationship could lead to a legal marriage.

However, the legislator cannot ignore what is apparent: society evolves in the way of shaping and recognizing the various models of coexistence; hence, the legislator can and even must act accordingly to avert any fracture between the rules and principles of the law and the values of a society whose relations it should regulate. In this respect, there is no doubt that present-day Spanish societal reality is much more plural, dynamic, and culturally rich than the society of the Civil Code of 1889. The cohabitation between partners of the same sex based on affection has certainly received increasingly social acceptance and recognition, thus overcoming deeply rooted prejudices and stigmatizations. It is now generally accepted that cohabitation of said couples provides a medium through which many individuals can fully and harmoniously develop their personality, a coexistence where both partners provide emotional and financial support to each other, but whose transcendence until now has been limited to that of a private relationship, due to the lack of formal recognition by the law.

This perception toward same-sex couples not only occurred in Spanish society, but also in broader areas, as we may see in the Resolution of the European Parliament executed on November 8, 1994, which expressly asks the European Commission to present a legislative proposal for putting an end to the prohibition of marriage between couples of the same sex, and to ensure them their full rights, together with the benefits of marriage.

II

History abounds with evidence of discrimination based on sexual orientation, a discrimination that the legislator has decided to eliminate. The establishment of a legal framework, allowing personal fulfillment to those that freely opt to express their sexual and affective inclination to persons of the same sex, so they can develop their personality and exercise their legal rights in conditions of equality, has become an important demand from Spanish citizens of our time, and therefore, this law attempts to respond to these concerns.

Certainly, the Constitution, by entrusting to the legislator the regulatory configuration of marriage, does not in any way exclude regulation with respect to partner relationships in a particularly different way from that which has existed up to the present; a regulation suitable to accommodate new forms of affective relationships. Moreover, the option expressed in the law herein has constitutional foundations that the legislator must consider. Hence, promoting complete citizenship and effective equality of rights for the unhindered development of human personality (Articles 9.2 and 10.1 of the Constitution), the preservation of freedom with respect to forms of cohabitation (Article 1.1 of the Constitution), as well as instituting a real framework of equality for the enjoyment of all rights without any discrimination based on sex, opinion, or any other individual or social conditions (Article 14 of the Constitution) are constitutionally protected values whose realization must be expressed through the regulation of the laws configuring the citizenship status in a plural, free, and open society.

Considering this broad perspective, the regulation of marriage that is hereby being instituted aims to fulfill a tangible reality, whose changes the Spanish society has adopted because of the activism of social groups that have been advocating for the absolute equality of rights for all, regardless of their sexual orientation, a reality that requires the formulation of a framework to determine the rights and obligations of all who would formalize their partner relationship.

Within the aforesaid context, the law grants that marriage be entered by persons of the same sex, as well as by persons of different sexes, with full equality of rights and obligations regardless of its composition. Consequently, the effects of matrimony shall continue in its entirety with respect to the substantive configuration of the institution of marriage. Correspondingly, those effects shall be the same irrespective of the sex of the prospective spouses, and they involve the entitlement to social benefits as well as the possibility of taking part in legal proceedings for adoption.

Furthermore, an essential terminological adaptation has taken place within the diverse Articles of the Civil Code concerning to or arising from marriage, in conjunction with several rules containing explicit references to the sex of its members.

In the first place, references to husband and wife have been replaced by mentioning spouses or partners. By the new wording in Article 44 of the Civil Code, the legal definition of spouse or consort shall be that of a person married to another, without considering whether they belong to the same or different sex.

There continue to exist, however, references to the coupling of husband and wife in Articles 116, 117, and 118 of the Civil Code, considering that the factual assumptions to which they relate can only take place in the cases of heterosexual marriages.

Moreover, and because of the First Additional Provision of the present law, all references to matrimony contained in our legal system shall be deemed equally applicable to marriages between two people of the same sex as to marriages of two people of different sexes.
Sole Article: *Amendment of the Civil Code in the matter of rights to contract marriage.*

The Civil Code has been amended in the following terms:

One: A second paragraph is added to Article 44 henceforth reading as follows:
"Marriage shall have the same requirements and effects whether the couple to be married is of the same or different sex".

Two: Article 66 shall read as follows:
"Article 66.
Both spouses are equal in rights and obligations."

Three: Article 67 shall read as follows:
"Article 67.
Both spouses must respect and assist one another and shall act in the best interest of the family."

Four: The first paragraph of Article 154 shall read as follows:
"Non-emancipated children shall remain under the parental responsibility of their parents."

Five: The first paragraph of Article 160 shall read as follows:
"Even if biological parents do not exercise their parental responsibility, they shall have the right to interact with their minor children, except for children that have been adopted or in compliance with the provisions of a Court order."

Six: Second Paragraph of Article 164 shall read as follows:
"2nd. Those acquired through inheritance in which one or both parents exercising their parental responsibility were fairly disinherited or considered not able to

inherit by reason of infamy; in this case, the administration shall be carried out by a designated person or otherwise and consecutively, by the other parent or by a specially appointed Court administrator."

Seven: Subsection 4 of Article 175 shall read as follows:

"4. No one can be adopted by more than one person, unless the adoption takes place jointly or successively by both spouses. If the marriage was entered after the adoption, it will allow the spouse to adopt the children of his or her consort. In the event of the death of the adoptive parent or if the adoptive parent is excluded by the provision in Article 179, a new adoption of the adoptee shall become possible."

Eight: Subsection 2 of Article 178 shall read as follows:

"2. By way of exception, the legal bonds with the family of the biological parents will continue:

1°. When the adoptee is the biological child of the spouse of the adoptive parent, even if the spouse is deceased.

2°. When only one of the biological parents has been lawfully determined, if such disposition has been requested by the adoptive parent, the adoptee over twelve years of age, and the biological parent whose bond will persist."

Nine: Second paragraph of Article 637 shall read as follows:

"Unless otherwise provided by the donor, this provision does not apply to donations made in favor of both spouses jointly, between which the accruing right shall take place."

Ten: Article 1323 shall read as follows:

"Article 1323.

The spouses will be able to transfer rights and property to one another by any title, as well as enter into agreements of any kind between themselves."

Eleven: Article 1344 shall read as follows:

"Article 1344.

Pursuant to community property, the earnings and benefits obtained by either spouse belong to both spouses jointly. In the event of dissolution of community property, all assets will be divided equally between the spouses."

Twelve: Article 1348 shall read as follows:

"Article 1348.

Provided that a credit which belongs exclusively to one of the spouses is set to be payable for a number of years, the amounts paid on the due date will not become joint property but rather they shall be counted as equity of the spouse who owns the credit."

Thirteen: Article 1351 shall read as follows:

"Article 1351.

Profits from gambling gained by either spouse or profits originated from other causes which are exempted from restitution shall belong to community property."

Fourteen: Article 1361 shall read as follows:
             "Article 1361.

Property, money, and all existing assets of a married couple are assumed community property until proven that they belong exclusively to one of the spouses."

Fifteen: Second Paragraph or Article 1365 shall read as follows:
             "2nd. In the normal exercise of the profession, skills, or occupation or during the normal administration of their own property. If one of the spouses is a merchant by occupation, he or she shall be subject to the Code of Commerce."

Sixteen: Article 1404 shall read as follows:
             "Article 1404.

Upon being effected these provisions in accordance with the foregoing Articles, the remaining balance will constitute the community property assets subject to equal partition and distribution between the spouses or their lawful heirs."

Seventeen: Article 1458 shall read as follows:
             "Article 1458.
             The spouses shall be entitled to sell property to one another."

First Additional Provision. *Scope of Legal Application.*
All statutory and regulatory provisions containing any reference to marriage shall be deemed applicable regardless of the sex of its participants.

Second Additional Provision. *Amendment of the Law of June 8, 1957 with regard to the Civil Registry.*
    First. Article 46 shall read as follows:
    "Article 46.

Provisions with respect to adoption, Court decisions regarding legal capacity, statements pertaining to bankruptcy proceedings, actions relating to nationality and domicile, and generally, all documentary proceedings subject to registration which are not set forth to be entered in a specific Register Section, shall be registered by means of a marginal note against the corresponding registry entry.

    All actions concerning parental authority, except for the death of the parents, shall be registered by means of a marginal note in the children's birth certificate."

Second. Article 48 shall read as follows:
    "Article 48.

Paternal or maternal filiation shall be recorded by means of a marginal note in the birth registration, by reference to the marriage registration of the parents, or against the registration of the acknowledgement of paternity."

Third. Article 53 shall read as follows:

"Article 53.

People shall be designated by their first name and the surnames corresponding to both parents, a right to which the Law bestows full protection."

First Final Provision. *Law-Making Power*

The Law hereby is enacted by the exclusive competence of the State in matters of civil law granted by Article 149.1.8a of the Spanish Constitution, without detriment to preservation, amendment, or development of the civil, regional, and special rights approved by the Autonomous Communities where they exist, as well as the regulations approved by said agency in the exercise of their competence in Civil Law.

Second Final Provision. *Effective Date*

This Law shall become effective on the next following day after its publication in the "Official State Bulletin".

Wherefore,

I hereby command all Spanish citizens and public authorities, to comply with this law and ensure its compliance.

Valencia, July 1st, 2005

JUAN CARLOS R.

José Luis Rodríguez Zapatero
Prime Minister

Questions for discussion

1. Do you think that marriage is a progressive way to legalize the union between same-sex couples? Explain your answer.

2. In what way did the approval of this law by the Spanish Government influence the rest of Hispano-American countries?

3. Why is there such a big opposition to equal civil rights for everybody when it comes to sexuality? Does a law make what it regulates mandatory for everyone?

4. Why is the name of the union between same-sex couples so important? Is the opposition to the name of marriage based on reasonable arguments? Explain the difference between "union" and "marriage."

MODULE 10
EMPIRES ACROSS OCEANS

ABSTRACT

The documents included in this module are intended to help understand Spain's role in the Atlantic crossings between Africa and the Americas over more than five centuries. The first text by Dominican friar Bartolomé de las Casas (1484–1566) provides a compelling view on the problems generated as the result of the encounter between Europeans and the peoples of the Americas in the sixteenth century. Las Casas' dissenting voice and criticism of the status quo highlights the existence of counter-discourses to colonization at the very inception of the Colombian discovery.

The texts which follow, by the Spanish politicians and intellectuals Emilio Castelar y Ripoll (1832–99) and Gumersindo Azcárate (1840–1917), demonstrate that those moments of contact retold by de las Casas were only the seeds of a long-lasting and volatile economic, social, and political relationship between three continents that would last until the early 1800s and the Latin America wars for independence. The ties that colonization in the Americas created, included all aspects of everyday life, and, like the Paternal Dissent Law included in this module shows, family affairs were an essential pillar of Spain's control over its colonies until the Spanish-American War of 1898.

DOCUMENT 1
BARTOLOMÉ DE LAS CASAS, *CHRISTOPHER COLUMBUS TRAVELS*, 1566–1600

A most significant figure within Spain's imperial enterprise in the sixteenth century, Dominican friar Bartolomé de las Casas (1484–1566) traveled with Christopher Columbus in his last trip to the New World. De las Casas was appointed by the Spanish crown with the initial task to make conversion to Catholicism an intrinsic part of the colonization of the New World. His *Diario de abordo*, was De las Casas' first comprehensive writing about the island Hispaniola, where he first landed in 1502. This work provided a description of the New World's population, which shaped Europeans' first impressions about these unknown lands. After years in the Antilles and Central America, Bartolomé de las Casas wrote harsh pieces about Spain's colonization process, such as the *History of the Destruction of the Indies* (1552) and a series of letters about the condition of indigenous people under Spain's rule. He was appointed Protector de Indios (Protector of Indians) by Cardinal Cisneros in 1516. Over the centuries, his critiques of Spain's methods of colonization and the exploitation of indigenous populations in mining and other labors were internationally known and widely used by Spain's European imperial opponents, contributing to the Black Legend of the Spanish Empire. In the twentieth century, Liberation Theology promoters also used his writings to denounce indigenous marginalization and economic exploitation in Latin America.

BARTOLOMÉ DE LAS CASAS, *CHRISTOPHER COLUMBUS TRAVELS*, 1566–1600

Prologue[1]

Most Christian and most exalted and powerful Princes, my Queen and King of the Spain and the islands of the sea, our Sovereign Lady and Lord:

In view of the fact that this current year 1492, after Your Royal Highnesses had brought an end to the war of the moors, who reigned over Europe entire, and to the war in the great city of Granada, where on the second of January of this current year I saw Your Highnesses' royal banners raised by force of arms atop the towers of the Alhambra, the fortress of the aforementioned city, where I also saw the king of the moors go out to the gates of the city and kiss Your Highnesses' hands and those of the Prince, my Lord;

Since later in that same month—because of information I had given Your Royal Highnesses about the lands of India, about the many times a sovereign known as the Great Khan (which in our parlance means King of Kings), as well as his predecessors, had sent to Rome for learned men that could instruct him in our great faith, men which the Holy Father had never sent, resulting in so many peoples becoming lost in idolatries and creeds of perdition—Your Royal Highnesses, being princely Christian Catholics devoted to the furtherance of the holy Christian faith, as well as enemies of the sect of Mohammed and all forms of heresy and idolatry, determined to send me, Christopher Columbus, to the aforesaid regions of the Indies, to see the aforesaid princes and peoples and lands, determine their nature and disposition, and establish the ways they could be converted to our holy faith;

(...) since you also ordered me not to go to the East by land, as is customary, save by way of the Western route which in good faith and to this day we remain uncertain anyone has ever traveled; (...) and since, having cast out all the Jews from your every kingdom and territory, Your Royal Highnesses ordered I sail in the same month of January with a sufficient armada to the aforesaid regions of the Indies, and to this end did great favors by me, ennobling me thenceforth with the title of Don, granting me the ranks of Major Admiral of the Ocean Sea and perpetual Viceroy and Governor of all the lands and islands that I discovered and won, as well as those thenceforth discovered and won in the aforementioned Ocean, decreeing also that my oldest son should succeed me in all these, and so on from generation to generation for all eternity, I left the city of Granada on Saturday the twelfth day of May of the same year 1492, and came to the town of Palos, a seaport.

There, half an hour before sunrise on Friday, the third of August of the aforementioned year, I gathered and equipped three ships well suited for such an enterprise. Amply stocked with numerous provisions and crewed with many seafarers, I set sail from the aforementioned port toward Your Royal Highnesses' Canary Islands, located in the aforementioned Ocean Sea, so that I could set course from there and sail until I reached the Indies, to deliver your Royal Highnesses' embassy to the Princes therein, and so carry out my orders.

To such an end, I have decided to set down in writing all that I did and saw, as well as all that transpired each day during this voyage, as will be seen in due course. Furthermore, my Lord and Lady, aside from writing each night what in each day transpired, and each day the distances traveled by night, I also intend to create a new navigational chart, in which I will lay out all the seas and lands encountered in their proper places and truest course. Finally, I intend to create a book, in which I will record everything according to its true semblance, its latitude from the Equator, and its longitude from the West. Above all, I must now forsake all sleep, and work to concentrate entirely on our navigation, for such is my duty and it will surely be no small task.

Friday, August 3rd
We left from the bar of Saltés at eight pm on Friday August 3rd, 1492. We sailed South with strong winds for sixty miles, which is equal to fifteen leagues, until the sunset. We then sailed southwest and south-southwest, which was the route to the Canary Islands.
(...)

Thursday, August 9th

It was Thursday before the Admiral could make Gomera Island, while he ordered Martín Alonso to stay on the coast of Grand Canary Island as he could not sail his ship. The Admiral then turned back to Canary Island and, along with Martín Alonso and others, repaired the Pinta with many pains and labors. Eventually they reached the Gomera and saw a great fire burning on the mountain of the Island of Tenerife, which is quite large. They outfitted the caravel Pinta with square sails because she was rigged with lateen sails and started to return to Gomera Island on Sunday, the second of September, having already repaired the ship.

According to the Admiral, many honorable Spanish men from the neighboring Island of Hierro—men who were on Gomera Island with Doña Inés Peraza, mother of Guillén Peraza, who later became the first Count of Gomera—swore that every year they would see land to the West of the Canary Islands, in the direction of the setting sun. Others from Gomera Island affirmed the very same thing under oath, and the Admiral remembered that while he was in Portugal, in the year 1484, a man from Madera Island came to request a caravel so as to travel to this land, which he had seen and swore he saw each year, always in the same way as the other men described. He also remembered how the same was said on the Island of Azores, where everyone described these sighted lands as being in the same direction, and having the same aspect and size.

Having brought aboard the water, firewood, meat and whatever else could be acquired by the men the Admiral had left at Gomera when he went to Canary Island to repair the Pinta, he finally set sail from Gomera with his three caravels on Thursday, the sixth of September.

Friday, October 5th

He kept his course. They traveled around eleven miles an hour, and must have traveled fifty-seven leagues in the course of a single day and night, as the winds picked up a bit at night, though he told his people they had traveled forty-five. The sea is calm and beautiful—"Thanks be to god", he says—and the air is sweet and temperate; no weeds at all but many shore birds to be seen, and flying fish fly onto the ship in great numbers.

Thursday, October 11th

He sailed West-Southwest. The sea was rough, much rougher than it had been throughout the entire voyage. They saw a few shore birds and a green rush next to the ship. The crew of the Pinta spotted a reed, and a branch, gathered another small twig that appeared to be carved with what looked like iron, another piece of reed, and various other plants that grow on land, along with a small wooden plank. The crew of the Niña also saw other signs of land and a small branch covered over by barnacles. Everyone rejoiced and breathed a sigh of relief at these signs. They traveled twenty-seven leagues until the sunset on this day.

After the sunset, he turned to his original course, due West. They must have traveled twelve miles an hour, and by two hours past midnight had probably made ninety miles, or about twenty-two and a half leagues. Since the Pinta sailed much faster and was ahead of the Admiral's ship, they were the ones to find land and give signal as the Admiral had instructed. It was a sailor by the name of Rodrigo de Triana who first sighted land. The Admiral had already seen a light from the poop deck at ten in the evening, but it was so unclear in the distance that he did not dare say in good faith. Still, he called Pedro Gutiérrez, the chamberlain of the King, and said there looked to be a light in the distance, asking him to look for himself, which he did, and he saw it. He also asked Rodrigo Sánchez of Segovia, whom the King and Queen had placed in the armada as inspector and overseer, but he saw nothing as he was not in a location from which he could see well. After the Admiral pointed it out, it was spotted once or twice, like a small wax candle rising and falling on the horizon, which to many did not seem at all a sign of land. Still, the Admiral was wholly certain he was close to land. As such, when the crew gathered to recite the salve, which all of the sailors said and sang in their own way, the Admiral urged and admonished them to keep a good lookout from the forecastle, and look out for any signs of land, adding that the first to tell him they had sighted land would later be rewarded with a doublet of silk, though he made no mention of the other rewards which the King and Queen had promised, such as the payment of ten thousand *maravedís*[2] to whatever man spotted land first.

Land was spotted two hours after midnight, and they must have been but two leagues from it. They shortened all the sails and kept the mainsail, which is the big one with no bonnets, and waited for daylight on Friday morning, when they finally reached a small island of the Lucayos, known as Guanahaní in the language of the Indians. Naked people started to arrive on the beach so the Admiral went ashore in an armed boat along with Martín Alonso Pinzón and Vicente Yáñez, his brother, who was Captain of La Niña. The Admiral brought out the royal banner and the Captains their two flags, which the Admiral had flown on all three ships, bearing the green cross and the letters F and Y with a crown above each letter on each side of the cross. Once on land they saw very many green trees, rivers and all manner of fruits. The Admiral called the two Captains and others who had gone to land, as well as Rodrigo Sánchez Segovia, and asked that they bear witness and faithful testimony before everyone that he would in their presence take, as indeed he did take, possession of said island on behalf of the King and Queen, his sovereigns, making all the necessary protestations, as has been already been set forth in writing, and in greater detail and length, in the testimonies made therein.

Many islanders were starting to gather 'round. The following is the Admiral's official account, recounted in the log of his first voyage and discovery of these islands. "In an effort to win their friendship and make their goodwill, and seeing that they were people best won and converted to our Holy Faith by tenderness instead of force, I gave some of them red caps, a few glass beads made for wearing on their necks, and other things of little value. This gave them such delight and made them so very much our friends that it was truly a marvel to observe. Later, these same people would swim up to the ship's boats, where we were, bringing us parrots, spools of cotton thread, darts and spears, and many other things to trade for other things we gave them, such as tiny beads of glass and small bells. In all, they took everything that was given them and gave amply of what they had in good faith. And yet, it seemed to me they were a very poor people with little to their name, walking around, as they did, naked as they came in this world—even the women, though I did not see more than a single beautiful one. Everyone I saw were young, not a single one older than thirty years. They were well built, of very beautiful bodies and fine features, their hair thick, and short, almost like horsetails; and they wear their hair just above the eyebrows, save for some long locks that fall behind their head and which they never cut. Although they are the color of Canary islanders, neither black nor white, some paint themselves black, and others white, red, and whatever other colors they make from what they find; some paint their faces and bodies, while others only the eyes or the nose. They do not carry weapons and have no knowledge of them for when I showed them our swords they would take them by the blade and cut themselves out of their own ignorance. They have no iron at all: their spears and darts are made of reeds without a metal tip, though some had fish-teeth and other such manner of things hanging from the very end. At a glance they are all well-made, of fine semblance, stature and size. Seeing some had scars and old wounds on their skin, I asked them what they were, and they showed me how people from nearby islands would often come, wanting to conquer them, and how they would defend themselves. I thought then and still think today that they come here from the mainland to enslave them. They must good servants make, as they seem smart and quick to repeat everything that is said to them; and I believe they would be easily converted to Christianity, as it seemed they had no creed of their own. In service to the Lord, I will take six of them with me, to see Your Royal Highnesses, so they can learn to speak. I have not seen a single animal of any sort on this island, save for parrots." This is all in the Admiral's own words.

Saturday, October 13th

"Soon after dawn, many of these men and women came to the beach. All were young, and very beautiful people of good stature, as I have mentioned before. Their hair is not curly, but straight and coarse like a horse's mane, their heads larger and their foreheads broader than any other race I have hitherto seen around these parts. Their eyes were very beautiful and not at all small, and not a single one of them was black, but the color of Canary islanders, which is to be expected since we are in a latitudinal line east-west of the Canary Island of Hierro. They are very well built: side-by-side their legs are very straight, and show no potbelly. They came to the ship in long boats made in one piece from tree-trunks and marvelously carved according to local customs. Some of these boats were quite large, with forty or forty-five men inside, while others were much smaller, with some only carrying a single man. They rowed with a baker's peel and moved marvelously across the water. If the boats somehow overturn, they all jump in and flip them over, baling them with empty pumpkin gourds they bring along. They brought us threaded cotton, parrots, darts, spears and so many other little things that it would be tedious to recount, and gave it all in exchange for whatsoever was given them. I was keen to know and tried to learn if there was any gold around, and I saw that some of them wore a little piece of it hanging from a hole in their nose. By way of signing and motions I was able to ascertain that to the South, or around the South side of the Island, lives a king who has gold by the cupfuls. I tried to get them to go there, but soon realized that they had no interest in going. I decided to wait until tomorrow afternoon and then set course to the Southwest to search for gold and precious jewels, since many of them pointed out that there were more islands to the South, Southwest and Northwest, the Northwestern ones being the ones that invaded them the most.

This island is quite large and flat, with very green trees, many a river, and a very big lake in the middle. There is not a mountain in sight. It is all so very green that it is truly a pleasure to behold, and these people so very gentle and tame. They desire our things, and fearing nothing will be given them when they have nothing to exchange, they take whatever things they can, even pieces of broken glassware and porcelain cups, and start swimming away. I even saw one of them exchange sixteen spools of cotton for three Portuguese *ceotisl* [Portuguese coins], which is equal to a *blanca* [penny or farthing] in Spain, when there must have been more than twenty-five pounds of threaded cotton among those spools. If there were plenty of this to be had, I would advise against such exchanges, forbid anybody from taking any of it for themselves, and save it all for Your Highnesses instead. It must surely grow on this island, but with such little time I could not confirm and say so in good faith; and the gold hanging from their nose can surely be found here too, but for the sake of time I want to go and see if I can find the island of Cipango. Now that the sun has set and night has fallen they have all gone back to land in their canoes."

(…)

Tuesday, October 23rd

"I'd like to set sail for the island of Cuba today, which I think must be Cipango from what these people have pointed out about the island's great size and its many riches. I will no longer delay here nor 'round these parts so that I may go swiftly to speak with this king or sovereign, as I had planned. Since I see there is no gold mine here, and sailing beyond these islands requires several strong winds that do not blow now as the men would like them to, I say the best way to avoid delays is to keep moving and stay our course until we reach more fruitful lands.

On the other hand, it is my understanding that this island is very rich in spices, though I have no knowledge of them. This causes me great grief for I see a thousand kinds of trees, each green and bearing their own distinctive fruit now, as in Spain in the month of June or May; and many thousands of herbs, all flowering now. Of all these we could identify but this aloe, which I arranged be brought aboard in large quantities today, to take back to your Royal Highnesses.

I have not, nor do I plan to, set sail for Cuba as there is no wind at all, just a dead calm, and it rains heavily. It rained yesterday too but it was not at all cold; to the contrary, it is hot during the day, while at night it is cold, like Andalucía in May."

[Expedition to Cuba]
December 25th, Christmas Day
They had been sailing since yesterday with very little wind, traveling from the sea of St. Tomé to Punta Santa and remaining about a league from the latter until after the first quarter—which must have been around eleven at night—so he decided to lay down to sleep, as he had not been able to do so in two whole days and a night. Since it was calm, the sailor who was in charge of the ship decided to also rest, leaving a young cabin boy in charge, something the Admiral had forbidden throughout the trip; that is, come rain or shine, no cabin boys should ever be left in charge of the ship. For the first and only time this entire voyage, the Admiral felt safe enough from rocks and embankments to

rest because when he sent his armed boats to land, to meet with the sovereign there, they had passed about three and a half leagues to the East of the aforementioned Punta Santa, and from there, having all three leagues of coast and shoals from Punta Santa to the East in sight, determined the route they could take to pass.

It was our Lord's will that soon after midnight all the men had gone to sleep, as they had seen the Admiral lay down to rest, and there was nothing but total calm, the sea as placid as water in a bowl. A young boy was left in charge of the rudder, and the running currents ran the ship aground, on to one of those embankments. It was nighttime, but the sea could be heard and seen crashing on the banks from a long league away. The ship went aground so softly that it could hardly be perceived. Since the young man felt the rudder shake and heard the crashes first, he shouted out, at which the Admiral came out, acting so swiftly that nobody had even realized they had run aground on the embankment.

Then the Ship Master, whose watch it was, came on deck, and the Admiral ordered him and the others to throw the small boat they were carrying and an anchor over the stern. The Ship Master jumped boarded the lifeboat along with several others. The Admiral thought they were obeying his orders, but they wanted only to escape to the caravel, which was half a league upwind. The caravel, acting judiciously and with good reason, would not allow them to board, so they returned to the lead ship; but the caravel's boat reached them first.

When the admiral saw that his own crewmen were fleeing in such a way, when he noticed the tide was receding and the ship was leaning broadside into the sea, he saw no other course: he ordered the mast be cut away and the ship lightened of as much of its load as could be carried out so they could try to get her out of the embankment. But nothing more could be done, as the water continued to recede. She fell broadside into the sea, though most of the water had already receded by then, and though her joints burst open, the ship remained in one piece.

The Admiral went to the caravel to bring the ship's crew back to safety aboard the caravel, but since there was a light breeze blowing from shore now, it was early in the night, and it was uncertain how far the embankments extended, he stationed her and waited for dawn. Then, at daybreak, he went back to the lead ship through the reef of the embankment. First, he sent a boat to shore commanded by Diego de Arana of Córdoba, bailiff of the fleet, and Pedro Gutiérrez, chamberlain of the Royal House, to inform the sovereign who on Saturday had invited us to bring our ships to his harbor and whose town was about a league and a half from the embankment. They say he wept the moment he heard the news, and sent all his people in a great number of large canoes, to unload the ship. They did so, certainly, and everything was unloaded from the decks in a very short span of time, such was the attentiveness and diligence shown by this sovereign. Even he himself, along with his brothers and relatives, actively assisted, and not only in unloading the ships but in caring for and protecting whatever was brought to land so that all might be kept safe and sound. Now and then, he sent one of his companions weeping to the Admiral, trying to console him and saying he must feel neither grief nor upset, for he would give of everything he had. The Admiral assured the Sovereigns that in no part of Castile would such good care of things have been taken that not even a single needle was missing. He ordered all the property be placed by some houses which said sovereign had placed at his disposal, and ordered some armed men to stand guard around them all night, while some things he wanted emptied were made available. "The king and all his people wept; and they are—says the Admiral—so kind and loving a people, so without avarice, and so willing and able to do anything, that I assure your Royal Highnesses that there are no better people or lands in the whole world. They love their neighbors as themselves, and they are soft and gentle in their speaking, and always smile, like nobody else in the world. Though both the men and women go as naked as they came into the world, Your Royal Highnesses will find that they are very good in their internal dealings; that the king is a man of such remarkable presence, and so sensible and sober in his manner, that it is a delight to behold; and will marvel at their memory, and the way they want to see everything, asking what it is and what it is used for". All this the Admiral set down in these words.

(…)

Monday, December 31st

Today the Admiral saw that water and firewood were brought on board, preparing for the voyage back to Spain, so as to give the Monarchs swift notice that they should send ships to discover whatever remains to be discovered, as "the enterprise seemed so astonishingly great and important that it is truly a Marvel," said the Admiral. Although he says he did not wish to return until he had seen all the land to the east, explored the entirety of the coast and found the best route to return to Castile so they could bring cattle and other things with them, he had but a single vessel left so it did not seem prudent to continue risking the dangers inherent to a voyage of discovery, and complained that all this trials and tribulations had resulted from his loss of the caravel Pinta.

Questions for discussion

1. Who would have wanted to read Bartolomé de las Casas' writings about sailing to the New World in the sixteenth century?

2. After visiting on several occasions and living in the New World, de las Casas denounced the mistreatment of Indians and their use as slaves. However, he did not raise the same concerns about black slaves. Discuss the reasons and consequences of this position, taking into consideration the triangular trading system in place between the Americas, Africa and Europe.

3. After taking Granada in 1492, the Catholic Monarchs also directed campaigns in North Africa. What were the differences between colonization campaigns in the New World and the campaigns in North Africa?

4. Travel between the Americas and Seville took months in the sixteenth century. Consider the routes and the difficulties of transatlantic travel in the sixteenth century.

DOCUMENT 2[3]
EMILIO CASTELAR RIPOLL, *DISCURSO PRONUNCIADO EN CONTRA DE LA ESCLAVITUD* (SPEECH AGAINST SLAVERY, 1870)[4]

Emilio Castelar y Ripoll (1832–99) was a Spanish politician known for his attacks on the royal privileges throughout the mid-nineteenth century and his negative views of Spain's imperial tradition. After 1868, Spain was fighting to maintain dominion over Cuba, while in Spain the different political factions were searching for a political formula that would end the violent military practice of *pronunciamientos* (coup d'état). The political involvement of the army represented a threat to the liberal state, while it remained also the only resort to fight against the ultra-conservative attacks throughout the nineteenth century in what is known as the Carlist wars.[5]

As a Professor of History and Philosophy, and as a journalist, Castelar became even more critical and outspoken about Spain's role in the colonies after the revolutionary events of 1868 that ended the reign of Isabel II and led to the brief reign of Italian Amadeo de Savoy and after his abdication in 1970 followed the proclamation of the First Republic. The republic lasted only an ephemeral and convulsive year.

To complicate matters further, the Cuban independence movement remained a most sensitive matter for politicians on both the left and the right of the Peninsula. Castelar's position, however, did not favor Cuban independence, but as the following excerpt shows, he advocated for a renovated and modernized relation with Spain's Atlantic possessions. He had been president of Spain's First Republic in 1873, which ended soon after General Arsenio Martínez-Campos' military coup allowed the Bourbon Restoration. After 1874, Cánovas del Castillo established the *turno politico* in government by which liberals and conservatives agreed to peacefully and alternatively be in office, through the control and manipulation of the electoral process.

EMILIO CASTELAR, SPEECH AGAINST SLAVERY, 1870

Congressmen: to understand the depth of my speech, you need to read the text of my amendment. It is fully deduced from all articles of the law and their meaning that the government wants abolition, but gradual abolition, and we call for abolition as well, but immediate abolition. The other evening, I mentioned that the abolition of slavery is discussed now from a different standpoint. In the past, abolition had enemies. Today, all of us absolutely want abolition;

(. . .) I do not give the government more time than necessary, considering the distance that separates us from the Antilles, to protect important civil rights, the civil rights of 400,000 men. (. . .)

Gentlemen, those who want to provide nations with great influence and great honor, need to inculcate a great idea. Nations grow, expand, shine, think and work with glory when they serve a progressive idea. Through ideas, the diverse greatness of races can be explained. The Arabian race, which today is just a corpse, spread to remote parts of Asia, and to the seas of Sicily, when it introduced monotheism to backward and polytheist races.

The great Latin race shone in the world when the principle of political or spiritual unity attracted all consciences. But from the moment that this principle broke, the scepter of the world passed to rationalist Germany, constitutional England, revolutionary France, and to Puritan and Republican America. Give people a big idea, and you give them power and wealth.

Well; what I come to ask today is that the Spanish nation rise up to the social principles, since, by serving civilization, serving progress, it will find strength, wealth, wellness, and it will influence humanity, just as it did in the past. The Spanish nation surprised the world at the beginning of the September revolution. (. . .)

There are three nations that seem to be dead, and these three nations were exceptionally great: the Greek nation, which led the world in philosophy and art; the Roman nation, which led the world in law and politics; the Spanish nation, which led the world in the fields of nature and creation. Spain held out its hands over the lonely Ocean and, in discovering America, doubled the world and widened space.

But, what has become of these three great nations? Today, Greece is a mount of ruins topped by crowns of nettles. Rome, instead of having its former political and civil rights, feels the absence of all civil and political life; poor, crippled, mute, stiff, over the ruin of its altars and cloisters.

As for us, as for the youngest and most fortunate of the three nations, with such a manly race that seems incapable of any decay; with colonies in all regions of the earth; with so recent and so glorious sacrifices, such as the sacrifice of the War for Independence; with institutions that are free, although corrupt; with our name, that name which was the talisman of Popes and Kings; that name whose echo shook the nations from the Far East to the end of the horizon.

Suddenly in September this nation rises; it expulses its old dynasty; breaks the yoke of religious intolerance, and announces to the world that it is ready to enter a democratic and law-abiding life. The oppressors paled; the oppressed waited. Yes; that nation had a great territory and population, performed radical social reforms, such as the abolition of slavery; that past nation can do without a historical dynasty, an official church, or a large army; that nation can exercise freedom of the press without scandal, the freedom of gathering without restraints, universal suffrage without Caesarism; that nation will be in Europe what the United States are in America: the ideal and the hope of all nations.

We could be, we should be that nation; the universal conscience will ask for accountability and the reasons why we have not become it. History will find that cause in the weakness that led us to take hold of dead ideas.

We are not only a European power; we have been, and always will be, an American power. There is immense significance in historical facts. The extraordinary ones are immanent. (. . .) The American policy is full of mistakes. Ah! the discovery of America. Imagine that this land disappears, and that only the peaks of the Andes are seen in the middle of the Atlantic; there on that peak the Spanish flag shall remain, and engraved as if by fire in those continents, no longer irretrievably lost material domain, but a great moral influence. What should we do to achieve this, gentlemen? We must give a great example to America. The Latin race needs us; it needs Spain to counter the momentum of the Saxon race: we need America to expand our spirit, to have large space to develop our pursuit, great objectives which correspond to our idea.

If America comes to one day form the confederation of confederations advised by Simón Bolívar, it will need to invoke its origin, which is the foundation of its unity, its language, its blood, its history, and in all these key elements of life, America will find the name of Spain. And, gentlemen, let us say frankly, it will not call upon the name if it does not shine with twinkling great ideas in the horizons of the world. What will free, independent, republican, and democratic America plead from us when it sees that there are Spanish territories where there is white and black slavery, colonial rule and the servile regime, which human conscience indignantly rejects?

Gentlemen, at the time of the September Revolution (and I do not want to reprimand anyone, because I start to recognize the patriotic motivation and feelings of convolution of September), we could have completely changed the way America views Spain by changing Spain's view of America. The reforms should have come as fast as light. The Providence had served us well. After ineffectual attempts and incomprehensible resistance, we reached the end of the cord, which was a kind of spine put on the planet, a new blood that infused all regions of the earth with the same feelings and the same ideas. The Leviathan had thrown to the bottom of the sea a country that had been chained up for so long. The greatest miracle of our industry was done. (. . .)

Cuba has been subject to military despotism; our kings, who were constitutional here, were absolute there; (. . .) And when the new Spanish world was starting, the domains of absolutism began (. . .) and the white decided the fate of slaves. Ah! The slaves, free without them and without us; free in spite of them and despite us; free against them and against us; free because they are children of God, sovereign in nature, members of humanity; and any power that ignores those primordial rights, no matter the law or pretext invoked, commits the murder of consciences, the murder of souls, a crime punished by divine wrath and that is purged with an eternal infamy in the eternal hell of history. [Applause].

I know the cause of our slow reforms in the West Indies. I know it, and will say it without offense to anyone, because I attribute this sluggishness to the ideas of the September Revolution that prevailed within the government. Was that just a single revolution? No; in the September Revolution there have been two movements: one akin to the French movement of 1830, and another akin to the French movement of 1848. There was, therefore, no unity of ideas, or conformity with the purposes of its core elements. The insolence of the Old Regime was so great that everyone, conservatives as well as radicals, decided to address it. So far there was unity regarding negations. But the difference was in the statements.

The Conservative Party wanted the renewal of the monarchy, the radical party wanted the nation's health; the Conservative Party wanted the progressive education of democracies, the radical party wanted the sudden advent of democracies; the Conservative Party wanted written law, the radical party wanted eternal law. (...) Ah, gentlemen! Property implies ownership. Prove to me that the black man is an object; prove to me that he is like your plow (...) that he has no personality, no soul, no conscience. (...)

I do not know sadder times in history than those of the gradual abolition of slavery. Emancipation has been attempted in a thousand places, and nowhere has it been achieved. (...)

No, there is no compromise: such evils cannot be tolerated; such serious evils flare up with useless palliatives, and need to be eradicated. That supreme remedy is the amendment that I have had the honor of introducing; this remedy is immediate abolition. (...)

Gentlemen, how many people from Cuba are free and how many are slaves? Per our census, there are 300,000 slaves and 700,000 freemen. How many people are slaves and how many are free in Puerto Rico? Per our census, 40,000 slaves and 350,000 freemen. What do you fear? A black insurrection? Well, you can rule out women, children, disabled individuals and domestic slaves, who tend to be peaceful in our islands of Cuba and Puerto Rico. How many fearsome slaves are we left with, after all, in Puerto Rico? We are left with 10,000, the 10,000 who cultivate the fields. And how many white men, or at least how many freemen are working alongside slaves? There are, gentlemen, 70,000 freemen, who have taken and paid their laborer's permit. What misgivings might you have when in Cuba free labor is at least equal to slave labor, and in Puerto Rico free labor far exceeds slave labor?

In addition, statistics have shown that slavery has disappeared in Puerto Rico, and wealth has increased. How much was the trade of the island of Puerto Rico in 1834? It was seven million *piastres*? And how much was the trade in Puerto Rico in 1860? It was thirteen million *piastres*.[6] (...) And the moral situation of Cuba and Puerto Rico is truly horrible!

Questions for discussion

1. Who is Emilio Castelar trying to persuade with his speech on slavery?
2. What is Emilio Castelar implying by providing population numbers in his speech? Why is he trying to appease fears of a rebellion?
3. The author of the speech is warning the parliament about the United States interfering in the Caribbean. What is his major point in this sense? How does he think that the United States is winning over in Cuba?
4. Abolition had just passed in the United States after the end of the American Civil War 1865. When did it happen elsewhere in the Americas? What were Spain's and other European powers role in the continents' abolition of slavery?

DOCUMENT 3[7]
MANIFESTO OF THE REVOLUTIONARY *JUNTA* OF THE ISLAND OF CUBA, ADDRESSED TO ITS COUNTRYMEN AND TO ALL NATIONS, 1898[8]

The independence of Cuba in 1898 came after a three-decade series of conflicts that began with a long war called the Guerra Grande (1868–78), then a one-year war between 1879 and 1880 called Guerra Chiquita (Little War), and the final Spanish American War in 1898. After all countries in Latin America had declared their independence in the early 1800s, Cuba and Puerto Rico remained colonies of Spain for one more century. Control over both islands' trade was among Spain's keenest interests, though by the end of the nineteenth century the relations between Cuba and Puerto Rico and the United States, and the North American economic involvement in the Caribbean had surpassed Spain and even other European nations control in the region. In February of 1895, another armed conflict between Spain's forces and Cuban soldiers began. This time, Cubans were heavily assisted by the United States. José Martí, a known Cuban independentist had been organizing the uprising from the United States since the end of the Guerra Grande in 1878. Twenty years later, the United States defeated the Spanish military forces, and both Puerto Rico and Cuba achieved their independence, but also a four-year US occupation of the islands. The first president of Cuba was José Miguel Gómez, who took office in 1902.

MANIFESTO OF THE REVOLUTIONARY *JUNTA* OF THE ISLAND OF CUBA, ADDRESSED TO ITS COUNTRYMEN AND TO ALL NATIONS

Through our armed rise against the oppression of the tyrannical Spanish government, following the custom established in all civilized countries, we declare to the world the causes that have forced us to take this step—to demand greater goods, which always produces inevitable turmoil—and the principles we want to build on the ruins of the present for future happiness.

Nobody ignores that Spain governs the island of Cuba with an iron-bloodied arm. Spain does not allow Cuba to secure their properties, it imposes taxes and contributions at will, and it deprives the island of all political, civil and religious liberty. As a consequence, their unfortunate children are expelled from their land to remote climates or executed without due process by military commissions established while in peace, while civilian power wanes. The right of assembly is denied, unless supervised by a military leader.

Cuba cannot request a remedy for its ills without being treated as a rebel, and has no other choice but to obey in silence.

The endless plague of voracious employees from Spain is overwhelming; it devours the product of our goods and our work. Under the despotic authority that the Spanish government places in their hands, they deprive our best countrymen of the public employment. A good government must possess the art of knowing where the destiny of a nation is headed. Supported by the restrictive education system it adopts, Spain wants us to be so ignorant that we have no knowledge of our sacred rights, and that if we do have knowledge of them, we cannot complain in any way if they are not respected.

This island is loved and appreciated by all nations that surround it. Since it has no enemies it has no need for an army or a permanent navy that require an enormous expense that would deplete its public and private sources of wealth. Yet, Spain imposes an army on our territory that serves the sole purpose of bending the neck to the iron yoke that degrades us.

Our valuable products are viewed with animosity by foreign countries due to Spain's customs system that halts commerce. Although Spain trades advantageously with other nations, here poor producers do not even make enough to cover their expenses. So, without the fertility of our land, we will perish in poverty.

In sum, the island of Cuba cannot prosper, because white immigration, the only immigration that suits us presently, is far from our shores due to the innumerable obstacles with which it is entangled and the prevention and animosity that it is targeted with.

Thus, Cubans cannot speak, cannot write, they cannot even think or receive with hospitality the guests sent to them by their brethren from other lands. Countless times Spain has offered to respect their rights, but so far it has not kept its promise; it has only left a vestige of representation, to conceal the single property tax enforced, and so large that it ruins our properties, already burdened by the other taxes.

Seeing ourselves on the verge of losing our assets, our lives and even our honor, we should risk them to re-conquer our rights as men; since we cannot achieve this with the power of the word in debate, we will use the power of arms in the battlefields.

When a nation reaches the degree of degradation and misery in which we find ourselves, no one can condemn it for taking up arms to get out of a state so full of infamy. The example of the greatest nations authorizes this last resort. The island of Cuba cannot be deprived of the rights enjoyed by other nations, and it cannot accept what is being told about the country: that it knows nothing but suffering. It is up to the other civilized nations to use their influence to release an innocent, enlightened, sensitive and generous nation from the clutches of an oppressive barbarian. We appeal to them and to the God of our conscience, with a hand over our heart. We are not misguided by grudges, we are not coaxed by ambitions, we just want to be free and equal, as the Creator made all men.

We consider these two venerable principles sacred: We believe that all men are equal, we love tolerance, order, and justice in all matters. We respect the lives and property of all peaceful citizens, even if they are Spaniards residing in this territory. We admire the universal suffrage that ensures the sovereignty of the nation. We wish for gradual emancipation with compensation of slavery, and for free trade with friendly nations that reciprocate, for national representation that passes laws and taxes, and, in general, we demand religious observance of the inalienable rights of man, making us an independent nation. All these will fulfill the greatness of our future destiny, and because we are sure that under the scepter of Spain we would never enjoy openly exercising our rights.

In view of our moderation, our poverty, and the reason that is within us, does a noble heart exist that does not beat with the same desire to obtain the sacrosanct goal that we are fighting for? What civilized nation will not condemn Spain's behavior, which has shed the blood of its bravest children in order to trample on the two rights? No, Cuba can no longer belong to a nation that, like Cain, kills its brothers and, like Saturn, devours its children. Cuba aspires to be a great and civilized nation, to give a friendly hand and a fraternal heart to all other nations, and if Spain agrees to leave it free and peaceful, it will stand by its side like a loving daughter of a good mother. But if it persists in its system of domination and extermination, it will sever all of our necks, and the necks of those who come after us before turning Cuba into a vile herd of slaves.

Therefore, we have agreed unanimously to name a single leader to direct operations with full power, and under his responsibility, especially authorized to appoint a second and other subordinates he may need in all branches of administration, during the state of war, which will most likely follow after the proclamation of the independence of Cuba. We have also appointed a five-member governmental committee to help the Commander in Chief in political, civil and other branches that are needed in the government of any well-regulated country. We also decree that from this moment on, all duties, taxes, contributions and other levies that have so far been claimed by the government of Spain are abolished, whatever the shape and the pretext that has been used to implement them. We propose a patriotic donation of five percent of present income to cover the expenses of the war, as is calculated this quarter. In case this was insufficient, the *juntas* will decide whether the tax should be raised, or a loan be requested.

We declare that all services rendered to the nation shall be duly paid. That in business, and in general, these laws, interpreted in the liberal sense, shall be observed until otherwise decided. And lastly, we declare that all arrangements are purely transitory, until the nation is free from its enemies, when it will be more widely represented and constituted in the manner and form it deems most successful.

Questions for discussion

1. What are the different aspects that the manifesto is pointing about Spaniards and Spain's control over Cuba? Who is the audience of this text?

2. There is hardly any mention of the United States in the text. After 1898, however, the US controlled different aspects of the island's political and economic life, and territory, such as the Guantanamo base. What were the reasons for Cubans to allow such influence?

3. The excerpt that you read refers to Cuba being isolated from civilization and progress. What are the *independentistas* implying?

4. Slavery in Cuba was abolished before the first armed conflict against Spain's control, in 1868. There were other reforms that Cubans achieved under Spain's rule during the nineteenth century, but why did Cubans continue to assure that Spain governed with an iron and bloody arm?

DOCUMENT 4[9]
LAW OF PATERNAL DISSENT IN CUBA AND PUERTO RICO, 1882[10]

The Paternal Dissent Law of 1882 was one of the final legislation introduced in the colonies by Madrid and it came at a crucial time in the process of nation-building in Europe and Latin America. The modern state was delineating its reach in different aspects of daily life, and one of them was the family. The Paternal Dissent Law changed some of the restrictions in place with regard to the father's authority within the family. It redefined what "*patria potestad*" meant, which was a term based in Roman law. It referred to the father's control over his underage heirs, their decisions about marriage, and their property. Spain's definition of "*patria potestad*" had changed in 1862, becoming slightly more open, and later in the 1880s the Spanish government implemented the Civil Code of 1889, another piece of legislation that defined the state's objectives to control family and civil life. Although the Paternal Dissent Law was modified after Cuba and Puerto Rico gained independence, other legislation to control family, civic, and commercial life was implemented over the course of the twentieth century. In Spain, the Civil Code of 1889 that prohibited divorce and regulated adultery, and restricted women's access to property within marriage, was not modified until the second half of the twentieth century with the reform of 1958 under the dictatorship of Francisco Franco.

LAW OF PATERNAL DISSENT IN CUBA AND PUERTO RICO 1882

Overseas Ministry
Exposition

Sir: The profound social and political transformation carried out in the West Indies through the abolition of slavery and the undoubted progress of ideas and customs in those provinces imperiously demand that legislation regulating the most momentous events of life also be transformed, beginning on those relating the establishment and organization of the family.

In the Peninsula, important changes were introduced regarding the Parental Dissent Act of June 20, 1862, whose application overseas has been under discussion since then. Undoubtedly, the requirements of the old decrees of late last century and beginnings of this present century, regarding what those laws called "irrational dissent from parents and known nobility or notorious blood cleansing," could not last and they cannot be upheld today.

(...)

Royal Decree
The son of a family who has not turned twenty years old and the daughter of a family who has not turned seventeen need parental consent to marry.

In those countries, such as the island of Cuba and Puerto Rico, where the application of civil marriage, or the marriage regulated only by civil law and by temporary authority, has not existed before, the union [marriage] which only has the direct and principal purpose of procreation and a religious and sacramental character, which leaves the ecclesiastical authority with the task of setting its constitutive and essential rules. The question arises whether the provision of Article 1 of this law fits within the jurisdiction of the civil legislator. (...) But at the same time, marriage is a legal institution that can not remain indifferent to human rights. It is a real contract from which consequences and effects on the civil order of society arise, therefore it is such civil order that is naturally called to determine and regulate marriage. (...)

On March 23, 1776, King Charles III issued a decree, enforcing the ancient laws of Castile regarding parental consent for marriages of the sons and daughters under the age of twenty-five, a consent which was declared necessary (...)

On April 10, 1803, King Charles IV issued another decree, commanding that neither sons under twenty-five years of age, nor daughters under twenty-three, belonging to any class, could marry without their fathers' permission. (...)

Family children are, legally, children subject to parental authority.

By parental authority it is understood the right or set of rights and the duty or set of duties—based in nature and confirmed by positive law, imitating nature—granted to parents to enable them to exercise authority and protection over their legitimate, legitimated, claimed and adopted children, regarding the latter, in the cases established by this law.

Under the old law of Castile, currently enforced in the Antilles, only parents enjoy parental authority. (...) Parental authority concludes—according to this ancient and Castilian law, still subsisting in Cuba and Puerto Rico—by death of the child or parent and by loss of nationality—since foreigners are subject to the Statute or Law of their new homeland—by religious profession of the father or the son, that creates links and duties of spiritual order, before which parental authority ceases. (...) Cuba and Puerto Rico will not be ruled by the new provisions under which the authority of the mother also holds over legitimate non emancipated children, in the absence of the father. And the emancipation law is implemented for the legitimate son when he comes of age. (...)

If it is true that women are weaker, so is the kind of education they receive, their predisposition to receive more submissively the father's and, above all, the mother's advice, and their inclination to worship that virtue called modesty.
(...)

Article 2
In the case of the preceding article, if the father is absent or is prevented from giving consent, the same right corresponds to the mother and successively in similar circumstances, to the paternal and maternal grandparent.
(...)

Article 3
In the absence of the mother and maternal and paternal grandfather, the authority to give consent for marriage corresponds to the testamentary guardian and the first instance trial judge, successively. The guardian will be considered incapable of giving consent when the future marriage involves one of their relatives within the fourth civil degree. Both the guardian and the judge shall proceed in conjunction with the next of kin and shall cease to obtain their consent, if those wishing to marry, regardless of their sex, have reached the age of seventeen. Regarding the negroes subject to patronage, while they are in this condition, and in the absence of a father, mother or paternal and maternal grandparents, consent shall be given by their master.

Article 4.
The board of relatives mentioned in the preceding article shall consist of:
   First, the ascendants of the minor.
   Second, his or her older brothers of legal age and husbands of the sisters in the same condition, if they were alive. In the absence of ascendants, brothers and husbands of sisters, or when these are less than three, the board will be reach the number of four members with close relatives, men of legal age, chosen equally between the two lines, beginning with the father. In cases of equal degree of kinship, older relatives will be preferred. The guardian, even if he is a relative, will not be counted in the number of those who shall form the board.

Article 5.
Attendance at the meeting of relatives will be mandatory for those residing in the orphan's home, or in another town that is no more than six leagues away from the point where the meeting is to be held; the absence, when there is no legitimate cause, shall be punished with a fine not exceeding 50 pesetas. Relatives residing outside of that radius, but within Cuba and Puerto Rico, will also be cited, although distance may serve them as a fair excuse. (. . .)

Article 6
In the absence of relatives, the board shall be formed with honorable neighbors chosen, if possible, among those who had been friends of the child's parents.

Article 7
The meeting will take place within a short period of time, which shall be scheduled in proportion to the distances, and those called shall appear personally or through a special representative, which may not represent more than one person. (. . .)

Article 12
Illegitimate children do not need the consent of the grandparents nor the intervention of relatives to marry when the guardian or the judge are called to give permission.

Article 13

The other illegitimate children will only be obliged to implore the consent of the mother. In the absence of the mother, the brother in law, if there was one; and finally the first instance judge. The relatives will not be summoned under any circumstances. The heads of the Foundling Houses will be considered for the purposes of this law as guardians of the illegitimate children accepted and educated in such institutions.

Article 14.

Persons authorized to give consent do not need to express their reasons to refuse it, and there shall be no appeal whatsoever given against their dissent.

Article 15

Legitimate sons over twenty years old and daughters over seventeen will seek advice regarding marriage from their parents or grandparents, in the order preset in the articles one and two. If the declaration were to not be favorable, they may not marry after three months elapsed from when the advice was first asked. The request of advice shall be established by a statement that shall be delivered to a notary public or ecclesiastical, or before the municipal judge, prior notification and personal appearance before such persons. Children who contravene the provisions of this Article shall incur the penalty marked in Article 611 of the Penal Code, in force in Cuba and Puerto Rico, and the priest who authorizes such a marriage shall incur a minor arrest.

Overseas Minister Fernando de León and Castillo
Gaceta de Madrid, February 8, 1882.

Questions for discussion

1. What was Madrid trying to accomplish by implementing this law during such a declining time of its colonizing history?
2. How does the law define *patria potestad*? How does it stand along with the principles of nineteenth-century liberalism?
3. What are the foreseen outcomes of the restrictions of this law?
4. What are the differences between a religious marriage and a civil marriage?

DOCUMENT 5[11]
GEDEÓN, 1898

The war of 1898, known as "*la guerra de Cuba*" meant a profound blow to Spanish national identity and her international standing in the imperial race at the dawn of the twentieth century. The defeat against the United States of America signaled the end of the Spanish empire, the loss of the remaining overseas colonies: Cuba, Puerto Rico and the Philippines made Spain turn back its attention to the Mediterranean and its possessions in Morocco. During the conflict with the United States, the yellow press on both sides of the Atlantic engaged in a battle of words as volatile as the one fought in the theater of war. The image included here is the cover of a Madrid weekly satirical newspaper called *Gedeón*. This periodical followed the style of its illustrated counterparts like *Punch* in England, or the *New York Morning Journal,* published by newspaperman William Randolph Hearst. Political cartoons had been a long-time tool for aggressive criticism of public figures and policies. In this image the artist portrays the different powers attending the peace treaty talks in Paris in early December 1898 to assign the spoils of the Spanish empire.

Figure 12. Political cartoon cover of *Gedeón*, 1898.

Questions for discussion

1. How does the artist portray the different countries in this image?
2. What famous national symbols are used to identify the United States?
3. Why do you think the picture is a representation of exchange of cargo?
4. Are there any European powers in the picture?

DOCUMENT 6[12]
GUMERSINDO DE AZCÁRATE, SPEECH ON SPAIN'S ECONOMIC AND POLITICAL INTERESTS IN MOROCCO, 1910[13]

Gumersindo de Azcárate (1840–1917) was a Spanish politician and an intellectual. He studied law in Oviedo and Madrid, and was a Professor at the Universidad Central in Madrid. Azcárate was a well-known reformist and progressive figure in Spanish politics, especially after he founded the *Institución Libre de Enseñanza* (Free Institution of Learning) in 1876 along with the Professors Francisco Giner de los Ríos (1839–1915) and Nicolás Salmerón (1838–1908). In 1903 he became the president of the *Instituto de Reformas Sociales* (Social Reforms Institute) where he pushed for the implementation of labor legislation. When Azcárate gave his speech about the Spanish-Morocco relations in 1884 at a meeting of the *Sociedad española de Africanistas y Colonistas*, Spain had secured its dominion of the cities of Ceuta and Melilla in northern Morocco after confronting France's and England's imperial quests. Spain's Protectorate, however, was not granted until 1912, and the area of influence included north Morocco with the cities of Tangier, Tetuan, Ceuta, and Melilla, and the southern part of the country, what became known as the Spanish Sahara. In his speech, Azcárate was not alluding to the military occupation of Morocco, but more to the cultural responsibilities of Spain as a Western nation in its colonies or occupied territories.

GUMERSINDO DE AZCÁRATE'S "SPEECH ON SPAIN'S ECONOMIC AND POLITICAL INTERESTS IN MOROCCO" 1910

Ladies and Gentlemen,

(...) A hunch, rather than a conviction that comes from the head (because I did not have time or opportunity to study the problems involved) brings me to this association: my heart tells me that Spain, which undoubtedly in past was the first colonizing nation, has to continue being so. If not today, it will happen some day, since this colonizing mission is in accordance with its vocation, its skills, and its history.

In this regard, our country's situation is like that of the individual who pursues science by vocation, only deals with it and is only surrounded by books, but he is later forced by the needs of life to pursue other activities (...) And if Spain has to go back to being a colonizing nation, even if not in the same way as in older times, how is it possible to ignore Africa, the Moroccan empire, which is the reason why this meeting is being held? We are all in agreement that Spain has that mission, but it will not be accomplished by means of war, and least of all by seeking it out without need, or forgetting that only in exceptional cases it is lawful to attempt an enterprise that cannot be achieved peacefully. A few years ago, Denmark went through a useless struggle, a fight against Austria and Prussia that they knew it was a lost battle; but Denmark had to defend a piece of its territory. In matters of honor, it is an obligation to fight, even if winning is not expected; fighting is enough to prove oneself. Even when we are not dealing with matters of honor, the individual can be adventurous, because when he allows himself to be guided by a hunch, he is the only one who is put in danger; but as one ascends within social circles, one must think more about the consequences of adventures and hunches, since family, country and humanity cannot be sacrificed the same way one sacrifices oneself. [*Very good, very good! Loud applause.*]

Therefore, if Spain must use peaceful means in the mission regarding Morocco, what are these? Only two: culture and trade. Regarding culture, Morocco does not have it today, we all know, but nothing gets in the way of being able to recover it; and I say recover it, gentlemen, because it has been good that tonight we are celebrating an act of reparation in honor of the Arab civilization. It is time we let go of those concerns that made us form misjudgments of that civilization, recalling the war between Moors and Christians; and if it is a duty for everyone, it is an elemental duty for those who live in Spain. It is not possible that those who once visited the Mosque of Cordoba, the Alcazar of Seville, the Alhambra in Granada and the farmland of Murcia and Valencia, do not feel obligated to do this justice. [*Very good, very good!*] The lack of culture of Moroccans today is indeed manifest; but there is still, gentlemen, a strong point where to support the lever with which must be wrought the miracle of their regeneration.

[*Ovation to the Alhambra.*]

But to fulfill our mission in Africa, there is another more powerful, more immediate way which has the great advantage of being accepted by everyone. Trade strikes a major chord everywhere, the chord of interest, and interest has the advantage that there is no *aqua regia* as powerful as the undoing of concerns [*laughs*]. Interest may end with some of those barriers that exist among Moroccans and that prevent closer relations between Morocco and Spain. It could even contribute to change absolutism; as well as the barbaric despotism that prevails there in all matters, but particularly in taxation; perhaps because the development of trade, by providing new resources to the Treasury, shall as a result produce relaxation in tax tyranny that has no rule or measure other than arbitrariness. (...)

So the example that our civilization gives to Moroccans could not be more excellent.

Melilla, until recently did not have cobbled streets, or even a school; but thanks to the intervention of one of those distinguished generals, who collected a small tax on consumer goods, soon could pave the streets, establish a school, and to build 80 meters of pier. So, you can see, gentlemen, that when there is a will, many things can be done which that at first glance is thought to be impossible. (...)

It could also contribute, and not just a little, to improve the current state of affairs in our Navy; because the Navy, by its nature, can fulfill part of its ministry equally in some seas as in others, equally in some points as in others, and part of its mission is to open the way to Commerce; because, gentlemen, the path that the warship opens in the sea, for the eyes of the body, as it happens, is cleared and closed as soon as the ship goes by. But in the eyes of the spirit, it is a path left open for the merchant ships that come back, and the path that merchant ships open is the path through which civilization and culture shall pass from one nation to another. So, I said. [*Very good! Very good! Enthusiastic and sustained applause.*]

Questions for Discussion:

1. Besides the actual attendees to the meeting, who is the audience of Azcárate's point of view?

2. Consider the idea of informal empire versus formal empire. Which are the tactics of each?

3. Spain continued to exercise formal authority over Western Sahara until 1975. It is still a disputed region between bordered countries like Algeria, Morocco, and the region's locals. Discuss the consequences of decolonization and Europe's role in Africa today.

4. Azcárate considers Morocco's culture as barbaric. What are the basis to support his argument? What does he think commerce can do about Morocco's undeveloped state? Compare this vision with other imperial projects in Europe and across the Atlantic.

NOTES

Introduction

1. Some of the Spanish scholars advancing the new cultural history in Spain are: Ricardo García Carcel, James S. Amelang, Antonio Castillo, Francisco Gimeno, Fernando Bouza, Mercedes García Arenal, and Tomás Mantecón, to name a few.

2. Jo Labanyi and Helen Graham edited a groundbreaking volume titled *Spanish Cultural Studies*, published by Oxford University Press in 1995, which remains one of the most important in the field, followed five years later by the establishment of the *Journal of Cultural Studies* founded by Paul Julian Smith and Jo Labanyi. Likewise, Peter Burke's work has had a very significant impact on Spanish historiography.

3. For an excellent overview of cultural history in Spanish historiography see: Justo Serna and Anaclet Pons, *La historia cultural: autores, obras, lugares* (Madrid: Akal, 2013).

4. Jacques Derrida and Eric Prenowitz, "Archive Fever: A Freudian Impression," *Diacritics* vol. 25, no. 2 (Summer, 1995): 9–63. Derrida continues in the first footnote explaining the significance of the political power of the archive: "*Forbidden Archives* (*Archives interdites: espeurs Françaises face a l'histoire contemporaine*. Albin Michel, 1994), p. 11, n. 1.

5. Derrida and Eric Prenowitz, "Archive Fever." As if in passing, Sonia Combe asks, in effect: "I hope to be pardoned for granting some credit to the following observation, but it does not seem to me to be due to pure chance that the corporation of well-known historians of contemporary France is essentially, apart from a few exceptions, masculine … But I hope to be understood also …" [315].

6. Derrida, "Archive Fever," 10.

7. For more on the theory of the archive see: Marlene Manoff, "Theories of the Archive from across the Disciplines," *Libraries and the Academy*, vol. 4, no. 1 (2004): 9–25; Richard Harvey Brown and Beth Davis-Brown, "The Making of Memory: The Politics of Archives, Libraries and Museums in the Construction of National Consciousness," *History of the Human Sciences* 11.4 (November 1998): 17–32; Antoinette Burton, ed., *Archive Stories: Facts, Fictions, and the Writing of History* (Durham: Duke University Press, 2006); and Francis X. Blouin and William Rosenberg, *Processing the Past: Contesting Authority in History and the Archives*, Oxford Series on History and Archives (Oxford: Oxford University Press, 2012).

Module 1

1. *"Converso"* (converted) refers to the Spanish Jews who became Christian after being persecuted by the Catholic church in the fourteenth and fifteenth centuries. Religious Jews were expelled from Spain in 1492 and in 1499 conversos were banned from holding public and ecclesiastical offices.

Notes

Module 2

1. All documents in this Module translated by Grabriela Báez and María Asunción Gómez.
2. The Pact of Madrid was an important, although controversial agreement, between Spain and the United States. After being isolated for more than a decade, Spain accepted US economic and military aid and, in exchange, allowed the installation of American air and naval bases on Spanish territory.
3. Source: Banco de Bilbao, *La Renta Nacional de España y su distribución provincial,* in *Estudios sociológicos sobre la situación social de España, 1975,* Madrid: Fundación FOESA, 1976 Prepared by Aurora Morcillo.

Module 3

1. Translated by María Asunción Gómez.
2. Among the diverse works that praise women, I will only quote a few. There is a very rare and old treaty, in Latin, by Fray Jacobo Felipe de Bergamo, entitled *De claris selectis que mulieribus,* Ferariae, typis Laur. De Rubeis 1949; Juan Pin de Tolosa: *De claris faeminis.* Parisiis 1521; *Dialogue in Praise of women,* entitled: *Ginaecepanos,* by Juan de Espinosa. Milan, in the office of Michel Tini, 1580. 4. The prologue is by Gerónimo Serrano, and it states that Espinosa was born in Belorado (Rioja); he served in Italy and he fought in Ravena, in Tunez and then became secretary of the Marquis Pedro González, Viceroy of Sicily; Joan Beverovicious: *De excellentia sexus faeminei* cum iconibus Cornelii Poy. Dordrecht 1639; Hilarion de Costa: *A Praise to the Queens and the Women Who Became Illustrious because of their Teaching,* in French, Paris 1642.
3. Translated by María Asunción Gómez.
4. Translated by Aurora Morcillo.
5. Some of the women who collaborated regularly included: As head editor was María A. Brisso and Jacoba Reclusa as secretary. Eminent lawyer and MP María Lejárraga (1874–1974), head of the Asociación Femenina de Educación Cívica y and Isabel Oyarzabal Smith (1878–1974); the prestigious ophthalmologists Elisa Soriano (1891–1964); Aurora Cáceres (1872–1978) whose pen name was Evangelina; Consuelo Bergés (1899–1988); dramatist María Francisca Clar Margarit (1888–1952), with the pen name Halma Angélico; María Doménech de Cañellas (1877–1952); Carmen Karr (1865–1943); Carmen Monturiol (1893–1966); Irene Lewy Rodríguez (1907–99), known as Irene Falcón; Encarnación Fuyola (1907–82); Elvira Serret de Fontanals, Antonia Torrents, Regina Oppisa, Eloina Malacheverría; María Luisa Navarro de Luzurriaga, Eulalia Vicenti o María del Valle Mantilla de los Ríos, funder of España Femenina. See, Biblioteca Nacional de España, http://bdh.bne.es/bnesearch/detalle/0003733915
6. *Cultura Integral Femenina.* January 15, 1933, num. 1 pp. 16–20.
7. Translated by María Asunción Gómez.
8. Translator's note: Lidia Falcón is quoting Karl Marx's *The Capital* from the Spanish edition, published by Grijalbo 1976. I am quoting from *Selected Writings,* by Karl Marx (edited, with introduction, by Lawrence H. Simon. Hackett Publishing, 1994. p. 234).

Module 4

1. Peter Burke, *Eyewitnessing: The Uses of Images as Historical Evidence* (London: Reaktion Books, 2001) Kindle Edition loc 153 of 4087.

2. http://cvc.cervantes.es/artes/muvap/sala1/hogar/defaultx.htm

3. *Flying Leaves* was an illustrated German magazine published in Munich between 1845 and 1944. In the same genre as the British satirical *Punch,* it published short stories and poetry for a middle class readership. By 1895 its circulation reached c. 95,000 copies.

4. Image provided courtesy of Mr. Ricard Terré.

5. Laura Terré, "Ricard Terré: el instante poético," http://www.ricardterre.com/cinst.html

6. http://www.carlosgimenez.com/menu.htm

7. http://www.bleedingcool.com/2015/02/05/idw-to-follow-corto-maltese-with-paracuellos-by-carlos-gimenez/

8. Translated by Aurora Morcillo.

Module 5

1. Juan Luis Vives, *The Education of a Christian Woman: A Sixteenth-Century Manual*, edited and translated by Charles Fantazzi (University of Chicago Press, 2007).

2. "Guidelines for the Creation of a Plan of Public Instruction to the Junta of This Matter, Being a Civil Servant of the Junta Suprema in Seville," in *Obras del Excelentísimo señor D. Gaspar Melchor de Jovellanos, Volume 4*, By Gaspar de Jovellanos, pp. 10–32. https://books.google.com/books?id=eTIJ1BceFuQC&printsec=frontcover#v=onepage&q&f=false

    For an excellent introduction to the life and works of Jovellanos, see: Angeles Galino Carrill, "Gaspar Melchor de Jovellanos (1744–1811)," *Prospects: The Quarterly Review of Comparative Education* (Paris, UNESCO: International Bureau of Education), vol. XXIII, no. 3/4 (1993): 741–56.

3. Translation by Aurora Morcillo. http://elgranerocomun.net/IMG/pdf/Ley_Moyano_de_Instruccion_Publica_1857_.pdf

4. Translated by Aurora Morcillo.

5. The distribution of competencies between the two main forces of the regime—the Catholic Church and Falange—in education would lead to the establishment of state organizations that enlisted teachers and intended to implement the Falangist principles among the faculty at every educational level. For example, SEPEM (Servicio Español de Profesorado de Enseñanza Media) was the organization for High School teachers. Other organizations included: SEM (Servicio Español de Magisterio) for Normal Schools faculty; SEPES (Servicio Español de Profesorado Superior); and SEPET (Servicio Español de Profesorado Técnico).

6. Translated by Aurora Morcillo.
    Text of the articles: http://www1.icsi.berkeley.edu/~chema/republica/constitucion.html

7. Text of the article: http://www.anpemadrid.com/uploads/Compilacion%20de%20leyes%20sobre%20educacon_1403774801.pdf

Module 6

1. Translated by María Asunción Gómez.

2. Translation provided by the *Tribunal Constitucional de España* (Spain's Constitutional Court) http://www.tribunalconstitucional.es/en/constitucion/Pages/ConstitucionIngles.aspx

Notes

3. Translated by María Asunción Gómez.

4. Translated by María Asunción Gómez.

5. Translated by María Asunción Gómez.

6. Translated by Aurora Morcillo. http://www.boe.es/boe/dias/2007/12/27/pdfs/A53410–53416. pdf

Module 7

1. See translation in https://treaties.un.org/doc/Publication/UNTS/Volume%201221/volume– 1221-II–874-English.pdf

2. There were three Carlist wars: 1833–9, 1846–9, and 1872–1876.

3. Translated by Aurora Morcillo.
    http://secviccentdocumentosoficiales.blogspot.com/2006/09/carta-colectiva-de-los-obispos.html

4. Translated by Aurora Morcillo.
    http://cardenaltarancon.burriana.es/descargas/pdf/pan_nuestro.pdf

5. FOESSA, *Estudios Sociológicos Sobre la Situación Social de España* (Madrid: Euramerica, 1976), pp. 536–7 and p. 681 (translated by Aurora Morcillo).

6. http://www.thegully.com/essays/gaymundo/020202_spain_gay_priest.html
    (Translated by Aurora Morcillo).

7. Translated by Aurora Morcillo.

Module 8

1. Translated by Paula de la Cruz Fernández (edita.us).

2. Translated by Paula de la Cruz Fernández (edita.us).

3. Refers to Alfonso X of Castile.

4. *Sideración* refers to a state of complete paralysis of the basic vital functions because of a shock.

5. Excerpt from Aurora Morcillo, *The Seduction of Modern Spain: The Female Body and the Francoist Body Politic* (Lewisburg: Bucknell University Press, 2010). Translated by Aurora Morcillo.

6. Translated by Aurora Morcillo.

7. Table translated by Claudia Battistel.

8. Fundación FOESSA, *Informe Sociológico sobre la situación social de España* (Madrid: Editorial de Euroamérica, 1966), 7.

9. FOESSA, *Estudios sociológicos sobre la situación social de España 1975* (Madrid: Editorial EUROAMERICA S.A., 1976), p. 413.

10. *Estudios sociológicos sobre la situación social de España, 1975* (Madrid, 1976), p. 423.

11. Translated by Claudia Battistel.

Module 9

1. Translated by María Asunción Gómez.

2. Gregorio Marañón. *La evolución de la sexualidad y los estados intersexuales,* 7

3. These inversions are of the psychological characters that largely correspond to the forms described by psychoanalysts as "latent or masked homosexualities," to which we referred before. We have affirmed that it does not seem fair to consider them as cases of homosexuality, because their instinct is correct, even if they have, perhaps, greater predisposition to inversion than abnormal cases.

4. I am obviously referring to the incapacity that otherwise normally endowed men have for struggle, due to the lack of these social skills; I am not referring to the mentally retarded, the sickly, or the sick.

5. The essential feature of sport is, in my opinion, the absence of creation as a consequence of effort. This distinguishes it radically from work, which is always creative.

6. In Spanish these men are called "*comineros*" (those who fuss about little details), "*refitoleros*" (natty) or "*cocinillas*" (men who enjoy cooking).

7. In the previous chapter we presented our concept of sexual timidity and its relationship with hypovirilism and homosexuality.

8. We have already seen the often abnormal and homosexual shades of the relationships that old men have with young girls.

9. We agree with psychoanalyst F. Boehm, when he states: "The more marked the heterosexual impulse is in a man, the more clear his monogamous tendency is; the more marked his homosexual impulse is, the bigger his polygamous tendencies."

10. Translated by María Asunción Gómez.

11. Robert Briffault, *The Mothers: The Matriarchal Theory of Social Origins,* first published in 1927 in three volumes.

12. *Gnaeus Domitius Annius Ulpianus*; c. AD 170–223, Roman jurist.

13. Translated by Aurora Morcillo.

14. Extract from the dissertation presented in the School of Law at the University of Granada by María Esperanza Vaello Esquerdo, on March 23, 1976. Translated by Claudia Battistel.

15. Translated by Claudia Battistel.

Module 10

1. Translated by José Villar-Portela.

2. Iberian gold and silver coin from the eleventh century until the nineteenth century.

3. Translated by Gabriela Báez and María Asunción Gómez.

4. Castelar, Emilio. *Discurso pronunciado en contra de la esclavitud*, Madrid, 1870. Slavery and Anti-Slavery. Gale. Florida International University. August 31, 2015.

5. The Carlist wars were the fight among the dynastic factions of Isabelinos and Carlistas since the coronation of Isabel II, daughter of Ferdinand VII. Her uncle Carlos de Borbón, claimed to be the rightful heir to the throne since there was a prohibition for women to be monarchs

under the Salic Law. However, Ferdinand VII eradicated this law through the Pragmatic Sanction in 1830, as he had no male heirs.

6. Currency unit.

7. Translated by Gabriela Báez and María Asunción Gómez.

8. Independence of Cuba. Wikisource. Commons.

9. Translated by Gabriela Báez and María Asunción Gómez.

10. Paternal dissent law applied to the islands of Cuba and Puerto Rico by royal decree of February 3, 1882, Madrid. Manuel G. Hernandez Printing. Freedom 16 duplicated, 1882. http://bdh-rd.bne.es/viewer.vm?id=0000077209&page=1

11. Translated by Gabriela Báez and María Asunción Gómez.

12. Translated by Gabriela Báez and María Asunción Gómez.

13. "Discurso de Don Gumersindo Azcárate sobre los intereses políticos y económicos de España en Marruecos," Barcelona: Imprenta de la Revista España en África, 1910.

FURTHER READING

Alvarez Junco, José, *Spanish Identity in the Age of Nations*, Manchester: Manchester University Press, 2013.

Armengol, Josep (ed.), *Queering Iberia: Iberian Masculinities at the Margins (Masculinity Studies)*, New York: Peter Lang Inc., 2012.

Bahamonde Magro, Angel, *Historia de España, siglo XIX*, Madrid: Cátedra, 1994.

Blackmore, Josiah and Hutcheson, Gregory S. (eds), *Queer Iberia: Sexualities, Cultures, and Crossings from the Middle Ages to the Renaissance*, Durham NC: Duke University Press, 1999.

Borggreen, Gunhild and Rune Gade (eds), *Performing Archives/Archives of Performance*, Copenhagen: Museum Tusculanum Press, 2013.

Burke, Peter, *Eyewitnessing. The Uses of Images as Historical Evidence*, London: Reaktion Books, 2001.

Burke, Peter, *What is Cultural History?* Malden, MA: Polity, 2010.

Callahan, William, *The Catholic Church in Spain 1875–1998*, Washington: The Catholic University of America Press, 2012.

Callahan, William, *Iglesia y poder en España 1570–1874*. Madrid: Nerea, 2000.

Carr, Raymond (ed.), *Spain, A History*, Oxford: Oxford University Press, 2000.

Casares Tortella, Gabriel, *The Development of Modern Spain: An Economic History of the Nineteenth and Twentieth Centuries*, Cambridge MA: Harvard University Press, 2000.

Cazorla Sánchez, Antonio, *Fear and Progress: Ordinary Lives in Franco's Spain, 1939–1975*, Oxford: Wiley-Blackwell, 2011.

Chambers, Sarah C., "Private Crimes, Public Order: Honor, Gender and the Law in Early Republican Perú," in Sueann Caufield, Sarah C. Chambers, and Lara Putnam (eds), *Honor, Status and the Law in Modern Latin America*. Durham, NC: Duke University Press, 2005.

Charnon-Deutsch, Lou, *Fictions of the Feminine in the Nineteenth-century Spanish Press*, University Park PA: Pennsylvania State University Press, 2000.

Chartier, Roger, *On the Edge of the Cliff: History, Language and Practices (Parallax: Re-visions of Culture and Society)*, Baltimore, Johns Hopkins University Press, 1996.

Clayton, Lawrence A., *Bartolome de las Casas*, Cambridge University Press, 2012.

Clouse, Michele L., *Medicine, Government and Public Health in Philip II's Spain: Shared Interests, Competing Authorities*, London: Routledge, 2011.

Crumbaugh, Justin, *Destination Dictatorship: The Spectacle of Spain's Tourist Boom and the Reinvention of Difference (SUNY Series in Latin American and Iberian Thought and Culture)*, Albany: State University of New York Press, 2010.

Cruz, Anne J., *Material and Symbolic Circulation between Spain and England, 1554–1604 (Transculturalisms, 1400–1700)*, London: Routledge, 2008.

Cruz, Anne J. and Caroll J. Johnson (eds), *Cervantes and His Postmodern Constituencies (Hispanic Issues)*, London: Routledge, 1998.

Cruz, Jesús *The Rise of Middle-Class Culture in Nineteenth-Century Spain*, Baton Rouge: Louisiana University Press, 2012.

Delgado, Elena, Pura Fernandez, and Jo Labanyi, (eds), *Engaging the Emotions in Spanish Culture and History*, Nashville: Vanderbilt University Press, 2016.

Dopico Black, Georgina, *Perfect Wives, Other Women: Adultery and Inquisition in Early Modern Spain*, Durham NC: Duke University Press, 2001.

Further Reading

"El segundo exilio liberal y el debate sobre la monarquía," in *La monarquía doceañista (1810–1837): Avatares, encomios, denuestos de una extraña forma de gobierno*, Madrid: Marcial Pons Ediciones de Historia, 2013, pp. 319–372.

Epps, Brad and Luis Fernandez Cifuente (eds), *Spain Beyond Spain: Modernity, Literary History, and National Identity*, Lewisburg: Bucknell University Press, 2005.

Erauso, Catalina De, *Lieutenant Nun: Memoir of a Basque Transvestite in the New World*, Boston: Beacon Press, 1997.

Esteban, Ángel (ed.), *Madrid habanece: Cuba y España en el punto de mira transatlántico*, Madrid: Iberoamericana, 2011.

Fernández Armesto, Felipe, *Pathfinders. A Global History of Exploration*, New York: W.W. Norton & Co., 2007.

Folguera, Pilar, "El franquismo. El retorno a la esfera privada (1939–1931)," and "Revolucion y Restauracion. La emergencia de los primeros ideales emancipadores (1868–1931)," in Elisa Garrido González (ed.), *Historia de las mujeres en España*, Madrid: Síntesis, 1997.

Gies, David T., *The Cambridge Companion to Modern Spanish Culture (Cambridge Companions to Culture)*, Cambridge: Cambridge University Press, 1999.

Green, Anna, *Cultural History*, New York: Palgrave Macmillan, 2008. http://www.lascasas.org/manissues.htm#BdeLasCasas:A Biography

Greer, Margaret, Walter Mignolo, and Maureen Quillian (eds), *Re-reading the Black Legend: The Discourses of Religious and Racial Difference in the Renaissance Empires*, Chicago: University of Chicago Press, 2008.

Grossman, Edith, *Why Translation Matters (Why X Matters series edition)*, New Haven: Yale University Press, 2011.

Herr, Richard, *Rural Change and Royal Finances in Spain at the End of the Old Regime*, Berkeley: University of California Press, 1989.

Herzog, Tamar, *Frontiers of Possession: Spain and Portugal in Europe and the Americas*, Cambridge MA: Harvard University Press, 2015.

Labanyi, Jo, *Constructing Identity in Twentieth-Century Spain: Theoretical Debates and Cultural Practice*, Oxford: Oxford University Press, 2002.

Labanyi, Jo and Helen Graham, *Spanish Cultural Studies: An Introduction. The Struggle for Modernity (Science Publications)*, Oxford: Oxford University Press, 1996.

Lombart, Vicent, *Campomanes: Economista y politico de Carlos III*, Madrid: Alianza, 1992.

Morcillo, Aurora G., *True Catholic Womanhood: Gender Ideology in Franco's Spain*, DeKalb: Northern Illinois University Press, 2008.

Morcillo, Aurora G., *The Seduction of Modern Spain. The Female Body and The Francoist Body Politic*, Lewisburg: Bucknell University Press, 2010.

Morcillo, Aurora G., (ed.), *Memory and Cultural History of the Spanish Civil War: Realms of Oblivion*, Leiden: Brill, 2014.

Nash, Mary, *Mujer, Familia y Trabajo en España (1875–1936)*, Barcelona: Anthropos, 1983.

Nash, Mary, *Defying Male Civilization: Women in the Spanish Civil War*, Denver: Arden Press, 1995.

Ofer, Inbal, *Señoritas in Blue: The Making of a Female Political Elite in Franco's Spain. The National Leadership of the Sección Femenina de la Falange (1936–1977), (Sussex Studies in Spanish History)*, Eastbourne: Sussex Academic Press, 2009.

Pack, Sasha D., *Tourism and Dictatorship: Europe's Peaceful Invasion of Franco's Spain*, New York: Palgrave MacMillan, 2006.

Parr, James and Lisa Vollendorf (eds), *Approaches to Teaching Cervantes's Don Quixote (Approaches to Teaching World Literature)*, New York: Modern Language Association of America, 2015.

Payne, Stanley, *Fascism in Spain 1923–1977*, Madison: University of Wisconsin Press, 1999.

Pérez, Louis A, *Cuba between Empires, 1878–1902*, Pittsburgh: University of Pittsburgh Press, 1983.

Pérez Sáchez, Gema, *Queer Transitions in Contemporary Spanish Culture: From Franco to La Movida (SUNY series in Latin American and Iberian Thought and Culture)*, Albany: State University of New York Press, 2012.

Perry, Mary Elizabeth, *The Handless Maiden: Moriscos and the Politics of Religion in Early Modern Spain (Jews, Christians, and Muslims from the Ancient to the Modern World)*, Princeton: Princeton University Press, 2007.

Perry, Mary Elizabeth, Nupur Chaudhuri, and J. Katz Sherry (eds), *Contesting Archives: Finding Women in the Sources*, Champaign: University of Illinois Press, 2010.

Phillips, Carla R. and William Phillips, *The Worlds of Christopher Columbus*. New York: Cambridge University Press, 1993.

Phillips, Carla R. and William Phillips, *A Concise History of Spain (Cambridge Concise Histories)*, Cambridge: Cambridge University Press, 2010.

Poska, Allyson M., *Gendered Crossings: Women and Migration in the Spanish Empire*, Albuquerque: University of New Mexico Press, 2016.

Preston, Paul, *Franco: A Biography*, London: Basic Books, 1996.

Preston, Paul, *The Spanish Holocaust: Inquisition and Extermination in Twentieth-Century Spain*, London: W.W. Norton & Company, 2013.

Quintero, María Cristina and Adrienne L. Martin (eds), *Perspectives on Early Modern Women in Iberia and the Americas: Studies in Law, Society, Art and Literature in Honor of Anne J. Cruz*, New York: Escribana Books, 2015.

Restall, Matthew, *Seven Myths of the Spanish Conquest*, Oxford: Oxford University Press, 2004.

Ribeiro de Menezes, Alison, *Embodying Memory in Contemporary Spain*, New York: Palgrave Macmillan, 2014.

Richards, Michael and Chris Ealham (eds), *The Splintering of Spain: Cultural History and the Spanish Civil War, 1936–1939*, Cambridge: Cambridge University Press, 2011.

Rodríguez Díaz, Laura, *Reforma e ilustración en la España del siglo XVIII: Pedro Rodríguez de Campomanes*, Madrid: Fundación Universitaria Española, 1975.

Serna Alonso, Justo and Anaclet Pons, *La historia cultural. Autores, obras, lugares.* Madrid: Akal, 2013.

Shubert, Adrian, *Death and Money in The Afternoon: A History of the Spanish Bullfight*, Oxford: Oxford University Press, 2001

Shubert, Adrian, *A Social History of Modern Spain*. London: Routledge. 2003.

Smith, Paul Julian, *Desire Unlimited: The Cinema of Pedro Almodovar*, London: Verso, 2014.

Stapell, Hamilton, *Remaking Madrid: Culture, Politics, and Identity after Franco*, New York: Palgrave Macmillan, 2010.

Steedman, Carolyn, *Dust. The Archive and Cultural History*. New Brunswick: Rutgers University Press, 2010.

Stepanek, Stephanie and Ilmanch, Frederick. *Goya: Order and Disorder*, Boston: Museum of Fine Arts Publications, 2014.

Surwillo, Lisa, "Mendizábal, García Gutiérrez, and the Property of Spanish Theater," *Arizona Journal of Hispanic Cultural Studies* 6, Department of Spanish and Portuguese, University of Arizona (2002): 43–56.

Terré Lozano, Laura, *Historia del Grupo Fotográfico Afal: 1956/1963*, Madrid: Photovision, 2006.

Valis, Nöel, *The Culture of Cursilería: Bad Taste, Kitsch, and Class in Modern Spain*, Durham NC: Duke University Press Books, 2002.

Vilá Reyes, Juan, *El atropello MATESA: toda la verdad sobre un caso abierto hace veintitrés años y que ni la dictadura ni la democracia han logrado cerrar*, Plaza y Janés/Cambio 16, 1992.

Vollendorf, Lisa, *The Lives of Women: A New History of Inquisitional Spain*, Nashville: Vanderbilt University Press, 2007.

Wright, Richard, *Pagan Spain*, New York: Harper Perennial Modern Classics, 2008.

INDEX

Index

Index

Index

Index

Index